Studying @ University

SAGE Essential Study Skills

Essential Study Skills is a series of books designed to help students and newly qualified professionals to develop their skills, capabilities, attitudes and qualities so that they can apply them intelligently and in ways which will benefit them on their courses and careers. The series includes accessible and user friendly guides to improving a range of essential life-long skills and abilities in a variety of areas, including:

- **Writing essays and reports,**

- **numeracy,**

- **presenting information,**

- **and communicating your ideas**

Essential Study Skills will be an invaluable aid to all students on a range of higher education courses and professionals who need to make presentations, write effective reports or search for relevant information.

Studying @ University

how to be a successful student

David McIlroy

SAGE Publications
London • Thousand Oaks • New Delhi

SAGE Publications Ltd
6 Bonhill Street
London EC2A 4PU

SAGE Publications Inc.
2455 Teller Road
Thousand Oaks, California 91320

SAGE Publications India Pvt Ltd
B-42, Panchsheel Enclave
Post Box 4109
New Delhi 100 017

British Library Cataloguing in Publication data

A catalogue record for this book is available
from the British Library

ISBN 0 7619 4706 X
ISBN 0 7619 4707 8 (pbk)

Library of Congress Control Number available

Typeset by C&M Digitals (P) Ltd., Chennai, India
Printed in Great Britain by The Cromwell Press Ltd, Trowbridge, Wiltshire

Contents

Foreword

This book, and the series of which it is a part, is designed to help you be successful on your course, your career and in your life.

What this book will give you

If you are just starting your course or thinking about improving your skills for work then this book will be an invaluable aid. It will help you to develop in an easy to use way skills and abilities in:

◆ **Writing essays and reports.**

◆ **Numeracy.**

◆ **Presenting information.**

◆ **Communicating your ideas.**

Using this book and others in the series will help you to gain more **confidence** in your writing, presentation skills and using computers. You will **learn how to learn** and to **transfer your skills** to new situations and problems in your studies and career.

Why an Essential Study Skills Series?

Academic and vocational courses at most universities make many competing demands on students. Further and higher education is very diverse and asks many things from students. Consider the following:

◆ **Most courses are now modularised. This means there is a diversity of methods for assessment which means different kinds of skills and qualities are demanded for success.**

- There is a greater emphasis on independent learning. This means more pressure on tutors who have little time to teach study skills and more pressure on students to take responsibility for their own learning.

- Information in the world's libraries and databases is doubling every five years. This requires an ability to manage information more efficiently for effective use in learning situations and for skills in literature searching.

- Regulatory bodies have set skills benchmarks. In the UK all courses of education have to set minimum benchmarks for transferable skills. These are built into the assessment criteria of modules and courses.

- Professionals are required to demonstrate continuing skills development. This means there is a need for skills books that are relevant to the modern world.

Students are required not only to be literate, numerate and have computer competency but to acquire and exhibit capabilities, attitudes and qualities necessary for inclusion in the modern world. This book and the others in the series will teach you the necessary skills and also provide you with the capabilities to think for yourself and the attitudes to apply your knowledge and qualities, which will define your character. Our approach to skills, which you can see in the following table, is one that includes acquiring technical abilities in terms of the development of you as a person for maximising opportunities during your studies and transferring these for success in the diverse, changing and competitive world beyond university.

The series has been designed to help you develop your skills, capabilities, attitudes and qualities so that you can apply them intelligently and in ways that will benefit you in your course and employment. Using the series from the start of your course and in your job will make your more effective, efficient, confident and more able to take on new and exciting challenges in your life.

Chris Hart
Series Editor

Standard expectations of the graduate

Skills	Capabilities	Attitudes	Qualities
Brevity and succinctness	Synthetical thinking	Proactive	Integrity
Budget construction	Analytical thinking	Responsive	Objectivity
Citation and attribution	Teaching and Instructing	Ethical	Honesty
Copy-editing	Facilitating	Positive	Leadership
Decision making	Argument analysis	Discretion	Self-confidence
Defining and classifying	Deductive and inductive	Trustworthy	Adaptability
Document design	Reasoning	Responsible	Assertiveness
Drafting and editing	Effective thinking	Persuasive	Openness
Essay writing	Information needs evaluation	Self-awareness	Determination
Financial management	Evaluation techniques	Visionary	Finisher
Indexing	Problem definition	Cultural awareness	Self-discipline
Information finding	Solution identification	Reflective practitioner	Sociability
Innovation	Setting criterion	Anthropological Research orientation	Empathetic understanding
Interpersonal communication	Managing change	Self-development	Motivator
Letter and memo writing	Managing projects	Self-control	Experimentation
Meeting deadlines	Team working	Inter-disciplinary	Sociological stance
Negotiation	Understanding group dynamics		Self-evaluative
Networking	Contextualising		Sense of humour
Non-verbal communication	Intuition and insightfulness		Playfulness
Numeracy and statistics	Understanding principles		Story telling
Oral presentation	Self-management		Consistency
	Concept mapping		

(Continued)

(Continued)

Skills	Capabilities	Attitudes	Qualities
Political awareness	Graphical		
Position paper	presentation		
writing	Self-marketing		
Problem solving	Stress recognition		
Proposal writing	and management		
Record keeping	Conflict resolution		
Report writing	Self-teaching		
Target setting	Understanding		
Time management	issues		
Use electronic	Giving and		
communication	receiving feedback		
Use ICT effectively	Consequence		
Write fluent and	assessment		
effective text	Concept		
	application		
	Theory application		
	Model use and		
	construction		
	Data management		
	Information		
	process		
	understanding		
	Information flow		
	understanding		

Introduction

The study guide has not been constructed as the typical heavy duty academic textbook, but has rather been designed to help students navigate their way through the many exacting tasks that face them throughout their academic life. It has been prepared as a 'companion guide' that students can use again and again at every phase in their undergraduate programme. The book can be read from cover to cover because of its applied and illustrative style, but can also be consulted for particular spheres of interest as the need arises.

A sad reality for many students is that they are only beginning to acquire the qualities that enable them to achieve personal excellence as their academic career is drawing to an end. Therefore the sooner students are alerted to the strategies that will help them maximise their potential, the better equipped they will be to seize the opportunities that seem to go as quickly as they come at university or college. An important aim in the book is to point students toward the full range of qualities that help turn an average student into a very good student, and also to highlight factors that will help in motivation toward achievement.

In the eleven chapters that follow, the student is presented with a journey through the academic life. Most of the material is generic to academia and is therefore useful to students from a wide range of academic disciplines. For example, all students need listening skills, communication skills, note-taking and writing abilities, computing competence, organisational skills, examination/test strategies and many may need to develop numeric fluency. Moreover, a recurrent theme in the book is the acquisition of qualities derived from the academic course which will enhance employment prospects. Undergraduates are encouraged throughout the book to cultivate, recognise and document the qualities that will give them the competitive edge in the job market after graduation. Chapter 1 will be particularly helpful for new students in making the adjustment to university/college life, but the practices inculcated will also be useful for more experienced students. Most study guides highlight benefiting from lectures, taking notes, reading, organisational skills and using the library. In addition to these this book also includes chapters on numeracy, computing, presentations, job applications, memory techniques, examination/test strategies and writing practical reports.

Sprinkled throughout the book are a series of simple exercises and these are contained in text boxes. These exercises may be attempted as they are encountered or alternatively left until the whole chapter has been read. However, some exercises require the student to use the library, email or to interact with other students. Again the aim has been to make the exercises as generic as possible so that they will appeal to the widest range of students. Moreover, the exercises are related to everyday life experiences and are generally well within the scope of students' repertoire of knowledge (although also designed to stretch and challenge!).

Other features of the book are the icons used throughout to highlight the illustrations, exercises, examples and guidelines. All illustrations are coded and are clearly related to a section heading. Text labelled 'example' either presents an example of the point under discussion or identifies some other important point to be emphasised. Finally, text highlighted in green is related to a central aim stated in the book – that is, it points to the path for success at university/college or identifies key skills for learning and achievement. Each chapter is also preceded by a list of key concepts that give a flavour of what the chapter is about, and concludes with summary boxes that present a synopsis of the chapter's content.

It is hoped that students who read the book will not only commit themselves to work hard at their studies, but will also discover the strategies that will help them channel their energies in the direction that facilitates economy of work and efficiency of performance. It is hoped that the book will be as enjoyable to read as it has been to write, and that the enjoyment derived from reading the book and attempting the exercises will spill over into enthusiasm for academic endeavours.

1 Getting Adjusted to University

In the beginning

WELCOME TO A NEW WORLD

The first message for new students is a welcome to a 'new world' that can now be adopted as your 'home from home' over the next few years. In many ways university is a world apart, a world of its own and is comprised of students from a wider range of backgrounds than you may have been previously accustomed to. There is also a diversity of staff – teaching, research, administration, technical, catering, cleaning and maintenance. In your three or four years at university you will probably be exposed to a diversity of teaching staff and each for only a short period of time.

For many students university will be the central point of their lives, with their living quarters in close proximity. The university becomes the hub around which all else rotates. However, the primary purpose for the university's existence is to be a centre of excellence in teaching, learning and assessment. It is there to prepare and equip students with a range of skills and expertise that will enable them to go on and fulfil a useful career. Presumably, most students who arrive at university have good motivation and high expectations. Although the end result for the new student may seem a long way off, the consistent testimony of students who have graduated is that they scarcely know where the time has gone. Welcome then to the new world of activity and aspiration, where there is a great buzz of excitement in the air!

CONGRATULATIONS ON YOUR ARRIVAL

Many do not make it to university either because they have not satisfied the entrance requirements or life's circumstances have not permitted them the luxury of a third level education. The university will only accept those they consider have what it takes to survive the rigours of a degree or diploma programme. Congratulations – you have passed the acid test and you should feel assured that you have been given the selectors' vote of confidence. There are likely to be moments when you doubt your own ability or tenacity to progress any further. At times like these it is important to remember the long, hard journey that brought you into third level education and the many daunting obstacles you successfully negotiated. Therefore, allow yourself to indulge in some self-congratulation. Of course there will be no room to rest smugly on your laurels, but it is good to remind yourself that you have had to develop considerably to reach the point where you are now at, and there should be no reason to doubt that your progress is set to continue.

THE FIRST DAY OF THE REST OF YOUR LIFE

In every new day that you face it can be said, 'today is the first day of the rest of your life'. However this saying is especially relevant to momentous occasions that mark the dawning of a new phase of life. That is certainly true of the student's arrival at university. There are new opportunities, new challenges, new people to meet and a whole set of novel circumstances to encounter. All previous achievements in one sense do not count for anything now, in that they do not contribute directly to degree classification. However they do count in that the student would not be at university without them, and all the solid habits learned in association with them will have continued usefulness. Moreover, there is now a fresh opportunity to remedy any weaknesses that may have previously impaired the fulfilment of potential. At the beginning of the new sports season, the team that won the league and the team that just avoided relegation in the previous season, both start in exactly the same position. Similarly, researchers have consistently found that in most disciplines, how students performed academically prior to university entrance is not a great predictor of their levels of achievement at undergraduate level (Peers & Johnston, 1994; Wolfe & Johnson, 1995).

Although university will present many novel situations and circumstances to the new student, there will also be many aspects of university life that will be familiar. If that were not the case, the new student would probably withdraw under the pressure of being entirely overwhelmed. Before arriving at university students will have already acquired experiences not unlike those they will encounter after university entrance. For example, they will have already sat tests, completed assignments, learned to read and quote from a variety of sources, worked to deadlines and have had some familiarity with the use of a library and a computer. Therefore the challenging new experiences will not be totally 'uncharted waters', and students can use their past accumulated experience as a reference point and guide to the less familiar. If the fear of the unknown is a trigger for anxiety, reference to past experience can become an antidote to it.

A cognitive schema

If you eat in a particular restaurant regularly, you will be well aware of all the procedures associated with taking your seat, reading the menu, ordering from the waitress, leaving a tip, paying for the meal etc. When you go to another restaurant, you may notice differences in the details of the procedure – for example, all courses ordered at once rather than at intervals, and different procedures associated with payment of bills. Various restaurants have differences in the procedures but this should not cause any consternation to patrons. Each patron has a mental map or cognitive schema for using restaurants and all that is required is some accommodation to a new situation. There is a clear advantage over the person who has never been in a restaurant in their life. Likewise your cognitive schema for teaching, learning and assessment will have to be adjusted at university to accommodate the novel aspects. You will have frames of reference from school, night school, technical college etc. that will act as a bridge to the less familiar and keep your anxieties under control.

I will survive

THE SWAMPED FACTOR

Within the first few weeks of the new student's experience at university, it is not uncommon to feel swamped or overwhelmed with much new material to assimilate and so many new situations to become accustomed to. Some new students may feel at first like a stranger in a strange land, and students prone to anxiety may feel that it is all a little too much for them. In the following paragraphs and in the remainder of the chapter, potential difficulties will be addressed one by one. For the present, the primary advice is to brace yourself for this kind of reaction and ensure that you do nothing rash. The feeling of being overwhelmed will come under control sooner rather than later. However, the more you are convinced that these feelings are controllable, the sooner you will actually find that they are. It is good to find a friend, family member or fellow student to talk to who will help to allay your fears and put your perceptions into perspective.

LECTURE THEATRES (EXCITEMENT AND APPREHENSION)

On my first day at university there were two lecturers that introduced the first module. Their introductory talk was in a lecture theatre that was filled almost to capacity with first year students who, like me, had just arrived at university. First year students from various disciplines shared common modules in the first year and then went their separate ways into their various specialities. There was an unforgettable feeling of excitement from being associated with those who had made it thus far and who were aspiring to work their way toward a satisfying, rewarding professional career. There was a detectable buzz of anticipation and an air of expectancy. However, these feelings were tempered with some apprehension about what was going to unfold in the next few weeks. There were questions in the minds of some of us such as, 'will I be able to keep up to speed with the demands of this course?' 'Will I be able to put the quality of work required into the assignments and within the deadlines imposed?' 'Would some of us end up feeling that we were out of place in this environment and realise that we had turned in the wrong direction in the pursuit of a career?' It is not unnatural for feelings of inadequacy and questions of uncertainty to enter the mind at this early stage at university. The antidote to these feelings is to resolve to prove yourself by planned study, concerted and committed endeavour and determination to persevere even when apparent setbacks occur.

OUTLINE OF THE MODULES

At the first lecture associated with each new module, there is likely to be a presentation of the planned outline for the module and a handout to accompany this. Every student should pull out all the stops to ensure attendance at the introductory lectures and to avail themselves of any handouts that are provided. These lectures are likely to furnish students with additional detail and they should therefore be ready to make supplementary notes. If lecturers make notes available on websites do not hesitate to access these and to extract all relevant learning material.

Plotting the way ahead

If you are determined to develop a good study strategy at university or college, then a good starting point would be to memorise the outline plan for each module. This should not be too difficult given that there may be around eight major topics within a module. The sequence in which the themes appear is likely to be ordered in a logical and coherent manner. Consider being given the task of navigating in a long car journey through many towns and villages with the use of a convenient road map. The best strategy might be to acquire an overall feel before the start of the journey for the direction you are likely to take. Some familiarity with the names of the main cities and towns you have to pass through would be a great advantage. As you arrive at each juncture you will be reassured that you are on track to reach your destination. You can continue to check your map at various points and stops in the journey. The whole task will have been made a lot less onerous by early familiarity with the map. By the time you come to making the return trip you will probably have a good 'cognitive map' of the route. In terms of university experience, the return journey can be likened to the period of revision. By the time you reach the revision stage, you should know where each of the subjects in the module fits into the overall scheme of things. Ensure, therefore, that you have a panorama of each module right from the outset and refer to it regularly along the journey.

LONG LIST OF REFERENCES

Prior to university entrance, many students may have only worked with a limited number of set text books which they were expected to treat as the Bible for a given subject. Perhaps all that was needed to master a subject was knowledge of the set book, and this may have required intensive effort. At university the strategy of reading within a limited range is left behind for the most part. However, the first year at university may not necessarily be more difficult than the final school year. Some students have claimed that their last year at school was more exacting and demanding in many ways than their first year at university. This may be because universities purposefully design the first year of their courses to allow students to ease into the new environment and learn the strategies required for optimal achievement in the degree programme. The ultimate aim is that students should be able to cite evidence and use references from a good variety of sources. This entails abandoning the practice of reading every textbook from cover to cover unless that has been specifically signalled. Moreover, students may not even need to read complete journal articles or book chapters – perhaps only one page, or a few paragraphs, or one abstract or table of results is essentially relevant to the point under discussion in a given assignment. Or if you read an article right through once you can learn to highlight the parts that you can refer to later. Economy and selectivity are of the essence in study at university. One of the keys to success at university is to learn not to spend excessive time reading superfluous material, no matter how much it may interest you. The secret is to read selectively and to condense the reading into carefully marshalled arguments. Therefore do not be intimidated by the long list of references for each module. Your tutor may guide you to some of the key articles that give a good overview of the entire subject.

DEADLINES FOR ASSIGNMENTS (IN SHORT SEMESTERS)

Many students do not fulfil their potential, not because of any deficiency in their ability, but because they fail to develop a sound study strategy. Even the most talented students will not achieve optimally if they, for example, attempt to begin and complete several assignments a few days before the deadlines. Most tutors will provide assignment titles and submission dates well in advance. Another aspect of the key to success is to make a note of these dates and begin to build a dossier of articles and notes as promptly as possible. Once you have the seeds of these articles embedded in your mind, you will be likely to attend to relevant information that you encounter in lectures or reading that other students may miss. In short, the road to underachievement is to let deadlines overtake you inadvertently so that you will not have the time, resources or knowledge-base to achieve the quality that you know you are capable of producing.

NEW WORDS, NEW TERMS, NEW JARGON

One of the most daunting elements in the first few weeks at university is the bombardment of new language that students have to learn. Every subject has its own jargon and students are expected to learn the correct terminology. Again it is a simple matter of remaining steady and being patient until you are familiar with the terms. When you have heard, read, written and spoken them a number of times they will become part of your natural repertoire of knowledge. Once they have been assimilated into your thought processes, you will find that they come back to you when you need them – such as in a test, examination, assignment or group discussion. Therefore the terms that may initially instil fear will become the tools for self-confidence and precise expression. The real problem arises when too many words are introduced within a short time frame, and the best strategy here is to learn them selectively in stages. It would certainly be useful to make a list of all the new terms and then to tick them off as they are learnt. At a later stage it will do your self-confidence no harm to look back at the lists previously mastered. This strategy will both boost your confidence and whet your appetite to learn more.

Using the university library

THE GUIDED TOUR

Library staff at the university will provide a guided tour at the start of the new academic semester. Students should attend as many scheduled events as possible in the first few weeks to ensure that they become familiar with all available resources and services. If attendance is not possible then students should make up the lost ground as soon as possible so that they do not suffer the knock-on disadvantages. Each library will have its own unique features related to duration of book loans (short-term and long-term), rules, fines etc. In the introductory tour you will learn how to trace and locate books and journal articles, as well as how to use inter-library loans and how to recall books already out on loan.

Photocopying is another important procedure to learn in association with library use. Students may not be permitted to remove journals or key textbooks where there are a limited number available for a large class. Therefore, it is essential to learn the system for using the photocopiers and this will probably be demonstrated in the introductory tour. One sound rule of thumb that should be applied to every new practice learnt at university is that students should go back and re-enact what they learned as soon as possible after learning it. Consolidation is one of the key elements in the road to success at university.

THE ELECTRONIC FACILITIES

In one class of third-year undergraduate students it was found in an informal survey that about half the students did not use the electronic facilities. This was a great shame and a real waste as these facilities allow students to access a wide variety of useful material and the little effort needed to master them will pay dividends. First and foremost, it is essential to learn how to use the university's electronic catalogue. These are designed to be user-friendly and are much less laborious than the old system of wading through large unwieldy catalogues. The computerised approach also means that records of stock can regularly be updated with ease and convenience. In the guided tour the library assistant will explain how to trace books and articles and how to place reservations on those books already on loan. Students will also learn how to find articles or books by authors' names and by keyword searches, and should ensure that they avail of any leaflets available that help to reinforce the lessons given in the guided tour.

Exercise — Library practice

Take a couple of friends and each of you go to separate locations within the library. Each take note of a few book titles, with authors and library reference numbers. Then rendezvous back at a library computer to exchange the information (except the library reference numbers). See if each can trace and then locate the books/articles suggested by the others. Motivation to do this exercise will be higher if you use a list of books and articles on your course and then divide the task equally between you. Try to practice this kind of use of the library on a regular basis. Allocation of tasks among friends and division of labour both enhances camaraderie and promotes efficient use of time.

It should be evident that knowing how to use the computerised library catalogue is indispensable. Moreover, the university will also provide electronic search bases that enable students to access either abstracts or full text facilities for journals. Some time and effort will be required in order to become familiar with these. Many students are daunted by the thought of using these and therefore never make the effort to master them. There will not be enough time in the initial tour to become thoroughly conversant with these facilities, but enquire if the university provides training seminars to familiarise students with their use. It should be a top priority of every student to book into one of these training sessions and then to make use of the facility as soon as possible afterwards. An additional advantage is the use of email, for the range of articles located in searches can be emailed to yourself and printed out later at a convenient time and place. Alternatively, articles can be saved on a floppy disk and later printed out from a PC. Remember that library assistants are there to help you and you must learn not to be shy about asking for assistance. It is important to build a good rapport with library staff and this involves some simple courtesies such as patience when they are busy, gratitude when they are helpful and apologies when you interrupt or inadvertently waste their time. A genuine and friendly smile and a teachable spirit will not do the cause of being helped one iota of harm!

Exercise — Operation regularity

It may be the case that in the first year of an undergraduate programme, the use of periodicals or journals is not an essential requirement. Some modules at this stage may be based primarily on standard textbooks. Students, therefore, may not have the motivation to use the electronic facilities for searching out these kinds of articles. Consequently when the time comes to use them, many are impeded in their progress. It's a good idea to get some practice with friends on the use of the electronic search bases from the outset of the course. A small circle of student friends can each find a topic of interest and try to trace aspects of this through the electronic services provided. This task will be more rewarding if a) the topic has been reasonably well-researched and there are substantial numbers of articles available on it or b) the topic is in some way related to your course so that you may be able to make use of what you find at a later stage and c) you set aside a regular period every week or so to engage in this practice so that what you learn does not lapse and d) you keep a folder to accumulate all the collected material. You can try to trace the subject matter through authors' names, keywords or particular journals that are likely to contain the topic. A good starting point would be to check the reference section in a fairly up-to-date textbook on your chosen subject.

SOME ETHICAL ISSUES

The quality of university libraries would be enhanced if all students complied with some basic ethical standards. It was previously stressed that library staff should be treated with courtesy and consideration and the same principles should be applied in other library situations. For example, some students appear to use the library as a centre for socialising in an environment where noise is distracting and 'silence is golden'. Most students will respond positively to a courteous request for silence but, if not, then you have a right to ask a library assistant for help.

A large problem in libraries is books not being returned to their proper place after being used within the library. This is most frustrating for other students who desperately need the books, and time consuming for library assistants who have to relocate them. It is not unknown for students to conceal a book deliberately or tear out a journal article so that they can have competitive advantage over others. However, a little reflection will show that such a reprehensible practice is soon obvious – other students complain that the book or article cannot be traced and yet one student has it referenced in their assignment. In general it is much wiser to be helpful to other students, and some of them will return the compliment.

Particular problems

FOR YOUNGER STUDENTS

Younger students are sometimes less confident than mature students because they have less experience of life and may not feel they have the social skills that would serve them well in interacting with others at university. One younger student observed that she felt intimidated by the mature students in her class who appeared to be confident and authoritative in their contributions to class discussions. In one sense this kind of confidence can only come with time, patience and practice and there is no short cut to it. On the other hand it may help to know that mature students often feel a little inferior to younger students because they reached university earlier and may be perceived as 'whiz kids'. The mature students may feel a little deficient in ability because they may not have had sufficient qualifications for university entrance after leaving school. Problems for younger students are often compounded by:

- Being severed from home and family ties, perhaps for the first time.

- Being in a new environment where they may not know anyone initially.

- Suddenly having the responsibility for managing a budget for the first time.

- Being secluded in a campus (perhaps outside town).

Four simple pieces of sound advice are:

- Try to make new friends as soon as possible and share your problems together.

- As soon as you see problems beginning to mount, contact student support services for advice and direction.

- Try to find an interest or hobby that you can pursue at university (all the better if you can attach yourself to some sports club etc. within the university).

- Never leave any problems until they are out of control.

FOR MATURE STUDENTS

The greatest problem for many mature students is trying to juggle a range of responsibilities (home, family, work, lectures) in order to accommodate regular study time. Such students are likely to be highly motivated and will already have developed coping strategies. The first piece of advice for mature students is simply to use the skills they have already acquired in relation to social interaction, time management etc. However there will be new insights in this book that will encourage mature students to develop their potential further. For many mature students sacrifices have to be made to go to university or college, so their eagerness to learn and achieve needs to be channelled into discrete strategies. Primary advice therefore is to develop sound strategies as early as possible in the course and to use whatever support services are available rather than let problems snowball out of control. The guidelines given throughout the book are meant for all students, but mature students may benefit especially from the sections on good time-management, selective reading, economic writing and good exam strategies. Mature students may not have as much recent experience in tests as younger students and therefore may derive benefit from close attention to Chapter 9, 'Doing justice to yourself in exams'.

STUDENTS WITH SPECIAL NEEDS

A range of disabilities/special needs is represented in contemporary universities, and the universities are required to demonstrate that they have made adequate provision for such students. However, the university cannot help students if they do not know about their particular needs. First, students with special needs should make themselves known to their course director, studies advisor or year tutor and ask if any processes have been put in place to deal with their particular problems. Second, these students should ask what support services and information services are available to assist them. Some students require special provision for access to essential parts of the university such as the library, computer labs etc., and some may need to sit near the front of a lecture theatre. Others may need special provision for sitting tests or examinations and the sooner these needs are made known, the better it will be for the student. Not all disabilities are clearly evident and therefore students can suffer in silence, bottle up their anxieties and disadvantage themselves in their academic performance. If students make their needs known at an early stage then adequate provision can be made in good time and they can be made aware of any support groups or special needs groups that exist, or at least have their attention drawn to the fact that such groups might be started.

FOREIGN STUDENTS

Students who take the trouble to uproot in order to study in a foreign land are likely to invest a huge effort in accomplishing their goals. Very often these students set examples to local students by their singular determination and concerted efforts toward excellence. Many foreign students will have friends already engaged in a course at the university of their choice. This is a great advantage for it is a good point of contact and provides the best possible introduction. In some courses there may be a tutor who is the contact person for foreign students and will guide them toward a comfortable initiation and adjustment into the university system. If you are coming to a university where you have no established friends, you should enquire if there is a tutor or person you can liaise with in order to make a smooth transition into university life. It will help if you can meet with friends of the same or similar ethnicity.

Moreover, it will be beneficial if you can, through time, widen your contacts and circle of friends, but allow yourself time to get accustomed to the new environment. Write to the university for any useful guidelines for foreign students, and it will also help if you can talk to someone who completed a course in the university (or at least country) that you are planning to move to. They will be familiar with all the problems you are likely to face and the best ways to negotiate them.

If you plan to come to an English-speaking university, and feel that your English needs improvement, you may find that the university provides a course on 'English for foreign students', or else they will be aware of the nearest available course. It is always easier to learn a foreign language when you are in the environment where it is spoken. Foreign students frequently become quite fluent in English after a short period in the university environment. First year at university is designed so that students can learn all the requisite skills for achieving a good degree. Therefore be patient with yourself for the first year and work at developing your English (if necessary) in parallel with the other knowledge you need to acquire.

SUPPORT SERVICES

Each university will have its own range of support services and there is likely to be full-time and part-time staff available to help you with your enquiries. It is not an inconvenience for them when you go and knock on their door and ask for help. Universities should have a range of advisors including welfare officer, solicitor, chaplain, counsellor, financial advisor and crèche service etc. If you knock on the wrong door for help then you will be referred to the right contact person. Ask for leaflets that give information about the range of support services available. Central points for leaflets are the library and the Students' Union. Find out where the Students' Union area is and take a look at the names on the doors and the services they represent. You do not know when you may suddenly need these services. Remember that problems should be nipped in the bud before they get out of control.

In addition to these services, each School or Department within the university may have its own particular provisions. Each course will have its own co-ordinator and there should be a tutor assigned to take overall responsibility for each level. Moreover, each student should be allocated a studies advisor and it may be the student's responsibility to go and introduce themselves to their advisor. Many students are afraid of being perceived as a nuisance, but you can share your problems in a manner that does not wear the listener down whilst getting some good advice that will help you bring them under control.

Many students suffer anxiety to a greater or lesser extent at one time or another at university or college. Anxiety can be an unpleasant state that is triggered by circumstances unrelated to the academic course, but the pervasive and recurrent activator for anxiety is more likely to be related to academic pressures. It is claimed that anxiety is more likely to kick in in situations where some performance is going to be evaluated, where the person entertains doubts about their own ability to complete the task successfully and where the consequences of failure are likely to be serious (Liebert & Morris, 1967; Deffenbacher, 1980; El-Zahhar & Hocevar, 1991). The good news is that anxiety can be brought under control, and it has been found that when anxiety is reduced, performance is likely to improve (Hembree, 1988). Chapter 9 is about developing strategies to maximise performance in tests or exams. This includes coping mechanisms for keeping anxiety under control and strategies that may help turn stress into advantage. Of course anxiety is not confined to testing situations but the strategies advocated will be adaptive for all anxiety-generating situations.

Ten reinforcements for a positive mindset

THREATS CAN BE INTERPRETED AS CHALLENGES

In the book '*The Pilgrim's Progress*' (Bunyan, 1622–88) the Christian traveller is confronted with two lions in his path. From a distance he wondered if he could get past them, but as his courage brought him nearer to them he noticed that each was tied to a post at opposite sides of the road. There was a gap in the middle of the path where he could safely pass through. The moral of the story is that when we confront problems head on, they are often not as debilitating as we previously envisaged, and usually there is some way through. John Bunyan also penned these words about the pilgrim: 'No lion can him fright, he'll with a giant fight, he will make good his right, to be a pilgrim.' The stress that you feel about a task that seems threatening may be converted into energy that can be used to face the challenge. Things are often not what they seem, and things that first appear to be stumbling blocks can become the stepping stones to great progress. For example, many students begin their course with a fear of statistics or computing and end up achieving a good standard in these disciplines. When students look at any task they have to perform under evaluative conditions, they can choose whether to perceive it primarily as a threat or a challenge – like the two men who looked out through prison bars – one saw mud and the other stars.

NEW STUDENTS SOON HABITUATE AT COLLEGE

In one experiment Zajonc (1968) found that people came to like what they were famil-iar with, even though the focus of familiarity was nothing more than nonsense sylla-bles! Many people would feel overwhelmed in a world where little was familiar or predictable. For many it appears that feelings of security only coexist with familiar surrounds and familiar people. Although that is likely to be true for many people, the simple fact is that the secure feeling of familiarity can be gradually extended to a range of diverse contexts. At first the university may seem almost a hostile environment because there are so many new features to address, but after a short time these will become part of your normal world.

Habituation

Through time and experience students 'habituate' to many aspects of university that initially appeared threatening. A lecturer once gave an example of what is meant by habituation – when a snail comes out of its shell and is gently touched by an object such as a pen, it rapidly recoils into the security of the shell. Next time this happens it will recoil again, but every time the touch is repeated the snail will recoil more slowly and emerge more quickly. If the action is repeated enough times the snail will only recoil a little and eventually will not recoil at all. In effect the snail learns that the stimulus is not a threat, and therefore habituates to its influence. So it is with accumulated experience at university – students learn that if they work steadily, their fear of failure diminishes, and the influences around them are found to be more benign than they had imagined.

FUN SIDE A – FRIENDS, SHARED EXPERIENCES, HUMOUR, SOCIAL EVENTS

One student said that he never wanted to leave university for he had come to enjoy the student life so much! A substantial aspect of university life is non-academic. There are coffee breaks, lunch breaks, periods between lectures, social events, sports activities etc. There are many opportunities to develop new friendships and meet interesting people from a variety of backgrounds. Even when the pressure is on, it is 'therapeutic' to be with people who have to face the same demands and deadlines. Students can share their problems and provide a primary source of support for each other.

University would be a morbid place if all students did was to lament their plight to one another. The Readers' Digest has a section entitled, 'Laughter: the best medicine'. In laughter our minds are pulled away from preoccupation with seemingly intractable problems. When we return to them, as we must, we often find that our thinking is clearer and more balanced. Children love funny characters who can make them laugh, and adults are often no different. Fun and humour are like valves that release pressure and diffuse tension. Ensure, therefore, that you find ways to laugh, have fun and enjoy relaxation. University should be remembered as a place where there were many harmless fun times and pleasurable occasions.

FUN SIDE B – LEARNING TO ENJOY YOUR ACADEMIC CAREER

When students involve themselves in fun activities and work at making good supportive friendships at university, these will help to shape within them a good positive perception of their academic institution. However, there is no good reason why this perception cannot be extended to include academic endeavours. The first thing to do is to plan out your study schedules well. Make out a plan that will cover the typical week – that should include lectures, seminars, labs, tutorials and all that is part of the weekly programme. Within the time frames that remain you should plan your personal study periods at home and in the library. Keep a diary for this purpose and don't give up the practice because some unexpected events arise at times to disrupt set plans. Ensure that you always schedule into your weekly programme times for relaxation, fun and socialising – these are 'the sanity factor!' By doing this kind of planning you will give yourself a good feeling of being in control of what is going on in your life, while at the same time being flexible enough to allow for any changes that arise.

Constructing outline points for assignments can also become fun. There is considerable satisfaction in devising your own little piece of handiwork as you hammer your headings and subheadings into shape. Contentment can be derived from eventually grasping the difficult problems you have grappled with and it is always gratifying to apply results/findings to real life situations and to find good illustrations to demonstrate some point more clearly. Students may derive a sense of achievement from engaging in a 'dialectic' approach to their essays – that is, propose a thesis, introduce an antithesis and then merge these into a synthesis. There is also satisfaction when students pass their assignments and tests and then look back on previous work to see how much the quality of their work has improved. Other sources of satisfaction include giving help to another student who is lagging behind and making a useful contribution to group or class discussions.

Exercise — Devising a schedule

See if you can write a plan for a week's activity at university (Monday to Friday) to include one day where there is no scheduled teaching etc. Include three lectures, two seminars, one tutorial and one computer lab. Also schedule in times for working on planning the next assignment and for reading over and tidying up any notes from lectures etc. Remember to allow for break times and fun times. Also allow time for preparatory reading before scheduled teaching and learning events. Finally leave time aside toward the end of the week when you can plan your diary for the following week. It you already possess your academic timetable, why not go to work on the 'real thing'?

COUNTER-CONDITIONING — A FEARED STIMULUS BECOMES
A PLEASANT STIMULUS

Experiments carried out by Pavlov (1927) demonstrated that dogs would learn to salivate in the anticipation of food merely at the sound of a bell. The noise of the bell was repeatedly paired with the appearance of an assistant who carried food to the dogs. Eventually the dogs associated the sound of the bell with the arrival of the food, and so all that was needed for the glands to salivate was the sound of the bell. The dogs had become 'classically conditioned' to respond to a stimulus (the bell) that was associated with the food even when the food wasn't present. This phenomenon has been used to explain some learning processes, including the acquisition of phobias and anxieties. It is not difficult to see how a process could kick in at university where a lecture room could be associated with confusion, an exam room with failure, a lab with anxiety or a library with intimidation etc.

Two things can happen to change the conditioning process and the first of these is 'extinction'. For example, if the bell in Pavlov's experiment had been rung repeatedly without the arrival of food (after the dogs had already become conditioned), the association between the bell and the food would become 'unlearned' and the dogs would cease to salivate. Similarly, many of the negative reactions to stimuli at university will just 'drop off' themselves over the process of time as students learn that the stimuli are not necessarily associated with failure, underachievement, frustration, low self-esteem etc. Alternatively steps can be taken to make the 'conditioned response' a pleasant rather than an unpleasant one. For example, children who fear furry animals can gradually be brought to love furry animals by a process known as counter-conditioning. Both teaching staff and students themselves can look at ways of making the learning environment more pleasurable and enjoyable so that students' reactions to the challenges they are presented with can be associated with positive energy.

Exercise — Altering negative perceptions

Imagine a person who intensely dislikes travelling as a passenger in a car. What factors might be introduced to make their travel more enjoyable and perhaps change their perception of car travel?

FINDING YOUR FEET BY CO-ORDINATING SKILLS — THE DRIVING ILLUSTRATION

I asserted earlier that good planning is the starting point for taking control over your own academic destiny. However, this is only the starting point and the next step is to get from the 'drawing board to the workshop'. How is it possible, it might be asked, to juggle with so many competing demands and to do justice to all of them? At times it may seem that the schedule is so congested that there is scarcely time to breathe. Students at the end of their degree programme will generally have acquired a wider range of skills compared to those who have just entered the third level educational system. The more experienced students will have learned how to select, to focus, to manage time, to 'cut to the chase' and to co-ordinate a range of skills that can be applied to the range of demands and deadlines. Therefore, when they graduate, they will not only have the accumulated repertoire of knowledge from their course, they will also possess the skills that can later be developed to fulfil a professional role.

Co-ordination in driving

Skilled co-ordination only comes with time, patience and practice.

Consider a simple analogy from the sphere of driving — the person who steps into a car to learn to drive for the first time may wonder how they will ever be able to handle being in rush hour traffic. Drivers have to maintain control over many things within the car itself such as accelerator, brakes, clutch, gears, indicators, lights, horn, mirrors, wipers and steering wheel. They also have to look at what is happening outside the car with reference to other traffic, pedestrians, traffic lights, speed limits, traffic signs, crossings, junctions, one way streets, roundabouts etc. How can all this mass of information be marshalled into safe, relaxed driving? In reality experienced drivers do not get into a car and mentally rehearse all they know about driving every time they take a journey. Rather, they take everything in their stride and as they face problems their background knowledge is applied. Moreover, their skills are so well learned that they can co-ordinate a range of activities in parallel with each other. There is an 'automaticity' factor that activates within drivers' minds once they begin to engage in their familiar driving routines. Similarly, students learn to develop and co-ordinate the skills that enable them to apply themselves successfully to lectures, seminars, tutorials, labs, essays, assignments, tests and exams, library use and private study without feeling overwhelmed by it all.

FIRST YEAR — DESIGNED TO GIVE TIME TO LEARN THE SKILLS

Results from the first year in a degree usually either do not contribute or make a small contribution toward eventual degree classification. What is normally required is to pass each module, although most students will want to do better than merely pass. However, it is clear that the first year has been designed to give students time to adjust to the university ethos, to learn the required skills and to profit from mistakes made. Of course it is the intention that this flexibility should induce steady progress rather than the development of maladaptive habits that will later be difficult to unlearn. Nevertheless, the fact that students can recover from first year slumps in performance should help to remove some of the anxiety that first year students can suffer. Each student should aim to develop good habits that will later equip him or her well in professional practice. An old adage crystallises how each small attitude and action combines to lead toward an end goal:

> Sow a deed, reap a habit;
> Sow a habit, reap a character;
> Sow a character, reap a destiny.

The foundational habits you cultivate will shape your progress and destiny during and after university.

COMPENSATION SYSTEMS AND SAFETY NETS TO KEEP YOU THERE

No university is given a quota of students that it has to fail every year. In contrast it is likely to be better for a university's image to be producing successful students rather than have substantial numbers of students who regularly drop out without completing their course. Moreover, it is better for the university from a financial standpoint that students remain within the system and it is great for the university's Teaching, Learning and Assessment evaluation if students are seen to improve steadily throughout their course. From every point of view it is better for the university if you remain within the system. Therefore, a number of safety nets will be placed under you to ensure that you do not fall easily out of the system. For example, if you fail an exam you can do a re-sit, and if you fail this you may be able to carry this failure with compensation from course work or other modules. A student who has failed marginally will probably not have to re-sit the failed test, and sometimes tests can be deferred due to extenuating circumstances. Extensions of time may be granted to students for completion of assignments where sickness or other problems have impeded their commitment to study. If the best strategy is to go back and repeat an academic year then this should be considered. The wisest strategy for students is to alert their tutor when potential problems are looming. Flexibility within the system has been designed to aid students who are overtaken with problems, but students with genuine problems are sometimes loath to use the system in case they are construed as opportunistic individuals. Whenever you need to use the flexibility in the system because of problems that have overtaken you through no fault of your own, you should not hesitate to do this without any feeling of stigma.

A NEW BEGINNING – LEAVING SCHOOL BEHIND

For younger students who have just arrived into university after leaving school, third level study marks a new approach to education where school has to be left behind once and for all. Many mature students may also have their former school days as the main perception of the educational process. At university or college students are ostensibly treated as adults and are expected to demonstrate more independence and maturity than students in the advanced secondary level. On the positive side, lecturers may prefer to be called by their first names and are likely to discourage students from referring to them as 'sir' or 'madam'! They are also more likely to be open to vigorous discussion or debate. On the negative side (which turns out to be not quite so negative), lecturers will not 'spoon-feed' students and tell them every word they should write. They will give credit for up-to-date research that students have taken the initiative to ascertain for themselves. Some will say that they are happy to see students disagree with them in an assignment provided they can adduce the evidence that supports their case. This does not imply that students should attempt to demean lecturers in public – there are courteous and respectful ways of asking awkward questions. In short, the 'rules of engagement' are likely to be quite different from those that students were accustomed to at school. If students demonstrate respect in all their interactions at university then they will both win respect from others and be able to respect themselves, especially because this road has been chosen without coercion. Effective interaction with others is part of the learning process which will prepare and equip students for their future career.

USING THE PAST AS A STEP TO THE FUTURE

Every student comes to university with a rich history of learned experiences and with some degree of successful achievement. All third level students step into an environment that has many novel features, but there is enough experience in each student's past to form a bridge to the less well-known. Students will have learned from their past that they can master difficult material, that they can give a good account of themselves when they are tested and they can emerge successful when a range of pressures envelop them. Briefly, students can take what they have acquired into novel situations and watch these skills develop further as they nurture them. Just as previous experience from school etc. serves to form links with practice at university, so university experience provides a bridge to the career that awaits the graduate. Best wishes with your new adventure at university. May it be a very rewarding adventure and may it lead to a useful, fulfilling and appropriate destiny!

SUMMARY

♦ Entrance to university or college marks the beginning of a new adventure.

♦ Pre-college experience will serve as a bridge to new challenges.

♦ New challenges that are initially daunting will soon become familiar and manageable.

♦ Every opportunity should be taken to become conversant with all aspects of the new environment.

♦ Good systematic planning is an essential ingredient on the path to success.

♦ Familiarity with support services will help form a buffer to anxiety.

♦ The cultivation of fun times and friendships will assist in forming a positive perception of the university.

♦ University academic programmes are designed to help students remain within the system.

♦ Learning adaptive attitudes and practices will assist in reinforcing a positive mindset at college.

♦ Qualities developed at university are preparatory and transferable to a subsequent career.

2 Profiting from Lectures, Seminars and Group Work

KEY CONCEPTS

● SALIENT POINTS ● BIRD'S EYE VIEW ● LECTURE RECONSTRUCTION ● LISTENING AND WRITING ● PERSONAL SHORTHAND ● CO-ORDINATED STRATEGY ● PREPARATION AND CONSOLIDATION ● ILLUSTRATIONS, APPLICATIONS AND QUESTIONS ● ACCESSIBLE MEMORIES ● STYLE DIVERSITY ● ATTRACTIVE, PRODUCTIVE, FUNCTIONAL AND INTERACTIVE ● COMPLEMENTARY LEARNING CHANNELS

Your presence makes a difference

AN INVALUABLE CHANNEL OF INFORMATION

Lectures should be regarded by undergraduates as a central channel of essential information. The content of lectures should guide students toward the material to focus on and away from irrelevant tangents. Students should also be guided selectively by the reading lists, the module outline and previous examination papers. However, the lectures are the starting point to build on for more detailed study. No student is going to remember every word spoken in every lecture, and some students claim that they remember very little from most lectures. In reality, students remember more than they imagine for in spite of thinking that they have forgotten what they heard, whenever they hear the same material again they immediately know that they have heard it before. Therefore it is profitable to attend lectures because the received information can be reinforced from other sources such as reading and seminars. At any rate lecturers have no inclination to see their material reproduced verbatim in a test or assignment. Conversely, they would not be pleased if the signals given in the lectures were totally ignored.

COPING WITH THE BOMBARDMENT OF FACTS

One problem that new students especially face is bombardment with a range of new terms and technical jargon that they may never have encountered before. In the first few weeks of term many feel that their minds are saturated and this anxiety is compounded by deadlines for the first batch of assignments. At such a time each student must persevere at reading and listening until the 'jawbreakers' become familiar. At primary school we were given lists of words to learn for spelling, and one day the word 'enthusiasm' appeared on the list. This word was new to all of us and we bandied it around all day like a new toy! When we became more familiar with it, the word lost all its mystical novelty appeal. This kind of gradual introduction to new words was fun, but the fun may disappear when many words have to be mastered in a short space of time. One simple strategy to cope with bombardment is to take regular breaks at set intervals. It is also sensible to try to engage in some relaxing pursuit such as a sports activity, walking, listening to music, watching a movie, socialising with friends etc. Another strategy is to switch to another subject for study, just for the variety. It may also help in building confidence to study something more familiar or revise a subject that you know you can comprehend.

BECOMING A NATURAL PART OF THINKING PROCESSES

When reading John Milton's poems, it is easy to become daunted by the copious references to Greek and Roman mythology, with such names as Zephyr, Aurora, Janus, Bacchaus etc. A commentator suggested that Milton had been brought up on these ideas as a boy and would have been as familiar with them as contemporary children are with cartoon figures. When some subject is almost entirely new to students, the first thing to do is to grasp enough of the central ideas to develop a working knowledge. At this point it is helpful to discuss it with other students. Later, the complexities and subtleties can be added one-by-one. Every time the subject is returned to it will become a little easier. With patience and perseverance you will become familiar with lecture material as you continue in your studies, and you will find yourself using terms effortlessly that have been woven into your natural thinking processes.

Exercise in reassurance

Think of some academic subject that you once knew little about but now have a reasonable grasp of. Make a list of all the central ideas associated with this subject. Now think of how encouraging this knowledge you have is in relation to learning new material. Try to recall how daunted you may once have felt at the sight and sound of all the new terms!

ACQUIRING A PANORAMIC VIEW

Many lecturers provide students with an outline of the module plan for the whole semester. This is very useful information to become familiar with because it enables students to keep a 'bird's eye view' of the overall material and the feel for where any given lecture fits into the total scheme of things. This outline should not be filed away and forgotten about, but should rather be kept to the forefront of the appropriate file and glanced at before each lecture. Do not underestimate the effect of a quick glance here and there. Moreover, it is beneficial to glance over the overall module outline before each lecture. This strategy will make the lecture a more satisfactory experience for you and will also assist in helping you to see where it fits into the overall development of the subject. An artist will prepare a painting so that the observer will be struck by the overall effect of the entire painting. However, he or she will also expect the observer to see the range of details in the painting. No appreciation of the painting is complete without both forms of observation. The same applies to evaluating your academic module and the relation of each lecture to the whole. It is necessary to be aware of the whole and where each of the parts fit into the whole.

Exercise — Visualising a garden

Think of all the things that might contribute to an attractive garden in terms of colour, smell, shape, size and sound. Try to describe both the overall picture and the parts. Consider the difference if all the parts were separated from each other and how much of the effectiveness of the garden is lost. Also consider how much your vision is enriched by inspecting the component parts that comprise the overall picture. An actual example to look at is van Gogh's painting of flowers and trees in a garden walk.

Extracting the essence from the lecture

FOCUSING ON WHAT YOU NEED TO REMEMBER

An important task for students in any lecture is to identify the salient points that are being made. No one can be expected to remember the whole lecture but students should be able to identify the central issues. It is said that the best way to remember a joke is to tell it as soon as possible after you have heard it. A good strategy for remembering the salient features in a lecture is to mention them to your friends at the coffee or lunch break. You could for instance say, 'I thought the important points in that lecture were … do you think I got it right?' If a lecturer highlights some point as being particularly important, then insert an asterisk in the margin adjacent to the point, and then later underline the point. There is an ancient biblical text that asserts that the ear tests words just as the mouth tests food. In terms of food we all quickly learn to discriminate in taste (with the added criterion of smell). For example, we will not normally consume some food product that has gone off because it has to pass the smell and taste tests. Similarly, students must learn to discriminate between the central and peripheral in study material.

THE VALUE OF REHASHING THE LECTURE

Lecturers may differ a lot in their presentation skills, and some lectures may not be as well structured as others. Sometimes students need to re-structure the lecture material in a manner that they will remember. This should not be perceived as a major task, it just means identifying a few key points and arranging them in a logical sequence. Ironically, if you do this judiciously, then the lectures that are poorest in presentation may be the ones you remember best because you have done a little work on them yourself! In contrast, there may be a danger that you do no immediate work on the lectures that are very well presented because you think they are so good that you leave them intact and tuck them away for future reference. A wise strategy is to glance over all your lecture skeletons in a regular and systematic manner. However, if you make this task too formidable for yourself, you are less likely to maintain the momentum of your commitment.

Exercise — Preparing for entertaining guests

Imagine that you have been asked to write a short article on the hospitality and entertainment of friends that you would invite round for an evening. Consider how you would juggle the following points into a sensible sequence that would flow and fit a successful evening's entertainment:

- Organisation and preparation of food (shopping and cooking)
- Choice and mixture of guests, and invitations with sufficient notice
- Choice of food, music and drinks to suit the taste of all guests
- Co-ordination of tending to each course whilst maintaining interaction with guests
- Co-ordination for guests' arrival and departure at staggered times
- Choice of rooms to use, seating arrangements etc.

FINDING A CO-ORDINATION STRATEGY FOR LISTENING AND WRITING

Many students grapple continually with the difficulty of trying to listen and take adequate notes at the same time. This problem may be largely resolved if lecturers provide handouts of the main headings and subheadings at the beginning of each lecture or on a website. Students can then augment these with their own supplementary notes. If a lecturer does not make this provision then try to ensure that you make a note of all the main headings and that these are clearly identified as such. The next task is to ensure that all the written material is under the correct headings. If you have any visual or hearing difficulties, it is essential to sit near the front of the lecture hall. Some students decide to do more listening than writing and others do the opposite – they write vigorously from start to finish. Moreover, some students try out various strategies over the course of their academic career. The more practice you get at taking notes in lectures, the more your skills will develop until you have found the system that is optimal for you. There is no tailor-made solution to the problem that will universally fit every student. Each student should find the strategy they are most comfortable with but should constantly examine whether the strategy they are using is optimal for them. Moreover, you may have to be flexible enough to adjust your style according to the lecturer's style. Some lecturers work their way through their material slowly, patiently and with repetition, but others give the impression that there is always a vast amount of material that they are never going to reach the end of!

There are, however, a few suggestions that should be helpful for all lecturing styles, and these have already been hinted at. The first is to do some preparatory reading before the lecture even if this is quite brief. This will familiarise you with any technical terms that are used, and that is a big advantage as it can be daunting to hear a lot of new jargon all at once. Second, it is important to consolidate what you have learned as soon as possible after the lecture and preferably on the same day. Take a few minutes to read over the notes and identify the main concepts. It is also useful to read these again close to the subsequent lecture. Not very much time or energy is required to do this and only a little discipline. Any investment that is made at this level will pay handsome dividends. Remember that it is not necessarily the most able students who achieve the best standards at university or college, it is most likely to be those students who are organised and methodical.

Practical procedures for maximising benefit

Another suggestion to help in note taking during lectures is the judicious use of your own form of shorthand. This is especially useful where long technical terms are repeatedly used such as 'Operational Definitions', which can be abbreviated to ODs, or 'Cool Temperate Oceanic Zone' (to CTOZ). Expressions like, 'that leads into the next point' can be simply represented by an arrow. The words 'positive' and 'negative' can be designated by the appropriate signs (+ and −), and illustrations can be remembered by the use of an adequate cover word or two. As an example, one lecturer came up with the idea of a falling apple to illustrate a causal chain. It can be argued that the apple fell to the ground because its connection with the tree was severed, or that it fell to the ground because someone below failed to catch it. However, the causal chain can be traced a couple of steps back to the operation of the law of gravity. This whole illustration and its application can be remembered by a simple summary such as, 'gravity/apple/causal chain illustration'. The use of abbreviations means that time is saved in writing and good recall is accessed in revision. Again it is stressed that memory is more readily accessed if material is consolidated shortly after initial learning. Summary notes in capsule form make it more likely that you will glance over the lecture outline on a regular basis.

It is useful to build up a good stockpile of abbreviations in association with particular subjects, and to take steps to ensure that you have reference to the meaning of these. This will also serve you well in revision for exams and in drawing up essay plans during exams. Moreover, it is essential to abbreviate in those lectures where the lecturer races through the material. Remember, however, that abbreviating the spoken material can be done in a variety of forms apart form shorthand – such as pictures, a few keywords or simply by condensing or paraphrasing what your hear.

Exercise – Paraphrasing

See if you can quickly paraphrase into a few words the following opening sentence from Jane Austin's (1775–1817) *Pride and Prejudice*:
'It is a truth universally acknowledged, that a single man in possession of a good fortune, must be in want of a wife' (p. 5).* One suggestion is provided at the end of this chapter.

Students often write so much material so rapidly during lectures that they are later unable to decipher their own scrawl, but the use of abbreviations reduces this problem. At a practical level it is an advantage to keep good margins on your notepad so that you have room to insert explanatory notes later, and it is also beneficial for this purpose to leave spaces between lines. If you build up a collection of abbreviations you should make a note at the beginning or end of your notepad that explains what all these mean.

ILLUSTRATIONS — MAKING THE MATERIAL ATTRACTIVE

It is said that a picture is worth a thousand words. Everyone loves to hear a story and stories are good ways of remembering important lessons. Even the dullest subjects can come alive by means of good illustrations. The illustration may be real or fictional or it may be a concrete application of what might otherwise be an abstract concept. For example, a group of postgraduate nursing students were not enamoured at being told that multiple regression analysis allows a researcher to use a series of independent variables (IVs) to predict an outcome on some dependent variable (DV). However when it was explained that coronary heart disease (DV) can be predicted by knowledge of diet, exercise, smoking, genetics, stress and personality (IVs), then they understood the message perfectly, and the statistics came alive to them. Therefore, if a lecturer uses an illustration to good effect, make sure you capitalise on this. If he or she does not, then it will be helpful if you can think of your own.

APPLICATIONS — MAKING THE MATERIAL PRODUCTIVE

Illustrations are useful for understanding abstract lecture material, and so are practical applications. Think of how the principles in the lecture can be applied to real life situations. Students sometimes demoralise themselves by asserting that they will never have any practical use for the academic material they accumulate. An important aspect of learning is to envisage how the principles on the drawing board can be applied at the workshop. For example, watching the effects of various reinforcement schedules on animals in a Skinner box (an experimental box used in labs to monitor the frequency of pigeons' key-pecking or rats' lever-pressing responses to food or liquid reinforcement) may seem a million miles away from the real world. If you can, however, see how some of these schedules can be applied to child-rearing practices or help explain gambling behaviours then you are more likely to remember the principles.

Exercise — Application for survival

The principle of infarction — light entering a prism does not pass through it in a straight line but veers off at an angle. Similarly, when we look into water, we do not see objects under the water in their true position. Can you think of how important an understanding of this principle might have been for the survival of our ancestors who may have depended on catching fish by use of spears? In this example it can be seen that understanding the principle of infarction may have contributed to the survival of our ancestors, and survival is usually a good motivator!

WORKED EXAMPLES — MAKING THE MATERIAL FUNCTIONAL

Applied mathematics

Subjects such as mathematics that appear more abstract than other subjects can have many applied aspects. It is clear that maths solutions are very useful to world championships darts players as they have to calculate the scores they need toward the end of each game or for shoppers who need to compare prices before a purchase. Moreover, the application of mathematical formulae is useful if you can work your way through examples. For example, Pythagorean theorem states that, in any right-angled triangle, the square on the hypotenuse is equal to the sum of the squares on the other two sides. If you are hearing that for the first time it may amount to nothing more than a fine piece of gobbledygook. The hypotenuse is the longest side on the right-angled triangle and if it is for example, 5 mm, and the other two sides are 4 mm and 3 mm you can easily work through the example. The square on the hypotenuse ($5^2 = 25$) is equal to the sum (added) of the squares on the other two sides $(4^2) + (3^2) = 16 + 9 = 25$. Therefore it is wise to use illustrations and worked examples because these make the subject interesting and enjoyable and demonstrate that it has relevance to life. If the lecturer uses worked examples, you should make note of these and try to supplement them with additional examples from textbooks or that you construct yourself. The statement of Pythagorean theorem is more likely to be remembered if you have worked through an example in practice.

Applied perception

It is claimed that Allied fighter planes travelling in the same direction used to be in danger of crashing into each other because of the illusion of distance. A pilot would think the plane in front was further away than it actually was. This illusion allegedly occurred because the two tail lights were close together giving the illusion of greater distance between the planes. The problem was rectified by moving the two tail lights as far apart as possible. This had the desired effect in that the pilots were no longer tricked into thinking falsely that there was a safe distance between the two planes. A story like this is a good illustration and application of how the human perceptual system can lead to erroneous conclusions because of inappropriate use of perceptual cues.

Exercise — Selecting key words

Imagine that you have just listened to the above story in a
lecture. You want to remember both the story and its relevance
to the lesson. What few keywords would you insert in the margin
that will later enable you to recall what you need?

One necessary word of caution – when using illustrations in assignments and tests,
ensure that you do not over-elaborate on them or forget that they are supporting aids
and not a means to an end. This is especially applicable if the question does not invite
you to apply or illustrate your answers. Always beware that you do not go off at a
tangent into a stream of unnecessary and irrelevant ramblings.

QUESTIONS – MAKING THE MATERIAL INTERACTIVE

An important way to engage effectively in a lecture is to ask questions that will
further clarify your understanding. These may be questions that you ask yourself
rather than address to the lecturer (although some lecturers may leave space for you
do this at the end). Whenever you ask questions this indicates that you are thinking
about the subject rather than merely attempting to learn it passively. Why is it that the
police frown on drivers using mobile phones while they are driving, whereas they
accept that drivers can listen to their radio or CD/DVD player? Apart from the obvious
response that one hand is likely to be engaged with the mobile phone, the other aspect
is that conversation is continuous and interactive, and requires a concerted level of
attention. For maximum benefit from a lecture, a student should not merely be the
passive recipient of facts, but should see the lecture as material to engage with and
develop further in seminars, essays and tests. Questions help stimulate and develop
thought and assist in processing the subject matter at a higher level than mechanical
memory work. The person who learns the most is likely to be the one who is curious,
and the one who wonders what is going to come next. Kipling's words are suggestive
of a good strategy for learning – 'I kept six honest serving men, they taught me all I
knew; their names are what and why and when, and how and where and who.'

When recording lecture notes there will be questions that occur to you as you listen
and write. You may find it helpful to insert a question mark in the margin and a word

or two to remind you of what puzzled you at the time. A simple rhetorical question may serve this purpose, for example, 'is this convincing?' or 'what kind of an explanation was that?' In short, make sure that you engage your mind interactively with the lecture material, and questions are an excellent way to facilitate this process.

Your studies being steered in the right direction

WHAT APPEARS FORGOTTEN IS OFTEN STILL ACCESSIBLE

Memory making a comeback

Sometimes students feel stupid because they cannot recollect some of the basic and essential material they thought they had learned so well. It is just like getting the message on your phone line, 'try again later, as the number you have dialled is busy at present'. You should not be demoralised because the facts you are trying to recall are not at your fingertips at that particular stage in the learning process. All that is needed is a little more consolidation. Sometimes the harder you try to remember something, the more elusive it seems to be, and then it may suddenly come to you when you stop consciously thinking about it. Two friends tried to remember the name of a heavy-weight boxer who had come out of retirement for a comeback fight with Frank Bruno. They tried to jog their memories by going through every letter of the alphabet to trigger the name. Alas, the memory stubbornly refused to be retrieved, but later when they had ceased to think about it at a conscious level, suddenly and unexpectedly it resurrected itself, as the name of Joe Bugner popped into the head of one of the friends, apparently out of nowhere! All of us can probably identify with this kind of process. Such experiences reassure us that we are not wasting our time when we read or listen to a lecture.

LECTURES COMPLEMENT OTHER FORMS OF LEARNING

It would not be wise to hope that one past deposit in the memory will be enough to bring back all the material needed to address an exam question. It is essential that you both consolidate what you have learned in your lectures and read similar material from books and journals, and that you interact in smaller groups in relation to the relevant subject matter. In this way students not only reinforce what they have learned, they also elaborate on the foundational material and gain a clear picture of how all the various parts dovetail together. Difficult points that students had not understood in a lecture may later be comprehended by reading. Moreover, participating in seminars may uncover other interpretations you had not conceived and correct misunderstandings that had been entertained.

POINTERS TO THE CENTRAL QUESTIONS

Lectures serve an all-important purpose in that they highlight all the central issues on the course, and they flag up the way ahead in your preparation for the end-of-semester exams. It is likely to be the case that the person who delivers the lectures is the one who has constructed the questions for your exams (at any rate the lecturer will endeavour to ensure that all the exam material is covered in the lectures). Therefore, if you listen carefully to what they say, you are not likely to be totally in the dark about what is probably going to arise in your tests. Moreover, lecturers sometimes give guidelines for your coursework, which in turn can feed into your test revision process. Although attendance at lectures may not be compulsory on your course, it is possible that you could miss vital hints and suggestions for exams by staying away. Lecturers also make students aware of the common pitfalls that former students have slipped into, and the last lecture before the exams is sometimes used to give special guidance for the exams. Some lecturers may do this, however, in an earlier lecture in order to 'wrong foot' those students who make a special guest appearance for the last lecture! It would be useful to start to write little bullet points soon after the lecture that will later help you as you commence your revision. Don't write these down on scrap paper but on a pocket notebook that you can carry around. Scrap paper is easily lost or may later give you the impression that the note you made was not important.

TAKING UP THE BATON

Lecturing is not interchangeable with spoon-feeding! The lecturer is introducing you to the important ideas in order to stimulate you to develop them further. Parents sometimes advise their children that they should leave the table with the feeling that they could eat a little more. Similarly, when you leave a lecture it should be with the awareness that there is more for you to do. You should therefore know, not only the questions that have been addressed, but also about any outstanding issues that remain unanswered. Tutors will not be expecting you to relay back all their points, illustrations and references without some complementary material. The practice of returning nothing more than you were given in lectures might be flattering to lecturers but will not be advantageous to you. What you need to present to your assessor in an assignment or exam paper is what amounts to your own creation. Although you have drawn your material from a variety of sources (including the lectures), you should skilfully weave the material into your own style. Someone once said that if you extract your material from one source only, that is copying. However, if you glean your material from a variety of sources, that is research!

PROFITING FROM A DIVERSITY OF STYLES

Finally, it will soon become evident to you that lecturers have styles that are divergent from each other. Some styles you may feel very comfortable with and others may take a little more time to feel at ease with. The good thing about third level education is that you are exposed to a good variety of approaches and this is likely to be a good preparation for your career beyond university. University life is largely about learning to adopt, adjust and make the best out of whatever comes your way. One student complained that she did not like the style of a particular person who was her inaugural 'baptism' lecturer. The wise response came from another tutor that one swallow does not make a summer. There are a wide variety of lecturers in third level institutions and you are usually only exposed to each for short periods, and so you must learn to adjust to this with all its advantages and disadvantages.

Approaching seminars beneficially

COMPLEMENTARY TO LECTURES

Seminars are frequently used to address topics directly or indirectly related to the lectures. The group in each seminar will doubtless be smaller than the full body of students in lectures, and there is more opportunity for informal interaction as well as scope to elaborate on lecture topics. It would be foolish to look upon these occasions as optional extras for they should be perceived as opportunities to reinforce and expand on knowledge received through lectures and reading. Like all other events in the academic curriculum, students will receive maximum benefit from seminars if they engage in a little preparatory work. For example, if required to discuss a chapter from a set textbook then it is essential to do the background reading beforehand. On the other hand, if this is neglected then the student will suffer the knock-on effects in trying to play 'catch-up'.

A SIMPLE PRESENTATION

If required to do a full presentation with visuals, carefully read Chapter 11, 'A Skilful Presentation'. However, if the presentation required is informal and without visuals then give attention to the following basic points:

Guidelines for an informal presentation

- Be conscious of time limits and keep within them.
- Write out the main points clearly on your notebook and space them out well.
- Use main headings and subheadings and arrange these in a sensible sequence, but do not have too many points.
- Do not move too rapidly through the material — this can happen if a student over prepares.
- Indicate briefly where the given topic fits in with the range of allocated topics or at least show how it relates to the previous or subsequent topic.
- Try to look intermittently at the informal group rather than just reading every word with eyes fixed to the manuscript.
- Use voice inflection and some appropriate movements to provide variety and avoid monotony.
- Give a brief synopsis of the main points at the end and any applications that might be inferred.

GIVING AND RECEIVING

Seminars often become the launching pad for an essay or practical report. Therefore in spite of each student's natural preoccupation with their own presentation, they should also attune their antennae for receiving useful and vital contribution from others. Although the individual student will not be expected to make vigorous and extensive notes as at a lecture, it would be wise to have pen and notepad at the ready so that remembering crucial points is not left to chance.

Leakage through seepage

A report into water loss in Northern Ireland (2001) estimated that one third of water supplies are lost by leakage throughout the infrastructure. Consumers are always called upon to conserve water supplies in times of shortage. However consumer wastage looks minuscule compared to the leaks in the system. Parallel application – how much invaluable information is lost at college or university because a few brief notes were not taken at the time of receiving the knowledge?

Working on group projects

PROS AND CONS

In some courses students are required to complete one or more group projects, and this offers the advantage of learning how to work in teams – good training for the future. For example, it offers a chance to learn how to work with people who have diverse personalities. Another advantage is that team members bring the fruits of their labours to the benefit of the whole team. The downside is that if some do not shoulder their share of responsibility then the whole project may suffer, and lethargic students may unjustly benefit from the industry of their fellow students. However students who refuse to apply themselves to group projects are very short-sighted and their results are likely to suffer in the long term, for bad practice has it own adverse knock-on effects. Nevertheless that may not be much consolation for conscientious students who are being impeded in their work.

DEVISING A PLAN

It might be expected that tutors would have the providence to anticipate problems that might arise in group work and set measures in place that would reduce or eliminate their negative effects. If not then students should discuss and form a consensual agreement on safeguards that should be built into the process. One of these could be that more than one person should be allocated to each task, so that if one is negligent then there should at least be some input from others. The first aspect of any group meeting might be a 'brainstorming' session, where all the suggestions deemed relevant are put forward and noted. These can then be integrated into central strands and the group should aim for consensus for the overall theme and the major topic divisions. If there is disagreement on some points then the group should take note of all the agreed points first of all (this will help group cohesion), and then consider either dropping or compromising on the other points. The next stage is to break the group down into smaller numbers with each smaller cell (two or three) being given a task to complete and a time to do it in, and the division will be most practical if there are the same number of cells as there are tasks to complete.

PREPARING A STRATEGY

Groups are often put together randomly or alphabetically by tutors without prior notice. Before anyone has a chance to think much about it, students may find themselves in the middle of a group with a topic to address and about 45 minutes to devise a strategy. It is likely that one natural leader/organiser will emerge (it may be better to nominate someone so that time is not wasted) but it is essential that notes are taken. Moreover, it is vital that focus and direction are maintained and that individuals who are prone to indulge in protracted monologues are curbed. Unless some control is taken over the proceedings then a lot of valuable time will be lost. Someone needs to ensure that due attention is paid to the division of time and that all required aspects of the topic are outlined. If the whole group is to perform the given task effectively then every individual should, if possible, go away from the first session with a clear vision of what they are to achieve. Everyone should also go away with clear knowledge of the overall aim and the range of objectives to be achieved.

REPORTING BACK TO THE GROUP

It should be decided at the end of the first session how many group meetings should be planned, when each one will be and how long they will last for. Each cell should have a clear specification of what its task is and what core issues need to be presented at the next meeting. The second meeting is crucial as it is designed for the exchange of essential preliminary information. Each cell should prepare handouts for every member of the entire group so that everyone will have a total picture of all that is going on. If there is practical work to be carried out (for example, survey, observation, experiment) then it will probably be best for the group not to meet again until this work is completed. Moreover, if a co-ordinator is appointed for each cell then informal consultation between groups can go on between scheduled meetings.

A FINAL RENDEZVOUS

Keeping full group meetings to a minimum is likely to be advantageous to the project, provided the time during the meetings is used profitably. The final meeting of the group is vitally important for after that all students must apply themselves to writing up their project. At the final meeting all the contributions from each cell are brought together. Initial aim and objectives should be restated and then the group should consider the extent to which these have been achieved. Any problems or inconsistencies should be ironed out. No cell should withhold any information that would be useful to the whole group. In the write-up it should be clear to the assessor that everyone in the group is 'singing from the same hymn sheet'. However there should be some evidence of individuality to indicate that there has not been plagiarism (unless a collective group report was specified). Individuals can stamp their seal on a project by the style in which they present it and by the way they interpret and apply the group findings.

SUMMARY

- Lectures help focus students' attention on the salient points in the module.

- Frequent cursory glances at the module outline instils a sense of 'modular panorama', and fits each lecture into its place in the overall framework.

- A little selective summary reading prior to each lecture facilitates ease of learning.

- Judicious reading soon after a lecture crystallises and consolidates cardinal points.

- An optimal form of personal shorthand is a useful strategy in note-taking.

- Lecture attendance should be supplemented by complementary learning from a variety of sources (seminars, tutorials, library work).

- Students can capitalise on lectures by reconstructing the material in their own preferred format.

- Study material can be given dynamism by use of illustrations, examples, applications and questions.

- Seminars should be used for both giving and receiving useful information.

- Group work is most profitable if plans, strategy and proper controls are pursued.

*Everyone knows that a rich single man needs a wife.

3 Cultivating Organisational Skills

Achievements require organisation and planning

A WIDE DIVERSITY OF EVIDENCE

In all spheres of life there is evidence of planning, for it is clear that little that is worthwhile can be accomplished without it. Archaeologists have unearthed masses of evidence that ancient civilisations were adept in planning and building their well-structured and efficiently functioning cities. Whether the enterprise is for the family's weekly menu or for the holiday next summer, planning always figures in the process. Sports teams plan for the new season but may be flexible enough to vary their tactics according to the opposition on a given occasion. The news media plan how they will arrange and present the news each day and those who control air traffic have to plan for arrival times, departure times, delays, diversions etc. for each runway.

Planning is of course of little avail unless the plans are carried out – there must be organisation and implementation, but planning is an essential starting point. Some people prefer to document their plans in a diary or notebook, but others opt to conceive and conceal their plans within their own minds. If individuals are likely to lose track of their plans, they would be best advised to keep a diary, and students can easily let plans lapse because of the multiple pressures within limited time frames. The purpose of a diary is defeated unless it is checked every day. Students who have arrived at college or university must have proved their planning and organising capabilities to some extent. However, fresh and renewed thought is likely to be needed in order to raise these qualities to the level where maximum benefit is returned for effort invested. Researchers have claimed that factors such as planning, organisation and motivation are the kinds of qualities that make the difference between good and poor students (Bouffard, Boisvert, Vezeau & Larouche, 1995)

Organisation saves frustration

Example

Some people regularly spend a lot of time looking for their keys before they leave their house! This problem can be simply remedied by choosing a place to hang the keys as soon as the individual enters the house. In that way time is not wasted and frustration is eliminated (both for the individuals concerned and those who may have to wait on them). It can be so easy to misplace a watch, a pen, a ring, a purse, a wallet etc. When this is happening regularly it is time to take measures to prevent it! At university students can save themselves a lot of time, frustration, waste and inefficiency by developing simple and regular habits. For example, a good filing system that keeps all relevant notes together in a logical order within one folder for each module will save endless exasperation. Or a little note enclosed in a textbook to remind a student of the page number, paragraph number and relevance of a particular passage may later prove priceless. If a student is working in the library and stumbles across an article that he or she knows will later be useful, then a careful note should be made about the title, author, reference and relevance of the article. This practice will be especially useful if the note is made in a notebook that is used for the module to which the article is relevant. Students may later waste precious revision time because they have lost track of an article that they desperately need. Moreover, a failure to 'fill in the blanks' from notes taken in a lecture at some point soon after the lecture may lead to the intent behind the shorthand being 'evaporated'. A key to success at university is applying the truth of the adage that 'A stitch in time saves nine'.

PLANNING ALLOWS FOR BREAKS AND MAXIMISES EFFICIENCY

Some students may fear being perceived by others as a drudge or 'nerd' or robot. This image projection can be avoided by taking some time to socialise, to enjoy some fun with others and by being supportive of other students in their studies. In reality the person who plans well and is sufficiently organised to carry out their plans, can find time to do things to supplement their academic life. However, this is all a matter of prioritising – it is necessary to resolve to be applied to academic work, and then to have fun in the time left over (not vice-versa). Too many late nights and too much over-indulgence too often may throw the whole body clock out of rhythm. Grades may suffer and career ambitions may not be realised if students are unable to regulate their lives.

On the other hand it is important to take breaks and to factor these into the planned scheme for each new week. A car will not continue to run efficiently unless it is given a regular service. No student will function to their potential unless they break from their studies, have times of relaxation and engage in pursuits that will take their mind away from their academic work. These times serve to 'recharge the battery' and then the student can return to study feeling fresh and reinvigorated. Students should ensure that they have a good break at holiday time, at weekends and some short breaks in between study periods. They can learn to alternate smoothly between study and rest, work and fun. Many contemporary students find it necessary to have part-time work, and although this has some disadvantages, it has the clear advantage of diverting the mind from academic pressures.

A lesson from the four seasons

In recent years there has been much discussion about the alleged effects of global warming on climate changes and the overlap in seasonal patterns. However, in spite of the alleged change to extremes in temperature, rainfall etc., it is still possible to observe the characteristic differences between the seasons. There are regular times in the year when the flowers start budding, the birds start nesting or when birds migrate or animals go into hibernation. Each season – autumn, winter, spring and summer – serves its purpose for the growth, renewal, decline and rejuvenation of nature. The animal kingdom knows how to adapt behaviours according to the season of the year. Likewise humankind also adapts according to the season in terms of dress, food, sport, leisure, work (for example, construction), holidays etc.

In a similar kind of way, various 'seasons' come and go in the academic calendar at university. First, there is the season of initiation when the student learns to get adjusted to the new world of academia, then there is the season of preparation for assignments when it seems that the student's whole life is preoccupied with beating deadlines. There are also shorter periods within the academic semester when practical/lab or field studies run or when tutorials and seminars are operational. Moreover, there is the all round 'run-of-the-mill' season when students are engrossed in listening, reading, learning, writing, accumulating and compiling information. Finally there is the season of exams (or tests) when all lectures have come to an end and the period of intense revision begins, culminating in the exams themselves. Students have to adapt and adjust their behaviours according to the particular 'season' they find themselves in. Each new phase comes and goes very rapidly. However, in spite of the changes in academic activity during each semester, it is necessary to keep a number of commitments running in parallel with each other. Just as nature benefits from the fluctuations in the seasons (buds, blossoms, blooms), so students can capitalise from using the opportunities that come and go to add usefully to their repertoire of knowledge.

MORE TO ACADEMIC ACHIEVEMENT THAN ABILITY

Researchers believe that students' academic achievement is a combination of ability, thinking styles, behavioural patterns, planning, discipline, motivation, organisation and self-concept (Purdie & Hattie, 1995). Students who obtained a good standard before entering university cannot afford to 'rest on their laurels', and students who were in the lower echelons of achievement prior to university entrance should not imagine that they are doomed to stay there. Some researchers have argued that the most capable students do not always turn out to be the best students, simply because there is more to achievement than ability, and these students do not always fulfil their potential. Given that students have enough ability to satisfy the university or college's entrance requirements, there is room to use and develop the kernel of ability that is there. Therefore it would be short-sighted to envisage future performance as entirely commensurate with past attainment.

Checklist

Are you an organised person? Insert a number in the space provided after each question according to the following code — 1 = Always   2 = Almost Always   3 = Frequently   4 = In-between   5 = Occasionally   6 = Seldom   7 = Never

1. Do you have to rush out each morning at the last minute? ....
2. Are you late for your scheduled appointments? ....
3. Do you plan your meals for each new day? ....
4. Do you leave your meetings with friends to chance? ....
5. Are you caught out with nothing clean to wear for scheduled events? ....
6. Can you account for how much you spend on any given week? ....
7. Do you know roughly how many hours that you will watch TV on any given week? ....
8. Can you make a list of the range of foods you eat in any given week? ....
9. Do important events (birthdays, anniversaries) overtake you before you are aware of them? ....
10. Do you lose time through misplacing items such as keys, watch, pen ? ....

Total score ....

Scoring key — Any score over 40 means that you are reasonably organised (the higher the score, the more organised you are). Any score below 40 means that you are less organised (the lower the score the less organised you are). The above questionnaire was designed for the present study guide.

Role of conscientiousness

IMPORTANT IN PERSONALITY AND EDUCATION

In the study of personality there are a number of theories that present different perspectives, but almost all have a central role for conscientiousness, although it may not always be explicitly labelled as such (Wolfe & Johnson, 1995). Personality theorists such as Cattell, Eber and Tatsuoka (1985), and Costa & McCrae (1992), distinctly label one of the factors in their system as 'conscientiousness.' Other theorists such as Eysenck do not have a factor in their system labelled as conscientiousness, but the content of their system contains the same concept within larger factors. Questionnaires associated with these perspectives have been designed to assess responses to each personality trait including conscientiousness. A trait implies that there is a stable underlying disposition in a person that gives rise to consistent behaviours over time and across situations. As one of these central traits in personality, conscientiousness is manifest in behaviours that are planned, acted on promptly, follow rules, show evidence of industry, discipline and organisation. This does not imply that every individual is at either one end or the other of two dichotomous poles of conscientiousness. It is better to think of conscientiousness as a continuum where few people are at either extreme and most are at some point on either side but not too far away from the centre. Moreover, people may be more conscientious in some behaviours than in others. Nevertheless, conscientiousness has emerged as an important trait in human personality that serves well in explaining individual differences in people's behaviours.

It comes as no surprise therefore that the role of conscientiousness has been assessed in relation to educational achievement, and it has been found to be one of the important variables in predicting students' performance. In other words when students' conscientious behaviours are assessed, the results are likely to be good indicators of those who will perform best and worst in exams and course work. Empirical studies have demonstrated that this is indeed the case (for example, Wolfe & Johnson, 1995; Colquitt & Simmering, 1998). Some researchers have assessed a form of general conscientiousness that encompasses the full spectrum of life and have then used these scores to predict academic performance. Others prefer to assess conscientious behaviours that are exclusively and specifically related to academic settings. Students should certainly aim to cultivate behaviours that are characteristic of conscientiousness within the academic context.

REFLECTED IN OVERT BEHAVIOURS

In a university-based study we constructed a simple questionnaire that can be completed in about one or two minutes. The total score for each student's response to this measure can then be used to indicate where each student lies on the continuum of academic conscientiousness. In constructing the measure we first examined what personality theorists said about the construct of conscientiousness and all the features that represent it. We attempted to incorporate their range of indicators including planning, organisation, regularity, rules, industry etc. Second, we took these principles and applied them to students' application to study, lectures, assignments and exams. Third, we explored what students and lecturers thought were the important behaviours in optimising academic performance. In the fourth place we carefully worded the items (questions) so that there would be no ambiguities for respondents. Finally, we ran the study and analysed students' responses both in themselves and in relation to their subsequent academic performance. We found that each item elicited a range of differences in students' self-reported responses. We also found that students who reported higher levels of conscientiousness were more likely to achieve a higher standard in both course work and examinations. If you have had some experience in third level education, you may find it helpful to complete the following questionnaire (or complete it based on what you think you would do with reference to your past experience). You can then score yourself based on the guidelines given in order to ascertain where you currently lie on the continuum of academic conscientiousness. Moreover, you will be able to see particular weaknesses and be better equipped to address these.

Academic conscientiousness scale

Directions: The following are the kinds of statements students sometimes use to describe themselves. Read each one carefully and respond to all items by encircling the number which best describes you according to the following code (try to avoid using Neutral if possible):

1 = Strongly Agree   2 = Agree   3 = Slightly Agree   4 = Neutral   5 = Slightly Disagree   6 = Disagree   7 = Strongly Disgree

1. I go to work on my assignments immediately after learning what the [essay] titles are. .... *
2. I always plan my study time as a top priority. .... *
3. I never lag behind other students in my application to study. .... *
4. I have a well-established pattern of regular and consistent study. .... *
5. No matter how good my intentions are, I usually end up leaving revision until near exam [test] time. ....

6. I normally try to consolidate what I have learned as soon as possible after lectures. .... *

7. If I miss out on my study time, I immediately apply myself to making up for the lost time. .... *

8. I seldom work as hard at my studies as I intend to. ....

9. I can clearly see vast room for improvement in my application to academic study. ....

10. I make every effort to attend all scheduled academic sessions at university. .... *

Total Score ....

* Denotes items to be reversed in scoring. The code for reversing is as follows: $1 = 7$, $2 = 6$, $3 = 5$, $4 = 4$, $5 = 3$, $6 = 2$ and $7 = 1$. First reverse score all the items with an asterisk, and then add up your total score. If you have a score above 40 then you are on the 'right' end of the academic conscientiousness continuum. If however your score is below 40 then your are on balance toward the lower end of the continuum. The further away from the midpoint (that is, 40) of the scale you are then the closer you are to the extreme points of the continuum. The lowest possible score is 10 and the highest possible score is 70 (provided all questions were completed).

A methodical approach to study

In the 18th century the movement known as 'Methodism' had its origins under the leadership of John and Charles Wesley. These founding members and others combined as students at Oxford University to form what was called 'The Holy Club'. This was comprised of a small number of students who resolved to meet regularly and to discipline their lives for holy living. Among the practices they committed themselves to were prayer, fasting, study, meditation, acts of charity, prison visits, visits to the sick etc. It is alleged that other students who observed their behaviours nicknamed them, 'Methodists', because their lives were so methodical. Later the movement was to spread rapidly throughout the British Isles and over to America. The fruits of John Wesley's efforts are still evident today whereas other pioneering names of the same era are largely forgotten.

It is claimed that the secret of John Wesley's effectiveness was his personal discipline and his great ability to organise. For instance, he was able to capitalise on all the enthusiasm of the new converts by organising them into small lay groups and by mobilising lay people into active participation in religious services. He did this in spite of not having all the facilities of the established churches such as buildings and an ordained ministry.

The lesson from the story of Methodism is that lasting achievements can only be attained by planned, systematic effort and by a disciplined, organised, methodical approach to given tasks. No student is likely to be successful within the sphere of academia unless there is a concerted attempt to address study on a continual basis. An occasional binge on a study spree when the mood dictates is definitely not the pathway to success at university. Study may not always be full of joy and excitement but the end result will bring much satisfaction and the passport to a professional career. Moreover students will be able to acquire skills that will be of much use to them in their later career.

Illustration

It is reported that Queen Victoria once complimented the great violinist, Paganini, as a genius. His response was that he may have been a genius, but he was also a drudge. It is no surprise that he said this, given that he was alleged to have practised each bar of music 50 times over! The result of his drudgery was the beautiful melody that allowed him to play before a queen. It is reassuring to know that the times of drudgery at university will rapidly come to an end and that they are leading the student toward a definite goal.

TRAINING FOR YOUR FUTURE CAREER

Many students are prone to complain about the multiple pressures they have to endure and the looming deadlines they have to negotiate. However, students should also realise that life will not necessarily become a lot easier after graduation. The media frequently highlight the stress many professions such as nurses, doctors, teachers, civil servants etc.

are under. In many ways therefore university is about much more than acquiring a degree or diploma – the road to attaining a professional qualification helps develop the qualities that will enable efficient functioning within a professional environment.

Example

Take as a typical example the responsibilities entailed in managing a clothes shop. This is a very extensive role and entails co-ordinating a range of tasks combined with the careful management of personnel. Managers may be responsible for completing tasks themselves or ensuring that they are done. The following list is not necessarily exhaustive:

1. Monitoring stocks and ensuring a steady flow of supplies.
2. Observing stock that moves and stock that is static.
3. Dealing with customer complaints.
4. Keeping an eye on the competition.
5. Trying to accommodate staff requests – sickness, leave, holidays etc.
6. Always at the ready for 'drop-in' inspections from higher management.
7. Keeping abreast of security issues, theft etc.
8. Dealing with disciplinary problems such as staff who do not shoulder their responsibility.
9. Endeavouring to ensure that staff morale is kept high.
10. Keeping accounts up-to-date and presenting reports of progress to management.
11. Conducting interviews and making decisions based on fair employment legislation.
12. Preparing for the rigours of special sales days and extra opening hours.

When a graduate has spent a few years in a role such as the one described above, the pressures they were under at university may not look quite so bad! Remember that university will help to prepare you for the world of professional practice, but you will still be expected to continue to develop. A similar scenario to the above might be written for hotel management, computer sales, car sales, book sales, medical work, teaching etc.

Exercise — Matching current skills to future career

A. Write down about three occupations that would be your first preferred professions.

B. Make a list of the essential qualities for each job — think of the multiple roles you would have to play.

C. Make a list of the ways in which your university experience will help prepare you for these roles.

D. List how your 'failure' experiences at university may be beneficial to your future career experience.

Balancing your budget of time

PARALLELS WITH THE CHANCELLOR'S BUDGET

Illustration

The UK chancellor presents a budget each year in the month of March. This speech essentially consists of a parliamentary address that is both retrospective and prospective. The chancellor trumpets the achievements of his government since they took power and particularly over the previous year, and also maps out the course for future fiscal policy. Tough decisions have to be made that sometimes include increasing taxes directly or indirectly. Overall the aim is ostensibly to enable the nation to be more prosperous and for each family to improve their lot.

Every student should at various stages engage in a parallel exercise such as a periodic review. It is always good to do this at the end of the first semester after exam results are available. For example, you may need to look at why you have done so well in two subjects but poorly in another. Try to do some 'troubleshooting' to see if you can locate where the problem (s) is (are). Perhaps you have done well in exams but not in course work or vice-versa. At the end of the full academic year you will be able to compare your performance across two semesters. There is an adage that says that 'if it isn't broke, don't fix it'. If strategies are working for you, then stay with them, but some retrospective analysis may help you rectify debilitating weaknesses.

Exercise — Periodic review

Below is a simple graph that plots out fictitious course work marks and exam results for an undergraduate student in semesters 1 and 2 of year one. Subjects are labelled A,B,C (semester 1) and D,E,F (semester 2). Marks achieved were in the range of 38 to 85.

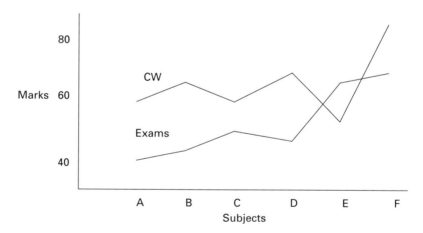

Figure 3.1 LINE GRAPH SHOWING EXAM AND COURSE WORK PERFORMANCE (CW) FOR 6 SUBJECTS OVER TWO SEMESTERS: ABC = SEMESTER 1. DEF = SEMESTER 2.

Questions:

✦ Is the student better at course work or exams?
✦ Has the student improved from semester 1 to semester 2?

- Should the slump in performance on course work at point E be a great cause for concern?
- How would you summarise the detailed trends overall in comparing within and between the two semesters with reference to both indexes of achievement?

LIMITED TIME TO EACH SEMESTER

Much activity is compressed into each academic semester, so there is no room for procrastination (which is said to be the thief of time). At the end of the academic year the student can enjoy a long break, and that will always come soon enough. An academic semester may only run over three months for teaching and one month for revision and exams. In each semester students may be expected to complete three full modules, each comprised of one or two items of course work and one test or examination. If there are six modules in an academic year this amounts to 18 pieces of work that are assessed (12 assignments and 6 exams). Since all these have to be completed within about an eight month period (this and the number of assignments and exams may vary from university to university), students need to learn to 'make hay while the sun is shining'. The opportunity to achieve goes as quickly as it comes. A two-edged sword of concerted effort and sound strategy should be applied. Some students always need to 'work harder' and others need to learn to 'work smarter' (a former advertising slogan). All students should be aware that they are battling against time. However, the strategies advocated throughout the book will help to keep anxiety under control and channel motivation into successful achievement.

THE DIVISION OF LABOUR

Self-perception theory claims that once individuals appropriate beliefs about themselves, they feel an unpleasant mental/emotional state of dissonance unless they act in a manner congruent with their beliefs (Aronson, Wilson & Akert, 1994). The up-side of this self-perception is that it can work in our favour if our self-beliefs are constructive and adaptive. For example, if students believe they can attain a good academic standard, then they will act accordingly. The down-side is that if students have negative self-perceptions they may entertain doubts about investing effort. They may, for instance, get fixated on the belief that they are good at course work but poor in exams or tests. Low expectation may lead to diminished investment of effort. Students should not therefore allow themselves to become fixated on such negative perceptions but should work toward developing all round abilities and skills. Labour needs to be divided between a whole range of academic activities including reading, listening, note-taking, consolidation, revision, interacting, computing, practical studies, maths/statistics and presentations. A key to success at university is to ensure that none of the range of required skills is left undeveloped but that every skill has been nurtured with care. Each student should give due attention to what they know is 'the weakest link' in their repertoire of skills.

TAKING TIME FOR LIVING

According to the late psychologist, Hans Eysenck (1998), extraverts love to party, to socialise, to be talkative and to be near others, even when they are studying. On the other hand, introverts prefer their own company and may spend much time in isolation with their books. He argues that a minority of people are at these two extremes but most of us are a mixture (that is, ambiverts) who are toward one side of the centre or the other between the two extremes. Either extreme in the continuum is not healthy for a student. This chapter has advocated the need for conscientiousness, industry, organisation, planning etc. However, when students leave university they should also be equipped with social and communication skills and with a settled awareness that they need friendships, breaks, fun and relaxation. Therefore it is vital that these provisions are factored into any disciplined regime.

Exercise and thought

It would be useful, at the end of each weekday, to take a moment to write a rough plan for the next day. Try to do this for a typical day at college, drafting out a plan that includes a lecture, lunch, library search, private study, rendezvous with friends, computing practice and some physical activity. For the evening you might want to plan time for preparing and eating a meal, relaxing with some music, recapping and revamping summary material that you have learned on the day and finishing with watching a video. This does not mean that each day necessarily has to be strictly regimented to the last minute, but on the other hand if you aim at nothing you have a good chance of hitting it! Planning can easily become a natural part of your daily behavioural repertoire.

Collating the study material

A FILING SYSTEM FOR EACH MODULE

From the outset of the new semester it is highly recommended that you acquire a folder or binder (according to personal preference) to file away all the notes, handouts and references for each module. If three modules are being taken then a separate folder should be used for each, and each folder should be clearly labelled and used exclusively for the material relevant to the labelled module. For further clarity of identification, the use of different colours for each folder would be advantageous. This makes it less likely that the 'wrong' study material will be lifted when rushing out in the morning. In addition the use of subject dividers would facilitate easy identification of a given topic within any module. Another useful practice is to list the range of topics at the beginning (or on the outside of the folder) in the sequence in which they are taught. A key to being well organised is getting into the habit of returning the material from each topic to its proper place after use.

A further aid to good referencing and efficient accessibility to study material is to keep a separate folder for course work and assignments. However, the same colour code can be used as the counterpart folder for a given module. All these practices will make the revision process a lot easier in terms of having all the material readily and easily available. Moreover, life will be made a lot easier in subsequent years when students inevitably need to refer back to their foundational studies.

BUILDING A SENSIBLE REPERTOIRE OF NOTES

For more detailed guidance on taking notes, refer to Chapter 2, 'Profiting from lectures, seminars and group work'. For now it is sufficient to observe that notes taken during lectures should not be filed away before being checked for clarity and comprehensiveness. This should be done as soon as possible after the lecture or else you will not be able to fill in the blanks and your memory of the words you cannot decipher will have dissipated. If a lot of material that has not been tidied up develops into a backlog, then much of important value will be lost from the lectures.

The process of building a reasonable repertoire of notes not only entails ensuring that they are clear and comprehensive, but also that the connected notes from diverse sources are collated within your filing system. For example, students accumulate notes from lectures, seminars, personal study at home, library textbooks, computer printouts, discussion groups and from keyword searches. Again it is essential to file these in the appropriate places. The full value of many study hours is often diminished because the notes taken from them have gone astray as they were not carefully filed away. When making notes, it is also essential to document the sources they are taken from. Make notes that include author, book title, year, library number, pages and publishers. Or if the article is from a journal then note author, article title, journal title, pages, volume number and library reference. These will be needed if the article is cited in an assignment or dissertation or if more information from the article is required or other supplementary references are needed.

USING PAST EXAM OR TEST PAPERS EARLY ON

Past exam or test papers are an invaluable source of information and no student who intends to achieve a good standard should ignore them. The university library should contain these and students will be permitted to borrow them on short-term loan so that they can be photocopied. Check with the tutor if any reference or library code is needed to trace the past papers. Also ask the tutor for guidance on how far back in time to go in using past papers. Some students convince themselves not to use these papers or to leave use of them until just prior to exams or tests. The second strategy is preferable to the first but the best strategy of all is to acquire a copy of the relevant papers at the beginning of each new semester and file them into the appropriate folders. Following this the relevant questions (for example, from the last five years) should be pondered over around the time that the lecturer addresses the corresponding topic. If students use this strategy they will get a clear feel for the kinds of questions that arise and the types of issues that emerge. They will also learn how to evaluate evidence and apply conclusions. Of course students should never bank on the same questions coming up again in an identical fashion, but they should practise the art of turning the subject over in their minds from a variety of angles. This kind of cognitive processing facilitates both good memory and sound understanding.

USING ASSIGNMENTS FOR EXAMS

Assignments are not completed under the same rigorous conditions as exams but they do require an enormous investment of effort. Students are expected to research the topic thoroughly, incorporate a good range of references, demonstrate an ability to engage in critical, analytical thinking and draw whatever conclusions and applications the essay title points to. Therefore it would be an extravagance to file the assignment away into unused archives after it has been assessed. Some researchers have claimed that material learned from course work is more likely to be recalled from long-term memory than material studied for tests. Students should ensure that they keep track of their assignments and make note of anything within them that is likely to be useful for exams. Moreover, past assignments may be useful for subsequent assignments and exams in later semesters and years. At the beginning of each new academic year, when given module outlines, it would be useful to have a cursory glance over assignments and revisions material from previous semesters and year(s).

Steps for handling difficult material

WHENEVER YOU GRIND TO A HALT

There will doubtless be times at university or college when students feel that their minds have run into a cul-de-sac. For example, an assignment may be required that is based on a journal article that is very difficult to comprehend and is replete with technical jargon that the author assumes the reader will be familiar with. There may be times when students face several problems like this simultaneously. Most students who have completed a course successfully can probably look back on times like these when they wondered if they would ever survive. In some ways a degree programme is like running a marathon – at particular junctures in the race, runners feel that they are at the end of their tether and the end appears a long way off. Some strength of character is required at these times, in the form of focusing on short-term and more immediate goals. Experienced runners know that they will get their 'second breath' and students should know that the 'gridlock' times pass and they soon get back into their regular flow.

COME BACK AGAIN WHEN FRESH

It is sometimes found that when a problem is slept on, the solution becomes clear the next morning. However, not all problems are solved overnight or in an instant. With some problems the solution only comes into focus gradually, like the emerging light in a dark room at dawning of a new day. Apparently intractable problems may only yield a solution after being addressed in a range of sessions with intervals between. It has been emphasised elsewhere in the book that the mind is like a machine in the sense that it needs 'resting for servicing and lubrication!' There comes a point in problem solving when the mind may feel saturated and at that point (or preferably before it) it is time to stop for a rest or to address a less exacting task. One of the keys to success at university is to allow sufficient time to address problems. If problematic exercises are left to the last possible moment, the recipe for underachievement is firmly in place.

DISMANTLE AND IDENTIFY KEY COMPONENTS

It may well be that upon returning to a problem, students will realise that their strategy for tackling it was wrong in the first instance. They may have tried to identify too many steps in the logical progression without seeing the connections between them. For example, trying to resolve the third stage of a problem without first grasping a key concept at stage two will frequently lead to confusion.

Learning a language

In learning a new language it is essential to learn the alphabet before attempting to master the vocabulary exercises. After that it would be useful to build some basic vocabulary before going on to attempt to translate simple sentences with subject, object and verb. Finally it might be easier to translate the new language into your native tongue before translating the other way round. Moreover, the best advice would be to read simple texts in the new language before attempting the more difficult works. This simple example illustrates the point that the correct steps should be followed in order to be able to solve the more complex problems. In short, troubleshooting means going back to the elementary principles in problems and identifying each component, and then tracing through the logical steps.

WORK THROUGH STEP BY STEP

On a church notice board some good words of advice were offered to passers-by: 'One step at a time – but keep on stepping!' Be prepared to work through your problems step by step but be prepared to be patient when you reach an impasse. Slowing down does not mean that you have stopped, it just means that you are preparing to accelerate again. Resolve that you will move on to the next phase of your problem once the deadlock is broken. In the game of golf, each player has to pot the ball into the designated hole before they can move on to the next nominated hole in the sequence. Sometimes professional players move very slowly through the holes but occasionally a ball goes astray into a bunker or the woods. In such instances they must patiently plot out in their minds how to get back on course with the minimum number of strokes. Aberrations like this may cost them the game unless they keep calm, avoid being rash and take whatever time is necessary to negotiate the hole successfully.

Two subjects that many students stumble over are statistics and mathematics. These subjects are often incremental in the way they have to be learned and it is therefore vital to understand each step in a process that leads to a solution. Therefore Chapters 6 and 7 in the book are devoted to the kinds of problems students may face in these disciplines and strategies for working through them are suggested.

BALANCE WITH MATERIAL THAT IS WELL KNOWN

When someone has toothache, they do not focus on the fact that the rest of their body is functioning well and is pain free! Whenever students run into an apparently intractable academic problem they may not naturally focus on the wide variety of problems they have previously mastered. Nevertheless that is precisely a good starting point to help bring an anxious mind under control. Moreover, in relation to the problem itself, it is always wisest to work from what is known toward what is not known. Going over points previously mastered will give a confident feeling of reassurance. Temporarily leaving a problem to one side is not an admission of defeat. In addition, in some subjects a good working knowledge can be acquired without necessarily comprehending every aspect of the subject. For example, you do not have to understand every word in a news broadcast to have a good grasp of the news content. Neither is it necessary to understand every rule of English grammar, and every exception to rules, in order to use the language effectively. In a nutshell, when students are frustrated at reaching an impasse in their studies, they should reassure themselves with the knowledge they already have, and work toward solutions from this knowledge base.

Preparing for revision

Preparation for revision essentially begins at the commencement of each new semester. Think of preparation as being like a bank account where money is deposited at regular intervals so that when the time comes it can be drawn out for the desired purpose such as a holiday. Take a lesson from squirrels that store up nuts for the winter and then have the benefits of previous labour at a time when food is scarce. It was previously suggested that past test papers are useful for alerting students to the issues that should be noted in preparation for exams. When these issues are embedded as a back-cloth in students' minds, the 'antennae' will be naturally attuned to important issues raised in lectures and seminars.

House construction

Whenever a new house is being built to specification for purchasers, the prospective occupants will pop round at various stages of construction to see how the work is progressing. Some like to take photographs at each stage so that they can later trace the development with friends at a house-warming party. There is no comparison when guests look around at the fully furnished house and then see a photograph of the bare foundation! The photographs are sometimes presented as slides to illustrate the gradual evolution toward the finished article. First, there is the brickwork to provide a basic shell and to this plumbing, joinery, electrical work, plastering, doors, windows, roof, tiles, floors, paint-work etc are gradually added. After all this is completed, the finishing touches provided by carpet, furniture and decoration make an enormous improvement. Clearly the beautiful edifice had to come through a gradual evolution before guests could be entertained within it!

Likewise when a student first looks at past examination papers, there is a considerable journey to take before they arrive at a position where they could do justice to the issue in a test or exam. They have to listen to the relevant lectures and reproduce the material in their own notes. Then they need to interact with others in seminars and reinforce what they have learned by reading books and periodicals. In addition they are required to discriminate between central and peripheral issues and to try to envisage various twists and turns in questions that might emerge in an exam. If students build up exam material steadily throughout the semester, by the time the test comes round, they will be ready to deliver the completed product with all the finishing touches!

SALIENT POINTS AND EXTENDED MATERIAL

The human skeleton

The essential structure in the human body is the skeleton. Bones serve a variety of vital functions and these include:

- Giving the body shape and stability.
- Protecting vital organs.
- Facilitating movement.
- Forming a foundation to which flesh can be attached.

Whenever students commit themselves to forming their subject matter into headings and subheadings, these become like the bones that will be used to address exam and essay questions. In a test these points serve to get you started and to settle your nerves in that they become the initial notes for your rough work. They also become the memory joggers you will need in order to elicit the more detailed information from memory archives. In addition they offer you protection in that they stop you 'freezing' on the spot and assist in getting your mind activated. They also preserve you from wandering aimlessly in your thoughts and writing. Finally they form the basis for a structured response to questions although you can vary the order and the emphasis according to the manner in which the question is worded.

Exercise — Public transport

Think of how you would write a letter that draws attention to
problems associated with your local public transport system.
Commend the good points and suggest improvements. See if you can think
of five aspects that need improvement and five aspects that are satisfactory. Imagine that
you later have to meet with your local council to discuss the issues you have raised more
fully. Consider how the outline points you have drafted up will then be used as a basis for
developing your arguments. Useful hint — for an exam it is best to be ready to note down
each point briefly (in a word or two) as rough work that can be expanded upon later.

USEFUL PHRASES AND WORDS

In an exam or test it should be the aim of students to convince the examiner that they
are the master of the subject. Therefore students should ensure that they become conversant with all the important words associated with the subject. If there are important researchers' names associated with the development of the topic then aim to
engage in all the right 'name dropping'. For example, if writing about the discovery of
penicillin it would be bizarre to omit the name of its discoverer Fleming. Under each
topic in the filing system, students should list all the important terms and names.
These can then be jotted down as part of rough work in an exam. It is an art form to
learn to weave all these skilfully together into an exam essay without making their
inclusion look disjointed, abrupt, intrusive or irrelevant. Some examiners will be very
keen to see if you have used material that is up-to-date. This is the kind of thing that
helps put the finishing touches on your masterpiece! Therefore, use up-to-date material if it is available.

Exercise — A familiar topic

Select any topic that you are quite familiar with and make a list
of all the key words and important names that are associated with it. Are
the origins of the topic associated with a particular name? Can you trace how the
topic has developed chronologically? Are you aware of the most recent research?

Can you think of how the topic may be applied to 'real life'? In what different ways might you be questioned in an exam about this topic? How have questions from previous papers been framed? Are there controversies associated with the topic that would need to be thrashed out in an exam setting?
(Note: Once writing has commenced, a flood of useful memories is often activated.)

SUMMARY

♦ Nothing of durable value in academia can be achieved without adequate planning and organisation.

♦ Ability without sound strategy and concerted commitment leads to unrealised potential.

♦ Learning to manage academic pressures helps develop qualities that make students employable.

♦ In order to maximise potential, students should learn time management strategies and tactics for the division of labour.

♦ Plotting out previous exam or test performance and course work results provides an effective diagnostic tool for troubleshooting.

♦ Fun and friendship times allows the mind to rejuvenate itself.

♦ An efficient filing system that is appropriately colour-coded and labelled is a useful prerequisite for an effective study strategy.

♦ Simple problem solving strategies should be held in readiness for times of impasse in study.

♦ Procrastination is the thief of time — always allow sufficient time to work through unforeseen problems that may arise.

4 Computers — Friends not Foes

KEY CONCEPTS

● COMPUTERS IN EDUCATION ● COMPUTERPHOBIA ● ATTITUDES AND BEHAVIOURS ● BACKGROUND IMPLICATIONS ● COMPUTER TERMINOLOGY ● SYMBOLS AND KEYS ● MOUSE, KEYBOARD AND SCREEN ● COMPUTING ADVANTAGES ● WORD PROCESSING ● INTERNET ● EMAIL ● BASIC ICONS ● MENU ● ELECTRONIC SEARCHES

Problems with perceptions

GROWING USE OF COMPUTERS IN EDUCATION

It has been suggested with some justification that information and communication technology is beginning to form the basis of extensive educational reform around the world (Selwyn, 2000). Given that computers are extensively used in occupational and educational settings (Colley, Gale & Harris, 1994), college students will not be exempted from the growing revolution in computing that has swept the modern world. Some students may come to university with the advantage of previous experience and even expertise in computing. Others may have little or no background experience and may have to spend a period of time 'playing catch-up'. This may not necessarily be a large disadvantage if some confidence building measures are appropriated, and research has indicated that some computer users develop worse attitudes to computers after engaging in difficult computer courses (Simpson, Premeaux & Mondy, 1986).

For some college students, minimal interaction with computers is their chosen route from the beginning of their course. It is, however, becoming difficult to resist the technological revolution in education, and all students should decide not to place themselves at a disadvantage through reticence in developing computing skills. For example, maximum benefit from using the library is forfeited by the failure to use the electronic facilities that are provided. Moreover, some universities in the USA specify that students are required to own a personal computer (Brosan, 1998).

Excercise — Initial confidence building

Below is a list of items — requiring computer-like skills — that you may have had some practise in using. Tick any items you have used before — it may surprise you to realise that you already possess skills that are readily adaptable to computer use. Sometimes such items are employed so regularly that users forget that they had to go through a learning process to use them effectively. This exercise should reassure you that you have already taken some steps toward acquiring computer skills.

Video recorder	....	Calculator	....
DVD player	....	Automatic Teller Machine	....
TV remote control	....	Mobile phone (& text)	....
Microwave oven	....	Alarm clock/watch	....
House alarm system	....	Domestic heating controls	....

EVIDENCE FOR WIDESPREAD COMPUTERPHOBIA

According to Pancer, George and Gebotys (1992) substantial numbers of people have expressed their anxieties and apprehensions about living in a computerised society. This may have serious repercussions for them given that 'the advent of computers is having important implications in the job market and in the field of education' (Levin & Gordon, 1989: 69). That statement is even more pertinent in the second decade after it was originally written. There is still a large volume of evidence to indicate that computerphobia hasn't gone away. Furthermore, the problem is so widely recognised that a number of self-report measures have been designed in order to elicit and pinpoint the exact levels and type of technophobia that respondents suffer from. It has been estimated that one-quarter to one-third of the general population suffer from some form of computerphobia (Brosan & Davidson, 1994). University students do not appear to have fared much better than the general population, with estimates of around 25 per cent of students reporting some degree of technophobia (Weil & Rosen, 1995).

It should be emphasised that computerphobia is not generally deemed to be a clinical condition or to be associated with a personality disorder. However, the state can range from mild to extreme and may relate either to anxious feelings or cognition or both (Brosan, 1998). Sometimes the term 'technophobia' is used interchangeably with 'computerphobia'. The problem associated with computer anxiety or negative perceptions about computers is that these attitudes or anxieties may restrict or thwart computer use. According to Paxton and Turner (1984), negative attitudes toward computers are more likely to lead to slower learning of computer tasks and more errors. Moreover, when these maladaptive attitudes are associated with high anxiety they may result in minimal involvement in or total avoidance of computing activity. However, for those totally new to computing it should be remembered that many activities engaged in for the first time generate an understandable anxiety that later subsides with practise (see Exercise below).

Exercise — Reassurance

In order to encourage you to overcome any negative or anxious attitudes you may have associated with the use of computers, see if you can list any other practices which initially generated some anxiety but have subsided with practice (for example, first time flying).

1..

2..

3..

FACTORS ASSOCIATED WITH COMPUTERPHOBIA

It would be foolish to be dogmatic about the precise causal mechanism implicated in the development of negative computing cognition and anxiety. Nevertheless, a growing body of empirical literature has demonstrated that a number of background factors are consistently associated with the development of maladaptive computing attitudes and behaviours (McIlroy, Bunting, Tierney & Gordon, 2001). For example, a user's first experience at the computer appears to be associated with the subsequent development of computing attitudes and behaviours. When respondents are asked the simple question, 'was your first experience with the computer positive or negative?', the answer is frequently indicative of their current computer phobia level. Second, whether respondents have regular access to and use of a computer at home also appears to be associated with positive attitudes and less anxiety toward computing than those who do not have such access. This may be because users are developing their confidence in non-evaluative conditions. Therefore taking these two elements together, computing attitudes and behaviours may be more likely to be adaptive if users can counteract negative initial experiences and if they can practise computing regularly in an environment in which they are not being assessed.

Another factor associated with the development of computerphobia relates to the person who introduced the user to computing (Brosan, 1998). If the person appears to be confident, competent and approachable this may mediate the development of good attitudes and practice for students. However, a teacher who appears diffident, incompetent and unapproachable may inadvertently assist in mediating the anxiety and negative perceptions that are a disincentive to learning computing. Students who feel that they have had this kind of 'computer baptism' should at least take some heart from the fact that part of the problem may not be attributable to them, and there is scope within the learning process to change their maladaptive attitudes and practices.

COMMON MYTHS ABOUT COMPUTERPHOBIA

Myths often have a self-generating and self-propagating dynamic that leaves them resistant to extinction even in the face of hard evidence. For example, it was earlier noted that students report almost as much computerphobia as the general population – some readers may have found this startling. Another common myth is that females are more computerphobic than males. Although females often do report higher levels of anxiety and negative perception than males, these apparent differences frequently disappear when past experience or current regularity of use is controlled for (Dyck & Smither, 1994). Moreover, mature students may feel that they have a greater disadvantage to younger students in using computers at college, but the empirical evidence demonstrates that younger students are just as likely to be technophobic (Rosen & Maguire, 1990). The problem with these myths is that students can see themselves as belonging to one of the disadvantaged groups and may consequently believe that they are inevitably destined to become poor computer users.

Changing negative perceptions

STEPS TO REDUCE ANXIETY AND NEGATIVE PERCEPTIONS

The first step is to be convinced that attitudes and perceptions can be changed, and the fact that an anxious person is reading this may be an indication of some level of belief in the possibility of change! A second aid to change is the willingness to wait and allow for the fact that change takes time. In the third place, it is encouraging that research has demonstrated that diffident and nervous students can become confident computer users (Wilson, 1999). Fourth, it is important to be convinced of the benefits of computing to a degree or diploma programme, and students should also realise that the acquisition of computing skills will make them more employable. Finally, it is useful to remember that a good working knowledge of computers does not necessitate knowing all there is to know about them. No one should be put off by observing the 'whiz kids' who appear to have limitless reservoirs of computing knowledge. Computing practice does not have to become an addiction to be useful, but a satisfactory command of computers does require a regular commitment and investment of work.

NO SUBSTITUTE FOR PRACTICE

One apparently alarming finding is that some users become more negative in their computing attitudes after a course than they were beforehand (Barrier & Margavio, 1993)! However, we have already suggested that inadequate teachers may be implicated in these problems. Furthermore, another important factor is the kind of course engaged in. For instance, the above researchers found that negativity was more likely to be engendered by computer programming courses than by more basic courses. At university the first introduction to computing is often as a component of some other discipline such as statistics and research methods. Statistics is a discipline that is in itself associated with high anxiety in many students (Onwuegbuzie & Daley, 1999). Students should therefore learn to try to dissociate computing from other factors that might be a dynamic trigger for their anxiety.

It is essential for students who are anxiety prone to acquire the right kind of experience in learning computing. Research has shown that those who have regular access to a computer outside of the university situation are more likely to develop positive attitudes and less anxiety in computing than those who do not. This may well be because those students who have regular access have opportunity to practise computing under non-evaluative conditions. In private, students are not being assessed and can therefore make as many mistakes as they please without the fear of embarrassment that may exist in a class situation. However, with others the fear of losing their way without recourse to immediate help may further extend their worries to private computing practise.

GETTING FAMILIAR WITH TERMINOLOGY

In learning any new subject there is always some new jargon to be mastered. When a lot of new terms are heard for the first time in one teaching session this can induce considerable anxiety. Within computing tutorials there may be a proliferation of new terms and students may feel overwhelmed at first. However, it is again the case that a computer can be used effectively without the user understanding all the terms, although it is advantageous to know the basics.

Exercise — Coming to terms with terminology

In your first few computer classes make a note of all the terms that are new to you, and gradually learn the meaning of each, one-by-one, between classes. Familiarity with terms will reduce anxiety and build a good platform for further learning. Learning will be more readily facilitated if you work with a friend in setting targets for learning together. Try to explain the terms to each other.

Have a look at the list of words contained in the box below – put a tick on the dotted line next to each term if you are familiar with it, and another tick if you can give a satisfactory explanation for it. After a few weeks in computer classes you might be pleasantly surprised at how many terms you have accumulated.

Exercise – Testing familiarity with jargon

Place a tick at the familiar terms and a double tick if you can explain the term.

Floppy disk ....   Hard drive ....   Screen ....   Mouse ....   Keyboard ....

Toolbar ....   Menu ....   Right click ....   Icon ....   Help system ....

Highlight ....   Copy and Paste ....   Delete ....   Save to disk ....   Window ....

Memory ....   Spell check ....   Desktop ....   Grammar check ....   Dialog box ......

Word count ....   Double click ....   Click and drag ....   Function keys ....

Export and Import ....   Arrow keys ....   Return key ....   Space bar ....

Tab ....   PC (Personal Computer) ....   Filename ....   Website ....

CONTROLLING THE KEYBOARD

The three main components that need to be mastered for competent computing practice are the keyboard, the screen and the mouse. Those who have completed an introductory word processing course have an advantage in relation to familiarity with the keyboard. The keyboard is comprised of all the letters of the alphabet, the numbers 0 to 9, and a series of special function keys (F1 to F12). In addition there is a return key (with a right angled line and an arrow), a space bar (long bar below the alphabet keys), a tab key with two arrows pointing in opposite directions and two shift keys with arrows pointing upwards. There is also a cluster of four arrow keys pointing in four directions and a series of keys above these for 'insert', 'delete', 'home', 'end', 'page up' and 'page down'. A few other important keys are 'control' and 'alt', and a delete key on the same line as the number keys is identified by a single arrow that points toward them. Students should learn where each of these is located, but should also understand that some keys will be more frequently used than others and some may never be used.

In some ways learning to type efficiently is like learning to play the piano – after some practise, the learner can 'feel' where the keys or notes are located without looking. Another illustration is entering a dark but familiar room, where with practise the light switch can be easily located even in the dark.

Below is a brief description of the various keys:

Example

Space bar — for creating a space between words (if one too may
is inserted use the left arrow key to get back).

Return key — for new lines, paragraphs or spaces between paragraphs.

Number keys — for adding numbers in the text file when word-processing or in a
grid-like data file.

Arrow keys — for ease of quick movement around the file in all directions.

Control (hold down) and home — to reach the top of the file rapidly.

Control (hold down) and end — to reach the bottom of the file rapidly.

Page Up and Page Down — to scroll up and down the file in blocks.

Control and Shift (hold down) and Arrow keys — to highlight more than one line
of text.

Click and drag on mouse (left button) — to highlight one word or line or more.

Caps Lock — to set all text for capitals (or upper case). Press again to return to
lower case.

Tab key — to indent text (for example, at the beginning of a paragraph) or to move
across file in 'jumps' at set intervals. This key is also useful for moving from cell to
cell in a table.

Shift key — To insert one upper case letter at a time or to use the upper symbol on
any key that has two symbols.

Escape key (top left) — allows the user to 'escape' from screens such as Print
Preview to revert back to working file.

Function keys (F1 to F12) — Different packages may have specific applications for
these, but most users prefer the alternative of the pull down menus on the screen.

Dual function keys — Some keys have two symbols, one in the lower half and the
other in the upper half (for example, a question mark [?] in the upper half and a
forward slash [/] in the lower half). Almost all the symbols will be recognisable on
sight but users can always try inserting them on the screen for practise. The keyboard will be set by default to the lower symbol, and holding down the shift key
enables access to the upper symbol.

THE TAMING OF THE MOUSE

The next component to master for acquiring computing expertise is the small move-able instrument known as the mouse, which is attached to the computer by a long lead and is placed alongside the keyboard on a pad. It has two buttons, right and left, which are used by a single click, a double click and by click, hold and drag (click and drag). The mouse controls the 'cursor' (flashing line or arrow) on the screen, which can be moved or dragged around by clicking or clicking and dragging on the left button on the mouse. The user can rest the cursor over the place where the next insertion is to be made. A right click will bring up a menu on the screen that allows the user to cut, copy, paste etc. but the left button is the one most frequently used. For example it is used for entering a package initially by clicking on an icon at the 'Desktop' (that is, the range of icons on the screen) or by going into 'Start' and then 'Programmes'. It is also used for entering existing files on the hard drive or floppy disk, and for pulling down menus and executing commands. Moreover, as previously indicated, the user can click and drag on the left button to highlight text. When text has been highlighted it can be deleted, moved, copied and pasted, changed to different font size or changed to bold, italics, underline etc.

Sometimes a double click in quick succession is required in order to activate a partic-ular command – for example, accessing a word processing package using the icon on the desktop. The simple golden rule to remember is that the user can try one click first and if this doesn't work then try the double click. However, users should be patient as some commands take longer than others. A little symbol that looks like an egg timer indicates that the command is active. The click and drag facility will allow students to move blocks of text around in their word processing document. 'Copy and paste' will allow the user to copy and transfer text, after highlighting, into another document, such as an assignment where its relevance is deemed appropriate. References can be copied and pasted in the same way, and this procedure will save much time as the course progresses.

NAVIGATING THE SCREEN

Finally, the third aspect of the computer to be negotiated is the screen or monitor. The most popular format is 'Windows' and this is very 'user friendly'. Computing is now much simpler because users do not have to learn complex commands to achieve their object. Ironically, users may learn much by making mistakes and finding solutions to these. Moreover, there is a Help system available and this is usually located on the menu at the top of the screen under 'Help'.

In the Windows format there is a 'Menu' at the top of the screen that will have a range of words such as 'File', 'Edit', 'View', 'Insert', 'Format' and 'Tools'. By resting the cursor on any one of these and then by a left click (all clicks referred to from now on will be left clicks unless otherwise stated) the user can access the contents for each menu. The required command can then be located and clicked. It would require a lengthy article to describe the function of each of these but users should browse over them from time to time to be aware of the potential that is available. Many users only employ a small range of the facilities available to them, but some practise by trial and error will repay the effort and add to the repertoire of computer knowledge. However, this point demonstrates that minimal knowledge is required for a basic working knowledge of the computer.

In addition to the basic menu there are also a few 'Toolbar' options that allow the user to execute commands by clicking on the appropriate symbol. In a good package users should be able to rest the cursor on the targeted icon and a word will appear to describe the function of that icon. The beauty of modern computers is that users do not need to wade through heavy instruction manuals before they can begin to use them efficiently. Everything that is needed is literally at the user's fingertips by resting the cursor on the targetted menu or icon, by trial and error and by use of the Help system. Help systems sometimes provide users with mini-tutorials and allow them to ask specific questions on a single issue. Moreover, once some general principles are learned they can be easily adopted and applied to other computing packages. For instance the Windows format has many common features across a range of different packages.

If a required tool bar is not visible on the screen it can become available by clicking on 'View' and then 'Toolbars' on the main menu. Toolbars can be switched on and off as required. Another facility in a good word processing package is a little toolbar for drawing at the bottom of the screen. If not available then click on 'View' and then 'Toolbar' followed by 'Drawing'. This will allow the user to draw circles, ellipses, rectangles, lines, lines with arrows, clip art etc. Simply click on the symbol and draw as required. Each time a new symbol or line is drawn there must be a new click for each one. Some examples are given below:

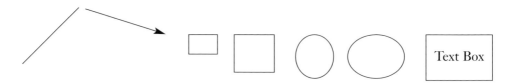

These symbols can be elongated by highlighting within the symbol, resting the cursor on the line and dragging to the required length. Try this out using the examples above. It is also possible to type text into a box as in 'text box' above. This is done after clicking on the symbol for text at the bottom bar and then clicking inside the targeted object. If the end product is not acceptable, the drawing can simply be highlighted, deleted and re-created. With some imagination the drawing symbols can be used to brighten up a dull textual presentation and make producing documents more satisfying. Text can also be coloured (only if a coloured printer is available) by highlighting the targeted text, and then clicking on 'Format' followed by 'Borders and Shading'. Take the option for 'Shading' and then click on the chosen colour, and then 'OK' this either for Text or Paragraph.

Exercise — Locating utilities

See if you can locate within the text menu the following functions (all of which will be of use for essays, assignments or presentations).

Word count	Toolbars	Bullet points	Draw table	Spelling and grammar		Select all
Paste	Paragraph	Page layout	Font	Header and footer	Copy	Print

A good word processing package will show up spelling mistakes as they are made by underlining them in red. If the cursor is positioned over the mis-spelled word and the right button on the mouse is clicked, the correct spelling will appear on the screen (sometimes several options appear). The user can then rest the cursor over the correct spelling and left click on the mouse. This will automatically change the mistake to the correct spelling. Try out the examples below (deliberately mis-spelled) and you can add some of your own if you wish.

Exercise — Spelling corrections

Correct the following spelling mistakes if you have a package that identifies them by red underlining. Rest the cursor over each word in turn and right click. Choose the correct spelling that appears and then left click.

Particualar	Objerct	Accomodate	Sysytem	Avalable	Knowlege	Sissors
Reticance	Sanguiine	Beatifc	Exploidt	Xenphobia	Infidality	Percentege

However, packages may be set either for American or Anglicised forms of spelling and this should be taken into account when looking at some spelling corrections (for example, center or centre, rationalize or rationalise). A facility to change from one language to the other can be found under 'Tools' and then 'Language'.

Another useful provision for students is the grammar check. When sentences are poorly or inaccurately constructed grammatically, they are underlined in green (or a particular word that should be changed is underlined in green). When the user right clicks over the underlined sentence or word, an alternative structure will be suggested on the screen. A left click over the suggested structure will then correct the mistake in the original sentence, or it may be preferable to reconstruct the sentence in another form. Sometimes the computer will merely indicate that it has no suggestions except that the sentence is very long. In this instance the user should consider devising two or more sentences as an alternative. As a simple exercise try typing in the following short sentences to see the green underline appear on the screen. Try to reconstruct the sentence following the procedures outlined above.

Exercise — Grammatical reconstruction

Reconstruct the following sentence using the grammar check on the computer:

1. We have went to that place many times before.
2. The two groups is at loggerheads with one another.
3. All that glitters is not gold, often has you heard this told.
4. I could speak properly when I was a children.

The spell check and grammar check are invaluable for students, as is the word count for keeping a check on essay length where word limits have been imposed. In order to ascertain the word count for text only (without references) then the text alone should be highlighted before the word count is requested.

USING THE COMPUTER FOR FUN

Research has demonstrated how some users become more negative about computing after completing a computer course than they were before the course began (Barrier & Margavio, 1993). The researchers suggested that the problematic attitudes may have developed because of what the computer course was associated with – for example, programming, statistics, mathematics, tests etc. Therefore it may be helpful to use the computer for some fun and light-hearted practise. This should not be restricted to computer games, but developed through experimenting with the icons, the graphics etc. and working on making presentations attractive. Another practice that can incorporate some fun is email (see later). A network of funny emails is always available and these frequently circulate around friends.

In addition to fun there can also be the sense of satisfaction that emerges from adding new abilities to basic computer knowledge, and discovering quicker ways of achieving objectives. Generally it is helpful to associate the computer with some fun, satisfaction, a lot of usefulness and a sense of having some control over the machine. However, it is important that the benefits derived from the fun times should be adapted to extend to the more serious computing practice. For example, some students who were comfortable with computer games, videos, cash machines etc. reported computerphobia in other domains (Weil & Rosen, 1995).

Recognising the benefits

ADVANTAGES OF WORD PROCESSING

Some of the advantages of word processing – access to spell check, grammar check and word count – have already been highlighted in this chapter. Another large advantage is that sentences and paragraphs can be moved around within the document by using the cut and paste facility, found under 'Edit' in the top menu bar. The text that is to be moved should be highlighted or selected by pressing, holding and dragging the left button on the mouse, and then this text (drawing or table) can be 'Cut' by using the icon for scissors in the icon bar at the top of the screen. Alternatively, 'Edit' and 'Cut' may be selected. The cursor should then be rested at the place where the moved object is to be inserted, the icon for 'Paste' (clipboard with script folded in corner) should then be clicked or use the procedure that allows you to click on 'Edit' and then 'Paste'. If the text is to be copied and pasted, there are again at least two routes that can be chosen. One is to work within 'Edit' after highlighting the targeted object, and the other is to work through the icons – the icon for 'Copy' is two scripts folded in the top right corner. A third possibility for cutting, copying and pasting is to use 'Control and X' for cutting, 'Control and C' for copying and 'Control and V' for pasting.

A further advantage for students in word processing is that neat presentations can be easily achieved and these can, if required, be worked at after all the typing is completed so that concentration is not diverted from essay content and structure. Users can play around with font size, headings, bold, italics, bullet points, line spacing, colour shading, underline, drawings, indentation etc. Moreover, even when radical changes have to be made to an assignment, the student does not have to start re-writing the whole script. In addition whole paragraphs and sections that are directly relevant can be imported from other essays, as can references.

TABULAR PRESENTATIONS OF DATA

Tables are easy to create within a word processing package, and if there are to be a lot of them, then much time is saved by means of the copy and paste procedure. The following example was drawn in Microsoft Word. To reproduce this example, click 'Table' at the top and then 'Insert Table'. Change the column and row settings to four and four, and then click OK. The table will then appear on the screen at the point where the cursor was flashing. The cursor can then be moved from cell to cell within the table by clicking or using the Tab key. If required, some words can be typed in the cells and numbers in other cells (as in the example below). Also practise 'stretching the lines' (by click, hold and drag on a targeted line) in order to make the cells for text a little larger. Also note that the text and data for Mean, Mode and Median have been centred in their respective columns. This can be done by highlighting all these and using the 'Centre' icon (the symbol with parallel lines that is close to the icons for bold, italic and underline).

When the table is satisfactorily completed, labelled and titled, the grid-like format below (Table 4.1) can be changed into a more presentable one. Simply click within the table and go to 'Table' in the menu. Click on 'Table AutoFormat' and select whichever one you prefer after you have looked through the options. The table presented in Table 4.2 is the first one available and is a popular choice.

Make sure that the tables are appropriately labelled and titled. If the table needs to be reproduced a number of times be sure to use 'Copy' and 'Paste'. This is a very useful approach when identical tables have to be reproduced a number of times. However, it is sometimes better to use copy and paste tables before using 'Table AutoFormat', because the lines might need to be adjusted. It is not difficult to imagine how much time and effort can be saved in compiling a report that includes a lot of data presented in many tables. Other forms of graphical presentation include pie charts, bar charts,

Table 4.1   AVERAGE YEARLY SALARY FOR COMPANY EMPLOYEES

	Mean	Mode	Median
Middle-management	£35,000	£34,000	£34,500
Shop-floor workers	£18,000	£20,000	£19,000
Clerical and administrative staff	£20,000	£22,000	£21,000

Table 4.2   AVERAGE YEARLY SALARY FOR COMPANY EMPLOYEES

	Mean	Mode	Median
Middle-management	£35,000	£34,000	£34,500
Shop floor workers	£18,000	£20,000	£19,000
Clerical and administrative staff	£20,000	£22,000	£21,000

histograms and scatterplots. Some of these can be created within a word processing package but may be better created within a statistical package (where all the data are stored) and then imported.

Practical hint

If the data file is opened over the word processing file — while the latter remains open — the graph can be created and edited within the data file. If the targeted graph or plot is then edited and highlighted, the data file can then be temporarily closed by moving it to the bottom of the screen. This can be done by clicking on the '_' symbol at the top right corner of the screen. The word processing file is then available on the screen, and the graph or plot can be pasted into the text file where the cursor is flashing and the file can then be saved. Ensure that all editing, titles and labelling have been completed before the transition is initiated.

TIME SAVING CALCULATIONS

In their first year at college students are often given lengthy calculations to work through for practise. This is a strategy that is designed to help develop fluency and confidence in numerical skills. Students may also be tested in exams in their ability to work through the calculations, although examiners are often more interested in seeing if logical step-by-step processes are followed and they will make allowances for some mistakes (the use of a calculator is normally permitted). They may be required to draw histograms based on given frequencies or to work their way through a chi-square calculation. Sometimes students may be required to work their way through the formulae and calculations for a statistical test such as a t-test or correlation. At a later stage they may look back and wonder why they had to go to all this trouble when these calculations can be done in seconds by a few clicks on the mouse! However, those who have been through both processes learn to value the computer for calculations and would never go back to the old style of tedious, laborious, painstaking hand calculations that were prone to errors at any rate. Nevertheless, any efforts made to learn the principles that lie behind statistical calculations done on the computer would pay dividends for the investment. According to Zeidner (1991), many college courses include a Statistics and Research Methods Module, so learning the procedures for statistical calculations may not be an optional extra for many, and the computer will make the process much easier than doing them by hand. Even degree programmes that are not heavily laden with statistics, may require students to conduct a statistical analysis in their final year project and this may have a bearing on their degree classification.

Simple steps to using the Internet

WIDE RANGE OF USES

Increasing numbers of people from diverse backgrounds are using the Internet on their home personal computer (PC) for shopping, booking holidays, booking travel, ordering goods, tracing required items, browsing websites, keeping up to speed with changes etc. If a user already has some experience with the Internet then the transition to university use should be straightforward. On the other hand if students have no experience in using the Internet, they should rest assured that they can learn the essentials very quickly. There is no need to wade through large manuals before beginning, as students can learn very quickly by practise. Some things are learned when a particular object is being searched for, but others may be learned quite inadvertently. Students should beware of getting side-tracked into time-consuming pursuits when time at the lab computer is restricted. Try to keep a healthy balance between searching for personal interests for fun and pursing material important for assignments.

CONSULT THE LIBRARY FOR TRAINING COURSES

The library at your college should provide you with leaflets about the electronic facilities available to you. They may also provide you with short training courses, which you will have to book to attend. In the initial tour of the library for new students, you will be given some basic information for obtaining books, locating journals, using photocopying machines etc. However, this will not be adequate for all your needs and you will be expected to build on the basic information you are given. Ensure that you attend any relevant course you are offered and always practise any practical directions that are given. If you haven't already done so, try out the exercises suggested under the library section of Chapter 3, 'Cultivating Organisational Skills'.

WORKING TOGETHER WITH A FRIEND

When two or more students agree about a time and place to meet in order to carry out some task, the task is more likely to be accomplished because a planned commitment has been made. This procedure will help all parties to articulate what they have learned and to receive constructive feedback from each other. It also means that the workload has been divided and time will be saved. On top of this, mutual weaknesses can be identified and corrected, and strengths can be underlined and reinforced. If a particular student has a tendency to be anxious at computer practise then he or she should work with someone they feel compatible with.

IN SEARCH OF YOUR OBJECT

One of the first things to locate in relation to the Internet is your university's 'Home Page'. This should be immediately accessible at library computers and perhaps lab computers by double clicking on an icon such as Internet Explorer. Once at the Home Page, the user has potential access to all the information about the university. There will be a number of headings such as 'Courses', 'Research', 'Staff' etc. If you are considering applying to a particular university, the section on courses will be of special interest. For students already at university, staff contact details may be of primary importance. Under this or a similar heading students will find room numbers, phone numbers and email addresses of staff members.

Prospective applicants not yet enrolled at university can also access the full range of information about a university by locating the appropriate Home Page. After clicking on the icon in the computer 'desktop' (that is, the range of icons for packages and short-cuts on the screen), the next step is to type in the university's website address in the address bar (Universal Resource Locator, or 'URL'), and then press the return key. If the precise address is not known then click on the facility marked 'Search'. You will then be able to type in whatever you know of the university – for example, 'Spoof University College'. After doing this press 'Go' (or some similar command such as 'Search') and then wait for the range of information that follows. Usually the user will then be able to single or double click on the relevant address and directly access the required Home Page, but several attempts may be needed. Users should not get anxious if a number of attempts are required before the desired goal is reached. From the comfort of your own PC at home you can browse through as many university websites as you please and find out as much information as you need.

LOCATING WEBSITE ADDRESSES

If you already know the website address then follow the procedure outlined above – type it in at the URL on your Home Page and press the return key. Alternatively, if the precise address is unknown, all you have to do to initiate the search process is to click on the 'Search' icon. Another address bar will then become available in which you can type in whatever words you know of the target address, and the computer will be set by default to a 'search engine' such as 'Alta Vista', 'Lycos' etc. If you cannot trace the required object on the default search engine then you can change to one of the alternative search engines by clicking on it. Sometimes users type in 'misleading' information that throws the search off in the wrong direction or throws up too much information to browse through. In this case, click on the icon at the top of the page that indicates 'Back' and resume the search with more accurate or appropriate wording.

SOME BASIC ICONS

The university's Internet icon facilities are simple to use and self-explanatory. No matter how far the user has searched from the starting point there are always 'Home' or 'Back' icons clearly labelled to enable the user to go back to the start either in one 'jump' or in a series of steps. By employing the step-by-step 'Next' or 'Back' provision, the user can stop and explore at any given point of interest. The process of moving forward one step at a time is usually pursued by selecting and clicking on a choice from a list of options as the user 'funnels' toward the final object. There is no substitute for some practise at this for 'a picture is worth a thousand words'.

Exercise – Tracing a university

Choose any university you want (other than your present one) and locate its website via the Search facility. Focus on a particular course you're interested in and then trace information about modules, research and staff by using the click and icon procedures.

BEEFING UP REFERENCES

In writing essays/assignments students are required to cite recent references from a variety of sources. One way to do this is to find where the journals are located in the university's library and scan through them to trace relevant articles. This is a commendable practice, and there is no substitute for the discipline of reading through a few key articles on a given subject in order to grasp the important central concepts and the relevant terminology. However, time restrictions and parallel pressures will limit the amount of in-depth reading that can be accomplished. Therefore, students should cultivate the habit of reading Abstracts and citing the central findings that are reported in order to 'beef up' the sources used. An excellent way to do this is by using the university's electronic facilities. These should provide up-to-date Abstracts and full articles that will give students speedy access to a good range of relevant information. Therefore ensure that you learn whatever you can about using these facilities, as they will assist you in improving your degree classification. After using these a few times, you will be amazed at how easy they are to access. The range of articles and Abstracts accessed at any sitting can either be saved to a floppy disk or sent to yourself by email (see later) and printed out from a PC. Any good study habit learned at university is always in danger of being lost through neglect. Once students master a particular skill, they should endeavour to maintain practise at regular intervals.

Getting started with electronic mail (email)

REGISTER AT YOUR UNIVERSITY OR COLLEGE

Students who already have access to the Internet through their home PC may already have an email address through 'Hotmail', 'Yahoo' etc. For those students who do not have this advantage, they should ensure that they registrar for email at the college without delay. Students who already have their own email address should also register on the college list – the advantages are that they will be more readily contactable because their name will also be on the university's email list. Moreover, the university's email facility can probably be used free of charge!

All a student may have to do to register for email is to go to Computer Services with their student registration card, or to Information to ascertain the necessary directions. On the initial guided tour of the library some directions may be given about procedures for email registration. Alternatively the university may have made provision for students to register themselves directly from the computer labs. Directions will be given either on the computer screen or on a chart on the wall of the lab or both. Students will need to have their student registration number at the ready and to follow the instructions step by step.

KEEPING IN TOUCH WITH FRIENDS

Some students have been known to register for email but that is the last respect they ever pay to it! There is little point registering if the facility is never used. It is repeatedly stressed throughout this book that an important step in the pathway to success at university for students is to get into the habit of practising what they have learned as soon as possible after they have learned it. A good incentive for using email is to keep in touch with friends who are both inside and outside college. A disincentive is to let the received email messages build up until it becomes daunting to reply to the large backlog. Therefore regular use is recommended and it will help if the emails sent are fairly short as a general rule. An exception to this might be in pursing a romantic attachment where there is clearly mutual consent! The facility can also be used for arranging a rendezvous with friends – it may not be possible to locate them by phone after arrival at the college on a given day. Email is another feature that can help to make university a more pleasant place to be, especially if it is used wisely. For example, it is good to keep in touch with other student friends who have gone to other universities at home or abroad. When you receive a surprise email from a good friend it can be a pleasant interlude in the usual routine of academic life at college. Moreover, by using email students are maintaining their computing skills and possibly increasing their employability.

Staff members are not always readily available when students need them and some staff members may prefer to do some of their work at home. Given that students' visits to the university may not always coincide with the presence of the required staff member, email is an excellent way to make an arrangement for a meeting. However, sometimes all that will be needed from the staff member is a short and simple reply and email may in itself suffice. For example, if a student just needs the title from an article and the name of the periodical where it can be obtained then this request can be satisfied by email alone. What students should avoid doing is sending lengthy emails to staff and messages that demand lengthy replies. An exception to this may be to prepare the way for a meeting, although even in this case it would be best policy to outline the central points that are to be discussed. In general, any enquiries to staff should be clear, concise, focused and non-trivial. This is the best strategy for eliciting clear replies that give authoritative guidelines! Emails or any other form of communication should always show courtesy and consideration. One teacher recounted how a student demanded an article that they wanted sent by post: 'I cannot get to university, send me such and such an article.' Such a demanding tone should always be avoided and all enquiries should be couched in courteous tones – this is often very effective in eliciting a prompt and appropriate response!

Exercise — A final year project

Imagine that you have decided on a final year project (which you should be thinking about and planning long before entering the final year) on 'Safety on Motorways'. You have already decided that you are going to approach a certain member of staff whom you think would be ideal to supervise you through this project. Your intention is to draft a preliminary email that would pave the way for a meeting. In the project you envisage addressing about five major questions that you would like to blend into a coherent whole. The intention is to interview police, motoring organisations and drivers and to elicit some information from traffic surveys. What you want to know from your chosen supervisor is, first of all, whether this is a feasible project. Can he or she give you any guidance on relevant literature and previous research? Are there any ethical considerations to be taken into account? How would any data collected be analysed? What are the major aims behind the project and how can these be blended together? Try to draft an email that would prepare the way — make the issues brief and to the point. You may want to choose a topic other than the one suggested above. In a real meeting you would need to have printed out a copy of the email you sent to your supervisor so that you can remember exactly what you have said. It is always useful to request 'Copy to self' when sending an important email so that the message can later be accessed when needed. This exercise will demonstrate to you how useful email is as a medium of communication with staff. These kinds of exercises will help you focus on the essentials and trim off peripherals and will also help lecturers to arm themselves in advance with some guidelines for you.

MULTIPLE COPIES OF ONE LETTER

In a job interview, applicants may be asked if they use email regularly. Interview panels do not expect interviewees to answer merely 'yes' or 'no' to each question, otherwise the interview would be over quite quickly and the applicant would almost certainly not get the job unless the vacancy was for the secret service! It is advantageous to elaborate a little bit on each answer and it would be beneficial to the applicant to enumerate a few aspects of email that are used, such as attachments and sending multiple copies of one letter. The latter practice can be done very simply after first typing out an email message that is to be sent, say, to three friends. Insert all their names at the top of the message – for example, Giles, Gale and Glenda. Type in the email address of one of these in the usual way and in the usual place. It is always good in all emails to type in a subject title even if these are comprised of only one or two words, such as 'latest news' or 'planned meeting'. Somewhere within the email facility there should be a designated 'Cc' that will allow the user to send one email to numerous recipients, either by typing in the addresses directly or by accessing the address book. Scroll down until you find the first address you need, and highlight this by clicking and use the paste option. Locate the next friend's address and follow the same procedure. Alternatively, the email address can be typed in at the Cc facility. When this is completed then press 'Send' and the same message will be sent to all three friends. The procedures and symbols outlined here may vary in different systems but the basic principles are the same, and you should ask an experienced user for help if you are stuck.

Multiple copies of one letter are very useful when students are engaged in a small group project (for example, about eight students). If all students in the group have an email address then they can all be sent the same message by anyone in the group. This would be very convenient for arranging meetings, providing updates on the progress of the study, issuing any new information that is available etc. However, all should agree beforehand to check their email regularly.

Exercise — Email multiple copies

If you have not used the multiple copies facility before then try out the following exercise for fun. The next time you are to meet your friends at college, decide beforehand to make the arrangements by email on a set day. On the given day send the proposed arrangement by multiple copies as outlined above. Each can take a turn at this at different times and each can send replies by multiple copies that all others can read. The practice can be further cultivated by sending simple things such as a book title, author and reference number. Ask your friends to reply just to ensure that the procedure has worked. If the practice is initiated amongst friends and not a lot is at stake, this should help to reduce the anxiety that may accompany learning something new.

SENDING ABSTRACTS TO YOURSELF

At the height of the 'busy season' in the academic environment, students may have to wait in a queue to use the computers in their college library. An obvious way to avoid this 'bottleneck' is to schedule library-computing activities for off-peak periods if possible. The material that can be garnered from electronic searches is so invaluable that students should not be daunted by queues in the library or lab, or by problems encountered in the process of learning to send abstracts to themselves by email. Undergraduates may initially need some guidance on this although some may be able to work out the procedures themselves by trail and error. An important key to success at university is to learn not to be daunted by mistakes but to profit from the lessons they bring. Relevant training courses should be attended but if this is not possible then try to learn from a friend who has mastered the art. Alternatively ask a library assistant to help when they are least busy or schedule a time when this can be done.

Each university will have its own particular system for searching electronic journals and abstracts, and each student should become conversant with the localised procedures that have to be mastered. It is impossible to provide general principles that will be a perfect fit for every situation that may be encountered but a few key points can be usefully adapted. For example students should be able to type into a search a journal title, an author's name or a keyword. An option is given to limit the search for to a particular year or years. Users should also be able to request an Abstract with or without references and perhaps a full journal article. The search may be for just one article or to build up a complete dossier of material from a good selection of articles. Any articles or Abstracts thrown up by the search may be designated as 'hits'.

As the user scrolls through the articles, all those deemed relevant can be checked by a click of the mouse on the article title. When the process is completed, there should be options for email and saving to disk at the end of the document. Students can email the material to themselves, or save to disk or both, and can later open up the material on a PC and print the documents out from there. The only way to learn these procedures effectively is to go and practise them. Students should first ensure that they have registered for email and then go to the library with some definite goals in view. For example, after being given the first few assignment titles at the beginning of the semester, the following exercise could be practised by several student friends.

Exercise – Electronic searches

1. Highlight journal titles that are relevant to a given assignment and find out which ones are available on the university's electronic facilities.
2. Select a journal and scroll through several of the most recent editions to find any relevant articles.
3. Also select any relevant Abstracts and request references with these.
4. At the end of the document try to email these to yourself.
5. Open and print the email at a convenient PC and ascertain if any of the references would be useful for further investigation and searches.
6. Try the procedure out again, only this time do an author search using an author's name that is prominent in relation to the designated topic. This option may help you to access articles and abstracts from diverse sources.
7. A final step is to choose central keywords or expressions and do searches based on these. The various strategies combined should throw up a rich variety of material from a range of sources.

ADVANTAGES IN USING ATTACHMENTS

An attachment to an email is a most useful facility for it allows users to send material they have previously typed into a word processing file or data file (although the attachment may not be able to handle very large files). Attachments can be used to send CVs for job applications, essays to tutors, first drafts of a dissertation, articles to a student magazine etc. Moreover, attachments are also useful for receiving information from others, and students often have important material to exchange with each other. Attachments bring a marked advantage to sending files over long distances and also serve well when a piece of work is being sent for corrections – these can be made on the file and then sent back as an attachment. An additional advantage is when several colleagues are working on a project, the fruits of their labour can be circulated to each other for final compilation.

TO OPEN ATTACHMENTS RECEIVED WITH AN EMAIL

A received attachment will come with an email and there will be a message to indicate that the email contains an attachment. Usually the email should be opened first and 'attachments' should be clicked or double clicked. When the attachment is double clicked, a number of options may become available such as 'View', 'Edit' and 'Save'. If 'View' is opened by clicking, this should allow the user to read, print and save the attachment. If there is more than one attachment, they can be opened one-by-one in turn. Some systems are simpler than this in that they just present an icon of the file beside or below the email and this should be double clicked to open.

TO SEND ATTACHMENTS WITH AN EMAIL

First, the name and location of the file to be attached must be noted. Second, type the email message and then click, 'Add Attachment' (or it may be under 'Insert' in some systems). A down arrow should then appear that when clicked allows the user to high-light and request the location of the file (for example, in A or C drive). If the file is saved in a folder, a few clicks will be needed until it has been traced. The cursor should then be rested on the designated file and double clicked. The file is then attached to the email message and the email with the attachment is now ready to send. When the file has been successfully attached there may be a symbol of a paper clip visible to the sender. If the system used differs from that described above try to adapt the principles as appropriate. The ability to send an email with attachments will serve a very useful purpose in your academic career and will furnish you with another skill.

Exercise — Attachments

Just for fun, type out a short story on a word processing file (if you cannot think of one, use one of the illustrations in this book). Save it on 'C' drive and send it as an attachment to a friend, following the guidelines given above. Try the same exercise again with another friend but work from 'A' drive on this occasion. Prepare your friend in advance so that he or she will know how to open the attachment. Then ask your friends to do the same for you — send you the story back with an attachment so that you can have some practise in opening attachments. Remember to try this out from time to time to keep the practice fresh. It would be useful to sit alongside your friends in the computer lab whilst you try out this exercise.

SUMMARY

♦ Computers presently have a central role in third level education and a working knowledge is essential for students.

♦ Mild to severe computerphobia is fairly common in the general population and in the student population, and may impede a student's academic progress if not addressed.

♦ Factors associated with computerphobia include a negative first experience, an inadequate teacher and learning computing along with another subject that is anxiety-generating such as statistics.

♦ Factors that might help to combat computerphobia include regular practise under non-evaluative conditions, associating the computer with satisfying activities and recognising the multi-valuable outcomes from regular computing practice.

♦ Students should learn to find their way around the screen, the keyboard and the mouse — well learned principles will generalise to a range of computer packages.

◆ Some marked advantages in computing at university include time saving, ease of corrections and presentation of work. Added advantages for assignments or essays include word counts, spell check and grammar check.

◆ Use of the college's library computers facilitate quick and easy tracing of targeted books and periodicals within the university's own library.

◆ The electronic facilities at the university allow students to access electronic journals for up-to-date articles and abstracts that will enhance the quality and relevance of subject matter used in course work and tests.

◆ The university may provide free email use for all its students. This can be used for communication with friends and staff, and can be used for sending and receiving attachments and for sending the same message to several people (for example, in small group studies).

5 Crafting an Essay

Initial steps in preparing an essay

GETTING YOUR MIND ENGAGED

People are likely to write best on the matters they feel most passionately about. Passion can help engage the mind and generate fresh ideas. However, the danger of being a crusader for a particular cause is that writers can become selective in the material they use and disregard or fail to do full justice to any issue that appears to weaken their personal standpoint. Therefore, in writing an essay, the essayist should attempt to engage with the subject without permitting his or her own sense of reality to be distorted. Subjects such as capital punishment and blood sports can be addressed passionately yet fairly. In contrast it may not always be possible to get passionately aroused about the essay titles given for assignments at college, but undergraduates should at least try to put themselves into the position of the various parties in a given argument. Students should initially endeavour to capture the main arguments for and against a set theme and then jot down a formative outline of the direction and preparation the debate will take.

Exercise — Engagement

To practise getting your mind engaged with the cardinal points in a subject, consider whether the use of cannabis should be legalised. Try to suggest three major arguments for and against:

For legalisation

1. ....

2. ....

3. ....

Against legalisation

1. ....

2. ....

3. ....

A SKILL TO BE CULTIVATED BY PRACTISE

Once the writer has sufficient interest in a subject to generate good, clear ideas, the essay becomes the medium for the message. The full impact of a message can be lost because of poor structure, inadequate balance, insufficient clarity and too many aberrations. Practise helps to cultivate the requisite skills for effective communication. Even a natural born poet has to have some formal training in the use of rhythm, metre etc. in order to present his or her work in an acceptable and effective format. Students can learn to pitch their expectations for producing a good essay at a realistic level in the early stages of their course. There can then be evolutionary progress in the ability to produce a good essay. Essay writing is an art to be cultivated through patience and practise. A tutor once claimed that students who received good marks without realising why they got them may later lose out because initially they stumbled into a good mark by chance. If students are prepared to accept gradual upward improvement in their efforts and achievements, then they will carry themselves toward a good standard in spite of some disappointments and setbacks. However, in cases where 'major surgery' is needed, undergraduates should work toward dramatic improvements. Great improvement can be made in a short time if a student is perceptive enough to follow good guidelines.

FIRST YEAR AT COLLEGE – A LEARNING OPPORTUNITY

This point has been thoroughly emphasised in Chapter 1, 'Getting Adjusted to University' but the general point is now specifically applied to the case of writing essays. The kind of essay required at college may be different from the type the student was used to in their pre-tertiary experience. Probably the most important thing to be said to students is that they should be prepared to listen and learn in relation to developing the structure, substance and style of their essays. This of course implies that things learned in the past should not be seen as 'set in stone', and students should be willing to change when change is needed. Learning is an ongoing process that should be operational at every stage of the course, but the first year is particularly important for making the transition to third level education. Moreover, learning is not merely about absorbing the facts related to a given subject, but also learning strategies for study and guidelines for optimal achievement. It is stressed in various places in the book that key transferable skills can be learned that will stand the student in good stead for all modules studied and at each level in the course. Good essay writing is indubitably one of the key transferable skills and it is therefore of paramount importance to devote adequate attention to developing the craft.

FEEDBACK FROM TUTORS AND USE OF STUDIES ADVISORS

Tutors are busy people and are not likely to provide students with extensive feedback comments on essays. Undergraduates do, however, have a right to expect more than the feedback one lecturer provided – 'Good discussion – 68 per cent'. This comment neither informed the student about why he had done well or what he could do to improve further. A few terse comments can be very instructive and if the same points are recurrent from various tutors then particular note of these should be taken. Some of the major points that should be addressed in an essay include content, structure, focus, expression and presentation. All students should consider whether they usually do justice to all these elements and if they have any clearly identifiable weaknesses in relation to them that ought to be addressed. Studies advisors and tutorial leaders should be able to provide more detailed commentary and guidance than the lecturer who has provided a few brief but pertinent comments. Points raised by a lecturer on a feedback script can be taken up by the student and worked out in more detail with a studies advisor or tutorial leader. If a number of students in a tutorial group have the same weaknesses then they have good grounds to ask their leader to provide common direction. Take the opportunities to meet with studies advisors and raise the points of weakness that have been highlighted in feedback. Much can be gleaned from a simple feedback script that has provided a few incisive comments. Take a look at the following fictitious feedback sheet, and ponder how much information about strengths and weaknesses can be gleaned from each of the terse comments.

Essay feedback sheet

Content	—	A good range of content was used but a couple of key references were not included.
Structure	—	A well structured essay with a good, gripping introduction. However, the conclusion did not reflect all the points discussed in the essay.
Focus	—	Generally reasonably good focus but I have highlighted two minor points that have been over elaborated.
Expression	—	Expression is on the whole fairly clear but I have asterisked a few sentences that are ambiguous and would need to be restructured.
Presentation	—	Some inconsistencies between the citations in the text and in the References at the end. Also spaces between paragraphs are needed to avoid the 'cramped look'. Headings used are very well chosen.

Not all tutors will provide you with this amount of feedback, but ensure that you glean what you can from whatever you are given, and especially from those who clearly have taken time to give you guidance. The aim of identifying weaknesses is to help students improve performance. If you feel that feedback is insufficient then ask your studies advisor for more elaboration. Moreover, if you are unhappy with a mark you have received you should address this in a diplomatic rather than in a militant fashion. Handling problems is also one of the skills that has to be learned to prepare students for the work environment. In approaching a lecturer about a mark you have received, you could say something like, 'I am not questioning your professional judgement. I just want to know if you can point me in the direction of improvement, as I would like to achieve a higher standard than I am presently at. What can I do to raise my standards?' Such an approach will both take the 'sting out of the tail' and put the onus on the lecturer to explain how your current standard can be improved.

REGULAR, CONSISTENT APPLICATION AND STEADY PROGRESS

An inspirational illustration

It has been claimed to have been demonstrated that a heavy metal block suspended from a ceiling can eventually be made to move by a little cork that is allowed to pound against it regularly. For a long time there appears to be no effect, but after some time elapses there is a very slight, hardly noticeable vibration. Eventually, it is claimed, the heavy weight can be brought to oscillate in full flow.

It is sometimes difficult for students themselves to monitor their own progress, but those who teach them at the beginning and end of their course can certainly notice the strides forward that they have made. It is only as students persevere at writing essays that they improve their skills in the use of content, structure, focus, expression and presentation. Often changes take place almost imperceptibly (see illustration above) as students absorb feedback from various sources. Some of the lessons learned may not come to full fruition until a later stage in the course. It is said that 'old habits die hard' and it may take bad writing habits a while to be eroded.

USING THE ESSAY TITLE TO FOCUS AND FILTER

Essay titles are sometimes given by tutors, but students are at other times left to construct their own. Either way, the titles should reflect the content of the essay and vice-versa. The title is a guideline to focus on in the quest for the material that is to be incorporated within the essay. Furthermore, the title should be used as a filter or gate-keeper to ensure that irrelevant material is excluded. Time should be spent working on the title to ensure that it is accurate, adequate and appropriate. If a tutor has given the title then much good will be served if it is memorised. By thinking carefully over the title, all the main ideas implicit within it can be unpacked one-by-one. There are no hard and fast rules about how long a title should be, but a few well-chosen key words can be very suggestive of an essay's content and orientation. For example, consider the heading of the present chapter – 'Crafting an Essay', and ponder how much is implied by the word 'crafting'. Ask questions about the nature of the essay – is it a review or critique, a discussion or description? Perhaps the intention is to have a strong applied element or maybe it is a contribution to an ongoing debate. Think over the purpose of the essay and check that the title reflects this. Do not necessarily stay with the first title that pops into your head, although this may sometimes prove to be the best.

Exercise – Constructing an essay title

Consider how the burgeoning increase in large shopping complexes may have changed the social behaviours and spending habits of people in recent years. In an essay like this you should weigh the advantages and disadvantages set by these shopping trends. Do the trends entail social engineering, and if so is this a bad thing? Is commercial exploitation going on and are people likely to lose control of their budget by piling up debts? Do the centres really have a friendly ethos (music, layout etc.) or is this all just a cynical attempt to extract more profit for large companies? What impact might shopping centres have on small shops and older people who cannot travel far? On the other hand, are such centres a good way for families to spend a few hours together away from TVs, videos, computers etc.? See if you can construct a title that would at least hint at the issues and outcomes involved.

*See end of chapter for one suggestion, preferably after you have constructed your own.

FAMILIARITY WITH CENTRAL CONCEPTS – USING SOURCE MATERIALS DISCREETLY

The essay title should be used for guidance in the pursuit of the material that will become the substance of the essay. Students must endeavour to discriminate between central and peripheral material, or else the flow of the essay will go off track. After the writer is clear about what all the central concepts are to be, all material that is gathered can be readily fitted into its appropriate place, or alternatively discarded. When the first draft of the essay has been completed, it can be screened for extraneous material that should be excluded.

Space and submarine travel

For example, an essay on first experience in space travel may make a few comparisons with what it is like to travel underwater by submarine for the first time. The inherent danger in such a comparison is that the experience described in the submarine may become a dominant theme within the essay in its own right. Therefore, the writer should take care to ensure that each point raised is like a tributary that feeds into the central stream of the essay.

As another example, consider writing the structure for an essay on 'the dynamics that contribute to the economic prosperity of a modern nation'. Some of the factors to be included in an initial draft structure might be:

- a well trained and highly motivated workforce

- minimum disruption through strikes, go-slows etc.

- good, steady trade with other nations

- an economy that is well managed by the government

- sufficient levels of inward investment

- a healthy balance between savings and spending

- keeping well abreast of developments in Information Technology

In such an essay the writer may want to mention briefly the advantages of economic prosperity, the problems associated with recession and the instability produced by a 'boom and bust' economy. However, these are not central to the intention announced in the essay title, and the writer must therefore guard against digressing from the main objectives. Moreover, too many small points that are not strictly relevant to the essay may become an annoyance to the assessor. Trainee drivers may pass their driving tests even after making a few minor mistakes. They can leave the examiner feeling that he or she has been driven by a 'good, safe pair of hands', and that the person behind the wheel has given the clear impression that they are in control of the vehicle. Similarly, the essay writers who demonstrate that they are in control of where the essay is going are likely to be awarded credit by the marker.

Finding your way in the dark

PUTTING TOGETHER YOUR OWN ORIGINAL CREATION

In the Hebrew language there are two words for create – one means to create out of nothing, but the other means to create out of existent material. God alone, in Hebrew thinking, could create in the former sense, but it was believed to be well within the power of humankind to create in the latter sense. Indeed, no human being can be entirely original in creation. Whether the artist is a poet, sculptor, carpenter, architect or essayist, each new idea is coloured by something that has gone before. No one is totally original in their 'creation', and all are likely to use non-original concepts even though the origins cannot always be traced.

The essay that a student writes for a prescribed assignment or exam is likely to be heavily laced with borrowed concepts. These will be, for instance, by direct and indirect quotations and repetition of ideas that are well rehearsed in the literature. Nevertheless, the essay can still be regarded as an original creation of the individual student in the sense that it has the stamp of their individual style upon it. The student will bring together a range of concepts from a variety of sources and will arrange them in a unique manner. He or she will then structure the essay in their own distinctive manner and will choose to place emphasis on particular points. The ideas that have been imbibed in learning will be filtered through the thought processes of the individual and will emerge in their own style.

AVOIDING THE TEMPTATION TO PLAGIARISE

Whenever a direct quotation has been used in an essay, this should be enclosed in quotation marks, and the author(s) should be cited, together with the year of publication and the page number as in the following fictitious example: 'Truth is unchanged, unchanging and unchangeable' (Bloggs, 2001: 32). The full reference for the author(s) and the publication should be cited in the list of References in proper alphabetical order by surname, so that readers can trace its source. It is also possible to cite a paraphrase of the quotation, which is not then a direct quotation. In this case the source is cited in the text and in the References, but there should be no quotation marks or page number in the text. Take for example, a paraphrase of the Bloggs quotation: according to Bloggs (2001), truth never has changed, never will change and never can change. Unless the source for the quotation or paraphrased quotation is cited, the writer has committed the 'crime' of plagiarism. That is, in effect, the writer has 'stolen' the concept from another and taken the credit for the originality of the idea.

Plagiarism can be heavily penalised at college, but only if it is found out! The form of plagiarism likely to be penalised is when students extracts large chunks of material from books or journals and use them verbatim without giving credit to the source, although when one student copies from another student, this is also deemed to be an infringement of rules. As a good rule of thumb it is preferable to use short quotes that blend well into the sense and direction of a given paragraph. Moreover, it should not be forgotten that a range of references well used help to enhance the quality and authority of an essay. A lecturer may be more likely to accept some controversial point from an empirical researcher than from a student! It is always possible that a writer will use ideas that are not always his or her own without being fully conscious of this. However, in the cases where a writer cannot remember their sources they should at least try to present the material in their own style and make some cover statement about sources.

Stamp of individuality

The story is told of an evangelist in New York who preached all week in a hectic schedule of meetings, but was left with no message for the Sunday morning service. As a last resort he lifted a book of sermons and choose an appropriate one from a famous London preacher. When the morning service arrived, and he was about to deliver his message, he noticed the famous London preacher in his congregation! The evangelist delivered the message in his own style and words. Afterwards the London preacher thanked the evangelist for the message. To this the evangelist responded, 'What! do you not recognise one of your own children when it is dressed up in someone else's clothes?' The moral of the story is that if students can present the good work of others in their own style, and with due acknowledgement, they will be given credit for their efforts.

In Chapter 4, 'Computers – Friends not Foes', there are sections that give guidance on using computers for a spell check and grammar check. Spelling, grammar, punctuation and structure are all important in as far as they are aids to clarity, fluency and accuracy. It is not helpful to a reader if a writer's spelling, grammar, punctuation and structure are so appalling that they become a distraction from the intent of the essay. However, students should be patient with themselves and be prepared to persevere until their writing skills are matured. Simple guide books on grammar or basic use of English are invaluable tools to consult for writing, especially if they provide exercises for practise.

As a general rule sentences should be kept short, simple and direct. A graduate told of how his professor at university used so many negatives and positives in his train of thought that the students had to write down the number of each as he went along in order to ascertain the final direction of the intended message! As a relevant aside to this point, it is useful to remember that two negatives make a positive. Take the following example: 'you are not the one who never comes here'. This can be a clumsy, awkward and confusing way to write, especially if it is done too often. A double negative can sometimes be effective if it used discreetly and sparingly, but its repeated use can be strenuous to the reader.

The golden rule in writing is to avoid ambiguities and obscurities. In order to achieve this goal, a sentence may have to be rewritten or restructured. Sometimes the adjustment is as simple as moving a word or two to another place in the sentence so that the word or words are no longer 'attracted' to a parallel idea that throws them off track.

Inappropriate sentence structures

An unfortunate choice of a word can throw the meaning of a sentence off course. A notice in a shop read, 'We are selling cigarettes no longer'. That could be taken to mean that the cigarettes being sold are the same lengths as they always were! Patrons of the shop of course clearly understood that the notice meant that the proprietor had ceased to sell cigarettes. There used to be a TV advert for a headache tablet that said, 'Nothing acts faster than Anadin'. A wit took up this idea and added, 'Nothing acts faster than Anadin, so use nothing: it acts faster!' These are humorous examples of where an unfortunate choice of a word can be misconstrued (in these instances a little mischievously).

When an essay has been completed it should be read over again to ensure that each sentence clearly communicates the writer's intended meaning. The writer should always use his or her critical eye to observe if each sentence is linked to the next, and if the cluster of sentences in a given paragraph constitute a coherent whole. In contrast to this 'post-check' approach, the structure of the essay should be decided before the essay is commenced, although hindsight sometimes demonstrates that some paragraphs may be better relocated to another position.

MOULDING THE ESSAY INTO SHAPE

Working toward a goal

It was said that whenever Michelangelo decided to carve a sculpture, he saw in his 'mind's eye' a picture of the figure he was about to 'set free' from the slab of marble he was to work on. He knew what his goal was before he started, and then he used his hammer and chisel to chip away until the perfect figure emerged from the marble. In the same way students should have some idea of where they are going when they commence writing an essay. It would be an unnecessary waste of time to set out on a journey if the traveller had no idea of directions. The story is told of a traveller who asked directions to Galway. A local man responded, 'Well, if I were going there, I wouldn't start from here!' When starting an essay, the student should begin at the right place, that is, with an outline plan. A good strategy is to write down all the main ideas even if these are only represented by one or two words. These brief capsules can later be expanded into full headings. In cases where headings are not required, they may still be useful for drafting plans, filtering and arranging material, and may then later be discarded.

Decisions should be made about which points are major, central headings and which are subsidiary, supportive points. The minor points can be clustered around the appropriate major headings, and the major headings should be arranged into the most logical and fluent sequence. A practice example is given in Chapter 11 'A Skilful Presentation', under the heading, 'Changes across the life-span'. Another example, requiring more work than the example just referred to, is provided below. The points given below are not headings as such, but basic ideas, in the form of questions, which can be formulated into headings and subheadings.

Excercise — Practice structuring an essay on 'The Role of The Media in Shaping Public Attitudes'. Address the following issues:

1. Do the media generally attempt to shape or reflect public attitudes?
2. Which forms of media are more likely to be influential?
3. Which sections of society may be more likely to be impressionable?
4. Does the way the media prioritise the news have any bearing on impression formation?
5. Do most people blindly accept or critically scrutinise media reports?
6. Does competition between various media serve a productive purpose?
7. Should the media engage in moral crusades?
8. Is there a danger that the public may sometimes 'shoot the messenger because of the message'?
9. Do the media ultimately have more power than politicians?

Drawing up plans

A SKELETON THAT REFLECTS AIMS AND DIRECTIONS

Example

The importance of outline points has already been highlighted and can be further emphasised with the analogy of a skeleton. A skeleton serves a number of important functions including giving shape to the body, facilitating movement for the body and protecting vital organs within the body. Although a skeleton on its own does not provide life, it does facilitate the important aspects of life highlighted above. In a similar manner the structure of the essay helps facilitate the range of evidence, quotes, anecdotes, applications etc. that help to make an essay 'pulsate with life'. An assessor will enjoy reading an essay that demonstrates understanding and enthusiasm, but that has also been structured in a manner that communicates these qualities in an efficient and economic manner.

Students sometimes allow their essay to become lopsided by giving too much attention to some points whilst failing to do justice to other equally important aspects. A good structure can help the student to see at a glance if the essay is sufficiently balanced and if appropriate weight has been given to each point. Excessive attention to and protracted treatment of a particular point, no matter how passionately the writer may feel about that point, can become tedious and irksome to the reader, and cause the essay to lose some of its dynamism.

WHEN THE SUBJECT MATTER BECOMES PART OF THE WRITER

A English-speaking friend who went to live in Austria told of his progress in mastering the German language. He felt that he had really got to grips with the language when he found himself thinking in German. At this stage there was no need for him to translate the words in his head before he understood his sequence of thought. The German vocabulary, sentence structure and characteristic style of thinking were becoming a natural part of his daily routine. Similarly, any subject that is new to a student may at first seem a little 'foreign'. However, when sufficient aspects of the subject become embedded in the mind, students will have the raw material to think clearly and fluently on the given subject. They will soon be able to form opinions, connect ideas in sequence and critically evaluate claims and counter-claims. Each student should develop the confidence to realise that they can formulate critical judgements on each subject on their curriculum. As previously noted, however, they must attempt to do justice to all aspects of an argument rather than allowing themselves to be driven by passionate prejudice (although strong feelings can be a good mechanism for triggering creative thought processes).

Sometimes students are diffident about developing their critical faculties, and this may be partly because they are given a short period of time in which to formulate mature and authoritative opinions on a given issue. Part of the path to success at university is learning to act promptly on assignment titles so that students become familiar with the issues in the shortest possible time. This may not be as difficult as it first appears and students will become more confident with practice.

A lesson in rapid familiarity

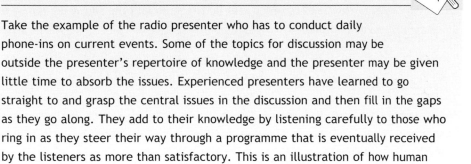

Take the example of the radio presenter who has to conduct daily phone-ins on current events. Some of the topics for discussion may be outside the presenter's repertoire of knowledge and the presenter may be given little time to absorb the issues. Experienced presenters have learned to go straight to and grasp the central issues in the discussion and then fill in the gaps as they go along. They add to their knowledge by listening carefully to those who ring in as they steer their way through a programme that is eventually received by the listeners as more than satisfactory. This is an illustration of how human nature can rise to the occasion and give a good account of itself when the time is limited and the pressure is on. There is no good reason to suppose that students are any different when given an unfamiliar topic for an essay. This kind of testing environment will help students develop the kinds of qualities that will later be beneficial in their chosen vocation.

USING A LITTLE INFORMATION EFFECTIVELY

No student will be successful at university without mastering the art of how to 'cut to the chase'. Time management is an important aspect of this but so is discrimination in selection of material. The task for the student is to harness the material that is related to the questions being addressed in the essay. This process involves both selective reading and focused use of summary notes. Some articles may only provide the student with one or two usable ideas, but these ideas may become a kernel that will develop into a more expansive point. When reading through an article or book it is essential to make a note of any quote or thought that strikes the reader as important. The inspiration of that particular moment can later evaporate, and so it is vital to get into the habit, without procrastinating, of capitalising on what is found. A pocket notebook should be carried around (along with a pen!) so that nothing important is missed or lost. Within a short period of time a good body of points can be built up that will give substance to the essay. When reading a journal article, the abstract or summary at the beginning will summarise all the central ideas, which the reader can then locate and from which they can extract useful notes. Books can be used in the same way by referring to chapter headings, subject index or authors' names. When a body of ideas from various sources has been collated in a notebook, these should be read over until the student is familiar with them. If this whole process is accomplished in a short period of time, the student will not need to refer back to all the articles and books from which the summary notes have been gleaned. Once the writing exercise begins, the ideas will begin to flow, the meaning will be triggered and the summary points will develop into a more comprehensive assignment that will soon be ready for submission.

BALANCED ARGUMENTS, SYMMETRICAL STRUCTURE AND SEDUCTIVE TANGENTS

Some points have already been made on this issue, but because of its importance further aspects of it are now addressed. In short, an essay should be well balanced, well rounded and should keep on track throughout. The temptation to digress is ever present and in an exam or test the lost time cannot be recovered. However, in course work assignments the irrelevant material can be cut out, but students should not leave addressing their assignments until the submission date is imminent. Allow sufficient time to read over the essay so that extraneous points can be removed or condensed. Tangents are often seductive to students, especially if they find them more interesting than the main issues in the essay. Some students prove to be quite determined to make a particular point in spite of knowing that it is not strictly relevant to the essay. Such intransigence only wastes time and space and guarantees reducing credit that could be given.

In the instances where students hold strong views on a particular subject, they may feel that they are betraying their own beliefs or convictions by articulating points that run counter to their own position. However, an essay should not be construed as a medium for crusading on a particular issue and students should not feel that they are compromising themselves by 'playing the devil's advocate'. Indeed, essay preparation and presentation are opportunities to try to understand a range of views and to represent each one as fairly as possible. This is part of the professional training that may later serve students well in their vocation. An essay that excludes important material will appear inadequate to anyone knowledgeable on the subject.

Students may hold strong views on issues like pre-marital sex, abortion, homosexuality, legalisation of cannabis, capital punishment, freedom fighters versus terrorist argument etc. Views held may be religious or non-religious, and some may feel so strongly that they would rather forfeit marks than betray their conscience. No student need feel that they are compromising their convictions by attempting to be fair to all aspects of an argument. The essay is intended to be a thorough discussion of all the issues and not a forum for one viewpoint. If students feel that what they hold is the absolute truth, then they should rest assured that the truth will be able to stand in spite of all the counter-arguments, and will look all the stronger when it does not fall after severe testing. Therefore if undergraduates are secure in their personal beliefs they should not fear allowing other viewpoints to be aired. Some examples provided for practise in this book use the argument/counter-argument approach to an essay. These include the legislation of cannabis (present chapter), corporal punishment of children (Chapter 8), smoking (Chapter 9) and the role of the media in shaping public attitudes (present chapter). An example that the reader may now want to develop is 'One person's terrorist is another person's freedom fighter'.

BUILDING UP A REPERTOIRE OF QUOTABLE QUOTES

Weaving suitable quotes into the tapestry of an essay is an art that can only be acquired by practise. First, quotes have to be noted at the reading stage of preparation. Some quotes are so good that they stand out and are best used in their original form, because they would be difficult to improve on. Other good quotes may be too long and need to be condensed into fewer words. When students are compelled to do this they should try not to dilute or exaggerate the author's intended meaning. Moreover, a text taken out of its context can become a pretext – and the same applies to a quote. An essay that is carefully sprinkled with appropriate quotes conveys the impression that it is founded on good authority, but an essay that has too many lengthy quotes may give the impression that it is merely a patchwork of other people's efforts.

An example of a short, simple, pithy quote is encapsulated in the words Shakespeare (1564–1616) put into the mouth of King Lear to express the wrenching emotion he felt at his daughter's untimely death: 'Thou'lt come no more, never, never, never, never, never'. (Act 5, Scene3, lines 307–8).

Or consider how Dickens (1812–1870) in *Great Expectations* gave words to Miss Havisham to reflect her tactics in influencing Estella to wreak vengeance on men. The words cited contain rhythm, express emotion, and evoke an atmosphere of their own: 'Break their hearts, my pride and joy, break their hearts.'

George Orwell (1903–1950) was a master of the English language and could carefully build up a terse collection of words that perfectly portrayed mood, atmosphere etc. For example, in describing the gloomy picture of the execution of prisoners in Burma, he described the day as 'a sodden morning of the rains', in which there was 'a sickly light'. It is not always possible to find quotes as effective as these but students should always be screening for short, suitable quotes to add body, flavour and authority to their essay.

Strengthening the essay with substance and style

USING AVAILABLE EVIDENCE TO SUPPORT ARGUMENTS

If the points raised in essays are to have any substance, it should be possible to demonstrate they are evidence-based. Even in applied subjects such as nursing, where clinical skills and hands-on experience are essential, researchers and practitioners look for evidence-based practice. Hoshmand and Polkinghorne (1992) argued cogently for the 'Science-Practitioner Model'. In this approach there is seen to be a continuous cycle of research informing practice and practice feeding back into research. Therefore, in essay writing it is useful to cite work that has proposed a model that has been tested in the field of practice. Conversely, some proposed models may be cited with the qualification that they have yet to be tested or convincingly proved in the sphere of practice. For example, Becker's (1963) 'labelling theory' proposed that 'deviants' such as cannabis users become more isolated from society because they are inappropriately labelled in a stigmatising manner. A claimed dynamic interactive process is initiated by the stigmatising label imposed by society on the deviants that in turn has a negative impact on the deviant group's perception of society. This leads to further polarisation between what Becker calls the sub-culture and mainstream society. The student might challenge the model by asking whether labelling is really the primary reason for the polarisation between the two groups, whether the proposed model can be tested in a scientifically rigorous manner and whether there is authoritative evidence available to substantiate the theory? Students should look at whether proposed theories are really testable, and if they cannot be, if the status of a theory is warranted for the proposed collection of ideas.

Students should come to realise that some 'evidence' cited in the literature is based on tenuous findings. This is not surprising given that the research process is always moving forward, and concepts are always refined whilst some old proposals have to be jettisoned. If students can at least add a sentence to show that the research they are citing has been questioned by other researchers, they will gain credit for demonstrating good awareness of the issues. In general the kinds of expressions that should be avoided are those such as, 'I have a hunch', 'my feeling is that' etc. A more authoritative approach is reflected in the following quotations – 'on the balance of the most up-to-date evidence, it can be concluded that …', or 'in the light of the available findings, it can be asserted that …'.

REPETITION THAT ISN'T REPETITIOUS

Repetition has a useful role to play both in teaching and in learning, and also has a place in essays. If the same concepts, however, are repeated in the same words, the repetition can degenerate into monotony. Moreover, the writer must not leave the impression that they are being repetitious in order to fill out the volume of the essay. Repetition should not be used as an excuse for lack of substance. Whenever ideas need to be repeated, the concepts do not have to be repeated in their full form every time. Some thought should be given to using a brief form of the concept after its initial use. For example, 'Newton's theory of relativity' can later be described variously as 'Newton's theory', 'relativity theory', 'theory of relativity' or just simply 'relativity'. The writer may need to use a little imagination to find variations of the expression, but the inherent danger with this practice is that an alternative word may dilute the original intention. On the other hand, if it is clear that the substitute word refers back to the original idea then no real damage may have necessarily been done. An injustice would be done to Newton if the writer referred to his theory as a mere hypothesis, but it would be acceptable to refer to 'Newton's concepts'.

There is no doubt that the wise use of repetition can serve to enhance the quality of an essay. For instance, if a series of subtle arguments are being used, it will help the reader follow the thread of the discussion if a brief recap of the progression of the points is made. Such a recap may be carefully introduced at the beginning of a new section, but it must be concise.

Exercise — Physical exercise summary

Imagine that you have just written the first section of an essay on the benefits and problems of physical exercise. If the exercise is, for example, jogging and is engaged in with friends, there may be clear social benefits, and if the jogging provides a break from a routine range of pressures, there will be psychological benefits. The physical benefits relate to breathing, circulation, muscles and weight control.

See if you can summarise the above benefits in a few words as you are about to address potential problems associated with jogging. You cannot rehearse all the arguments again in full so try to find one 'umbrella' term that would cover each of the three domains. This is an example of using brief summaries that repeat the overall ideas without describing the full detail each time.

IDENTIFYING AND ADDRESSING WEAKNESSES

In an earlier part of this chapter it was suggested that an important aspect of correcting weaknesses in students' academic habits is by reference to studies advisors and tutors. In the final analysis, the student has to make his or her own decision about what improvements should be made. Sometimes educators differ in the advice they give to students and this can be confusing. Students should therefore try to develop their own system of troubleshooting that takes into account the feedback they receive from tutors. A subtle aspect of achieving success at university is learning to give each tutor exactly what they want (we will keep this as our secret!). This is not as difficult as it may first appear, for when lecturers set an assignment they should provide some guidance about length, content, style, sections etc. Some may prefer an extended literature review and some may like headings whilst others may not like these features in an essay. Students must learn to vary their style according to the requirements for any given assignment. However, some general points that students should always keep under review are the five essentials already mentioned – content, structure, focus, expression and presentation. In addition each student should examine their own ability to structure sentences clearly, use words effectively and construct paragraphs appropriately. As was previously noted, if successive tutors recurrently notice a particular weakness, this must not be neglected. A general point is that no student should be unwillingly to change their style or to imagine that their approach to writing cannot be improved. The summary section at the end of this chapter can be used as an exercise for students in troubleshooting.

THE EARLY BIRD CATCHES THE WORM

It has been said that the road to hell is paved with good intentions. No successful student has ever kept their intentions at the level of inactivated plans. The path to a good level of achievement at university is characterised by the habit of acting early in the discharge of study commitments. If responsibilities are continually shelved away, the growing mountain of commitments become more and more daunting. The workload can then become so enormous that students settle beforehand for a lesser standard. Some will feel that they have the insurance to make up lost ground at a latter stage. In reality, however, habits are being formed that become increasingly difficult to break, and early slackness leads to later pressure and diminished quality. On the other hand, immediate application to assignments, followed by steady, consistent levels of effort result in a diminution of pressure and fuller opportunities to accumulate a richer range of content. Furthermore, once the mind has focused on the subject matter for an essay, the student will be able to pick up comments in lectures, seminars and tutorials that will help enrich the assignment. Other students who have not started preparing for their assignments will fail to grasp these opportunities. Whenever the mind has become engaged with a particular subject, relevant thought processes will be triggered from time to time that will enable students to develop and mature their thinking. This will often happen quite spontaneously and often outside of scheduled study periods. A good starting point for an assignment is to read some key article or book chapter associated with it as soon as possible and to make sure that the essay title is clearly embedded in the mind.

ASCERTAIN THE FLOW OF THE WORK

Attention has been given in this chapter to ensuring that the content, structure, focus, expression and presentation are all intact. It is also important, however, to read the completed essay right through from start to finish to ascertain if it flows well without hindrance or obstruction. When this exercise has been undertaken, it may be found that a paragraph is out of place and would fit better elsewhere or that a particular paragraph serves no real purpose and could be justifiably deleted. Anything from a sentence to a paragraph or a whole section that disrupts the flow should be modified to blend with the essay. It may also prove useful to have someone else read through the essay to ensure that it does read clearly all the way through. The student does not have to accept criticism of their own work from someone who is reading over the essay for them. No changes should be made unless the person making the criticism can provide valid reasons for their judgements. Even within all the parameters of guidance given in this chapter, there still remains much room for students to develop their own style and to stamp the mark of their individuality upon their own work. If other people's criticisms merely embody their own style preferences, they can be politely ignored. Beware of punctilious critics who appear to spend their lives attempting to destroy the creative style of others. Nevertheless, students should welcome constructive guidance that helps improve accuracy, fluency, economy and clarity.

CHECKING THE INTRODUCTION

Whenever the first draft of an essay has been completed, the student should look again at the introduction to ascertain if it is an appropriate preface to the work that follows. The purpose of the introduction should be to arouse the reader's interest in the subject, to make a summary statement about the background to the essay, to state what the aims of the essay are and to map out briefly how the aims are to be achieved. Let us again take the example of physical exercise, and delineate the points that might be used in an introduction:

Introductory statement — Over the last couple of decades, physical exercise has increased in popularity for a wide range of groups from various backgrounds.

Background statement — Researchers have focused on the social, physical and psychological benefits of exercise, but have not perhaps given sufficient attention to short-term and long-term problems associated with some forms of exercise.

Aim of essay — The primary aim of the essay is to assess both advantages and disadvantages, short-term and long-term, from the perspectives of the triple aspects previously stated: social, physical and psychological.

Method — Each of these three aspects will be examined in turn, and the advantages and disadvantages of exercise related to each will be addressed, first in the short-term and then in the long-term.

The headings used above were inserted for clarity but these are not normally used in the introduction to an essay. Concepts expressed above should be woven into fluent sentences but the suggested outline is not intended to be an introductory structure that is set in stone. The procedure for laying out points in the introduction should be flexible enough to be compatible with the subject matter of the essay.

EVALUATING THE CONCLUSION

The conclusion of the essay should be seen as at least as important as the introduction. Neither part of the essay should be thrown together in an impetuous manner. In the conclusion the author has the opportunity to bring together all the important points in summary form and to present the reader with a bird's eye view and synopsis of all the main arguments. A defence lawyer and a prosecution lawyer have both to summarise their perspectives at the end of a trial. At the conclusion of an essay, a student has to act as defence, prosecution and judge. A good strategy to finish an essay with is, first, to state the points of certainty that can be extracted from the ground that has been covered. Second, the student can highlight the issues that remain unresolved. Third, the student may suggest directions to guide future research (see example on 'Depression' at the end of this chapter). The example of physical exercise is used again below, this time to demonstrate how a conclusion might be presented. For the sake of brevity, the short-term and long-term factors are combined.

Advantages — Exercise helps to break the cycle of life's stresses and pressures, and gives a sense of achievement (psychological advantages). It also assists circulation, respiration, muscles, weight control and insomnia (physical advantages). Finally, interaction with others who exercise increases communication and social networks (social advantages).

Disadvantages — Some forms of exercise, such as jogging, may cause physical problems to the joints. Psychological benefits may be reversed if the activity is stopped or if the participant does not reach the standards they set for themselves. Finally, exercise may become so addictive that it disrupts other important aspects of life.

Overall conclusion — a) Long-term rigorous exercise on hard surfaces may store up physical problems for the future. b) More attention should be given to studying the adverse effects of protracted and excessive exercise. c) If a form of exercise can be chosen that is enjoyable to the participant, it is more likely to be beneficial and enduring. d) Those who exercise should ensure that they do not foreclose other important events in their lives. e) Maximum benefit from exercise is likely to be obtained if simple rules are followed. f) Lack of exercise is believed to be associated with a range of health problems. g) A decision either to exercise or not to exercise is likely to involve a trade-off between advantages and disadvantages.

SUMMARY

◆ Writing a good essay is a skill to be cultivated by practise, and students can use the first year at college as an opportunity to develop the craft.

◆ Attention to feedback from lecturers, tutors and studies advisors is an essential aspect of the learning process in writing, especially when a consensus emerges about recurrent weaknesses.

◆ Five general points that are recognised as impacting on the quality of any essay are content, focus, structure, expression and presentation.

◆ The title of an essay should be carefully chosen and must reflect the content and orientation of the essay. Moreover, it provides the basis for the student to focus and filter in the selection of material.

◆ Outline plans with headings and subheadings enable the student to arrange garnered material into a fluent and coherent structure.

◆ Plagiarism should be avoided at all costs, but the essay will appear authoritative if it is sprinkled with a variety of quotes and source references. As a general rule quotes should not be too lengthy and should be blended naturally into the text.

◆ Each sentence should read clearly and a paragraph is to be comprised of a coherent cluster of sentences. Students should ensure that they are not 'seduced' by tangents that are secondary or irrelevant to the central aim(s) of the essay.

◆ Personal prejudice should not be allowed to distort the use of evidence, and the various points and counterpoints should be woven into a symmetrical presentation. However, strong feelings on a given topic can be a good generator for productive thought and can be harnessed for effective use.

♦ Grammar, spelling, punctuation and sentence structure are important in that they facilitate clarity, accuracy and fluency. It is, however, important that students develop their own writing style.

♦ Books on basic grammar should be consulted, especially those that are readable and give worked examples. Attention to feedback from tutors will facilitate efficient learning.

♦ Attention should be devoted to working on an assignment as soon as possible after the essay title is known.

♦ Particular attention should be given to the introduction and conclusion in order to ensure that they are adequate and appropriate for the essay.

♦ It may be helpful to have a friendly critic read over the essay before it is submitted so that glaring 'howlers' missed by the writer can be identified and rectified.

*Suggested essay title for exercise: 'An evaluation of the social and economic impact of modern shopping complexes in shaping family and community trends.'

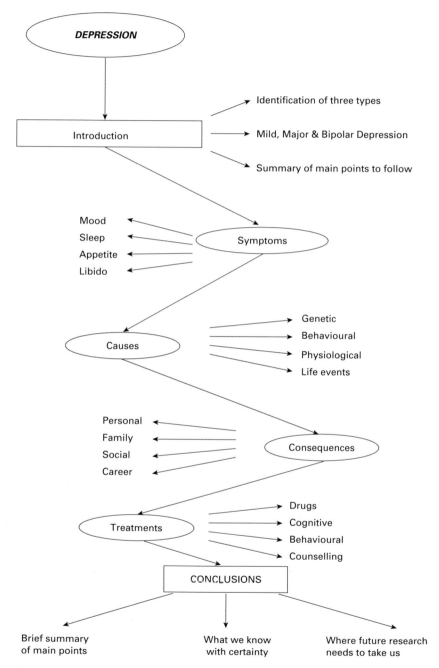

Figure 5.1 EXAMPLE OF HOW AN ESSAY PLAN MIGHT BE DRAWN UP: 'WRITE AN ESSAY THAT EVALUATES DEPRESSION: ITS SYMPTOMS, CAUSES, CONSEQUENCES AND TREATMENTS'

6 Writing a Practical Report

First things first — essential principles

THE BEGINNING AT THE END — THE ABSTRACT

The first section of a practical report after the title is the abstract. It is best to write the abstract after you have finished writing the full report because it is a summary of the entire report (the abstract is sometimes called the 'summary'). Tutors usually impose a word limit on the abstract and it does therefore have to be written succinctly. You may have to make a number of attempts at writing the abstract before you get it right. Abstracts usually start with an introductory statement about the background to the study, followed by a brief description of the sample (denoted by 'n') and where the study was carried out, for example, 'The study was carried out at the University of Bloggs with a sample of undergraduate engineering and nursing students' ($n = 180$).

At this point a brief mention can be made of any materials or apparatus that were used in the experiment/survey (this can be elaborated upon in the method section). For example, it may be stated that students completed a range of established self-report measures that relate to academic performance, such as self-efficacy, conscientiousness and test anxiety. All trimmings and trappings should be removed from the abstract in order to 'cut to the chase'. It can then be stated that the measures were analysed (cite statistics used, for example, t-tests and correlations) in relation to students' subsequent achievement in course work and examinations. After this the main findings in the results can be summarised in a few brief sentences along with a statement about whether they were what was expected. A final section should incorporate any conclusions from the results and implications for future research and/or practice. Tutors may be flexible about the order in which some of the above details are presented. As a good rule of thumb they should follow the same sequence presented in the report itself.

Exercise – Gender bias

Read the background to the following study on Gender Bias and Social Gender Cues in Children. Then attempt to write a brief Abstract (in about 100 words) that covers a) a background statement, b) sample description, c) method used to carry out study, d) what the simple statistics were, e) what implications the study may have.

In Japan it may be difficult to identify the gender of children in the four to nine age group because their hair styles and clothing are similar. In a study carried out in Japan most participants were able to identify the gender of most children. However when participants had to guess, they tended to opt for the female gender. In a similar study in a western university*, 400 students were asked to identify the gender of 200 children from photographs that were fed into a computer. Both the student sample and the photographs were split 50/50 on gender. However the photographs were trimmed so that the participants could not see length and style of hair and style of clothes (typical western social gender cues). The students had to select or guess the gender for each photo by pressing a designated computer key. Moreover, the children were deliberately chosen from a pre-puberty age so that there were no developmental cues related to the onset of puberty. Results demonstrated that all the participants got at least 50 per cent responses correct and most got around 58-72 per cent correct. However, when students guessed the answer they tended to opt for the male gender (in contrast to the Japanese sample).

*The above example has used fictitious data based on a western university experiment.

CARRIED OUT UNDER GUIDANCE

If you are writing up a practical report at university it will probably be in tandem with an experiment or survey you are carrying out. Your tutor will give you some guidance, or will point you to the literature that does, with respect to the rationale behind the study and why it has been designed in a particular manner. However, it is important for you to try to grapple with these facts yourself rather than blindly following where you are being led. It is part of the scientific process to identify weaknesses and suggest new directions, for true science ought to be self-correcting. Lecturers usually do not appreciate their own work returned to them verbatim by students, they prefer to see the student's fresh thinking in the practical report. This does not imply that bizarre and reckless speculation should be engaged in, but innovative thinking within the guidance given is refreshing for assessors.

INSERTING THE STUDY INTO THE SCHEME OF THINGS

Unless you are commencing a study that is totally new, there should be a body of literature to which you can refer. One of the drawbacks with a completely original study is that a good literature background cannot be provided, and this is something that should be taken into account especially before committing yourself to an important project.

Compulsory practical reports at university usually have strict word limits imposed, and therefore the literature review has to be selective and succinct. What should be aimed for are the key relevant articles and those most up-to-date. It is most useful to look out for the articles described as 'a review' in the title, or those described as 'a meta-analytic investigation'. These kinds of studies will save a lot of time and effort and will give a good panorama of the way a subject has developed over many years. For example a meta-analysis and review by Hembree (1988), examined 562 studies that had looked at test anxiety! These types of studies will enable students to acquire a good grasp of a subject quickly and will point to all the important landmark works on the subject. Another important tool is the use of computer-based word studies that will help you trace relevant studies through the Internet (see Chapter 4, 'Computers: Friends not Foes').

The next task is to present the findings to date in a structured, succinct and chronological manner, in order to show where the study being conducted fits into the overall scheme of things. It is important to emphasise that you are not merely replicating previous studies (unless that is the intention). More than likely there will be some new twist to the study that is designed to take the research process further forward.

In a literature review it is beneficial to incorporate a few useful quotes, but not too many and they shouldn't be too long. Useful quotes that summarise material in a nutshell are particularly effective. With a verbatim quote you should use name(s) of author(s) and page number(s), and incorporate the quote in quotation marks. As an example, Ramsden (2000) asserted that 'students will study what they think will be assessed' (p. 70). Alternatively, it is acceptable to summarise the quote in your own words without the use of quotation marks or page number. For example, a literature review in a brief practical report is rather like the abstract – it should be focused, comprehensive and concise. Always avoid the temptation to introduce points that are tangential to the running theme in the report.

A SCIENTIFIC REPORT

Practical reports, sometimes referred to as 'lab reports', are intended to be scientific in nature and therefore should be written in a style that is consistent with a scientific approach. This means that the researcher is not following hunches or intuition but is rigorously testing some hypothesis or hypotheses. If results are expected in a particular direction then there should be a clearly stated basis for these expectations. Conversely if there was no expectation of which way the results would emerge, it should be stated that the test was open-ended. The whole report should be presented in the tenor of testing and evaluating evidence rigorously. Limitations in the study should be identified toward the end of the discussion: this indicates that the researcher is making a contribution toward an ongoing accumulation of evidence.

A statement that highlights limitations should not, however, leave the impression that the writer has nothing authoritative to tell the reader. Students sometimes make the mistake of 'selling themselves short'. The wrong kinds of statements at the end can leave the impression that the experiment or survey was a pointless exercise (which may then reflect a poor design). Academic journals favour publishing articles that make some important contribution to knowledge. Your practical report should be based on an empirical study that has been designed in such a way as to make a contribution to the knowledge base in a particular domain. Studies that don't turn out as expected may also contribute to knowledge because they can guide researchers away from a cul-de-sac. Moreover, studies that refute previous findings may also be useful, especially if reasons can be suggested for the inconclusive results.

In the previous paragraph the word 'empirical' was introduced, and this is a very important word in scientific reporting. It refers to practical studies that have been carried out with proper rigour and control in order to test some hypothesis. Results presented in such a study have usually been tested by appropriate statistical analyses so that readers will know the degree of confidence that can be placed in the findings. Whenever literature is being cited that is based on empirical studies it can be said that the authors of the report 'found' or their results 'indicate' some conclusion. However, if the authors place a particular interpretation on their results, it would be better to say that they 'claimed' or 'interpreted' their results to draw some conclusion. Moreover, if citing an author who makes assertions based on some assumed premise rather than on a solid empirical study, it is useful to make this clear.

In practical report writing it is accepted practice to avoid the use of first person pronouns such as 'I', 'me' or 'we'. For example, instead of saying 'we found', you can use a substitute such as 'the findings suggest' or 'these findings indicate' or 'it can be concluded from these findings' etc. Another development over the last decade has been to refer to the people who participated in the study as 'participants' rather than 'subjects'. Writers should also avoid the repeated use of gendered language that might be construed as sexist, for example, constantly using only male or female third person pronouns, such as 'he' or 'she'. Both can be used alternately or use a plural form that incorporates both genders. A good rule of thumb when choosing the tense to use is to be consistent when referring to empirical studies and citations from these. Some prefer the past tense because the studies referred to were carried out in the past, for example, 'Hembree (1988) asserted that ...' in preference to 'Hembree (1988) asserts that ...'. This is a matter where you need to ascertain what your tutor's preference is as he or she is the one who will mark your assignment!

Thinking in a world of hypotheses

In every part of the report the impression should be conveyed that the report is going somewhere and everything that has been incorporated is relevant. When all is completed the report should be read over a few times to ensure that all unnecessary 'padding' is deleted and that every aspect is a tributary that leads into the main stream. The literature review follows on after the abstract and should be concluded with a paragraph that frames what was expected in the results. Most studies in the empirical literature will contain a series of expectations that are formalised into hypotheses. When expectations are rendered in the form of hypotheses, this indicates that a statistical test (a null hypothesis test, see next section) will be given to each hypothesis. The foundation for the hypotheses should have already been laid by showing how each arose from the literature review. In the final paragraph of the introduction, the series of hypotheses can be carefully woven together in a coherent paragraph. Some researchers prefer to state how each hypothesis is to be analysed statistically at this stage, but others leave this until the method section.

UNDERSTANDING THE NULL HYPOTHESIS TEST

The null hypothesis states that any apparent effect that has been detected in the experiment or survey does not differ significantly from zero (or null). Any difference is assumed to be due to chance factors alone and is not statistically significant. The difference tested for may be between two different groups of people (or animals), or between the same group at two different points in time (for example, before and after some treatment or intervention), giving rise to a 'repeated measures design'. Zero is taken as the assumed value for the general population on any given measure after the values have been 'standardised' (that is, made to range between a mean of 0 and standard deviation of 1). If a sample is taken from the population and tested on a given value (for example, self-esteem), the null hypothesis will assume that the sample is no different from the population (that is, does not differ significantly from 0). However, if the sample is far enough away from 0, then a significant difference is reported.

Illustration — Using IQ

The average or mean IQ score within the general population is 100.
Two thirds of the population fall within 15 points below or above this score (that is, within a range of 85 to 115). These two values are one 'standard deviation' below and above the mean respectively. In a statistical test the mean and standard deviation (refers to variation from the mean) are standardised to 0 and 1 respectively.

If 100 people are sampled at random and given an IQ test, and then the average of all these is taken, we can then test whether they differ significantly from 100 (or 0 when standardised). From one sample to another we would expect some fluctuation above and below the mean. For example it might be a score of 103 in our first sample and 98 in our second sample. We might conclude that these differences were not statistically significant, that is they are explained by random fluctuation around the mean.

However, let us suppose that we test two groups after we have given some specialised tuition to one group. In this case we might find that the 'control' group did not differ significantly from the mean (with this group we cannot reject the null hypothesis). With the 'treatment' group we might find that after a statistical test there is a significant difference between the mean and the group score. In this case we reject the null hypothesis and accept the alternative or experimental hypothesis. The two hypotheses can be written formally as follows: a) The null hypothesis (symbol H_0) is that neither of the groups will differ significantly from the IQ score in the general population. b) The experimental hypothesis (symbol H_1) is that the treatment group will differ significantly from the general population in the IQ score.

When a null hypothesis test is used this involves 'inferential' statistics as opposed to 'descriptive' statistics, which describe patterns and trends in the data. With inferential statistics, inferences are drawn from the data based on the null hypothesis test.

In another example you might test whether dental anxiety is reduced in a group that are tested before and after an intervention. Let us suppose we measure the anxiety levels of 50 people in a dentist's waiting room without any intervention. Fifteen minutes later we measure their anxiety levels again after we have let them hear relaxing background music and a short comedy video that has them all in fits of laughter. The next step is to apply an inferential statistical test between scores at time one and at time two. If the anxiety levels have reduced in a statistically significant manner, it can be 'inferred' that the treatment has worked.

GETTING TO GRIPS WITH THE ELUSIVE P–VALUES

The *p*–values (or significance values) follow the same principles no matter what statistic is used (for example, t-test, chi-square, correlation etc.). A statistically significant result is one where the p–value is less than (symbol <) .05. This means that there is less than 5 per cent of a probability of the results having occurred by chance. For example if a t-test is applied in the above example related to the dentist's waiting room, let us suppose that the difference in scores at times one and two results in a t–value of 2.7, and a p–value of .02. It can be concluded that the result is statistically significant because the p–value is less than .05 (and therefore that the treatment worked). If the statistic had not been significant then the p–value would have been greater than (symbol >) .05. A good rule of thumb is that as the test statistic gets higher, the p–value will get lower and the result will be statistically significant when the p–value falls below .05. If the researcher is looking for a statistically significant result then she or he will be hoping that the t–value (or any other test statistic) will be high. Statistical tests are less likely to be significant with small samples, because the test has less power to detect the differences or associations, and that is why it is always preferable to get a good-sized sample. If the independent variable (the variable we manipulate) had no effect on the dependent variable (the outcome we measure) and the researcher has detected a result that has occurred randomly, this is known as a 'type 1 error'. Conversely, if there is an effect but the test has failed to pick this up, this is known as a 'type 2 error' (Robson, 1994).

Initially it is important just to grasp that a statistic is either significant or not significant, and the p–value (or significance value) that marks the cut off point for this decision is .05. When the statistic is significant, the accompanying p–value will be less than (<) .05, and when the statistic is not significant the p–value will be greater than (>) .05. It should be noted that many students are prone to get confused between .5 and .05. In computer output, the p–values are often listed under the heading, 'Significance'. Because many students struggle to grasp and remember the above points they are summarised succinctly below:

1. The cut off point for deciding if a statistic is significant or not is .05. The statistic is significant if the accompanying p–value is below this, and non-significant if the related p–value is above this.

2. Significance (or p–values) are used with a whole range of inferential statistics (t-tests, correlation, chi-square etc.).

3. p–values go 'down' as the test statistic goes 'up' (that is, the higher the value of the t-test or correlation, the lower will be the accompanying significance or p–value).

4. A statistic that is significant with a large sample may not be significant with a small sample.

5. Two basic errors can be committed with statistical tests — a type 1 error occurs when an apparent effect or association is observed that has happened randomly, and a type 2 error occurs when a real effect or association has not been detected.

Exercise — Testing for arachnophobia

Two groups of people were tested for arachnophobia (spider phobia). Half the sample ($n = 50$) reported high levels of arachnophobia and the other half ($n = 50$) reported none. Each individual was left in a room to watch a short video and was made aware that a tarantula was in the room safely enclosed in a glass case. It was expected that those who reported high levels of arachnophobia would look much more frequently over at the glass case than those who reported no fear of spiders. Results demonstrated that there was a difference in scores between the two groups, and as expected the spider phobic group (group A) looked much more frequently toward the glass case. A t-test for independent groups was carried out to ascertain if the difference was statistically significant. The result was:

$$t = 3.926, p = .008$$

1. Was the result statistically significant?
2. What would H_0 and H_1 have been in this study?

A month later the above two groups were tested in exactly the same way again. The result was

$$t = 4.231, p = .002$$

Was this result statistically significant?
Another t-test was then applied to ascertain if group A was more or less spider phobic at time 2 (this was a related t-test because it was with the same group at two different points in time). The result was

$$t = 1.481, p = .141$$

Was the result statistically significant?
A final t-test was then applied to the non-phobic group (group B) to ascertain if they looked toward the tarantula more or less often than they had done at time 1. The result was

$$t = 1.943, p = .061$$

Was the result statistically significant?
If you have not worked it out, the first two tests above are statistically significant, but the second two are not. The above example is based on a university experiment although the data are fictitious.

STATING EXPECTATIONS FOR DESCRIPTIVE STATISTICS

As previously stated, the null hypothesis test relates to inferential statistics, but there are also descriptive statistics to grapple with. These do what they say in that they describe the data rather than draw inferences from them. Descriptive statistics have the advantage of allowing the reader to see the patterns, trends and shape in the data. Chapter 7 'Acquiring Numeracy Skills' examines one form of descriptive statistics known as 'frequencies'. Another useful descriptive statistic is the mean (sometimes described as the 'arithmetic average'). An 'X' with a bar above it represents the mean ($\bar{X}$). This statistic is calculated by adding all the numbers in a data set and then dividing these by their composite number. For example the mean of 3, 4, 5, and 6 is $3 + 4 + 5 + 6 = 18$ divided by (symbol /) $4 = 4.5$. The mode is another form of average, and is the most frequently recurring number in a data set. The third form of average is the median, which is the central number in a data set. Together the three averages are described as 'measures of central tendency'. Each of these can be requested within a statistical package or they can be calculated by hand or identified by eye (only the mode and median) in a data set. Any of the three measures of central tendency can be misused to give a false impression. For example if it is said that the average salary is £30,000 in a company (because 10 people earn that wage – the mode is used), and 100 people within the company earn between £15,000 and £20,000, then a very misleading impression is given. It is therefore often useful to present all three measures of central tendency.

Exercise — Central tendency statistics

In the simple data set below, see if you can identify the mode
and the median, and calculate the mean

2 3 4 5 5 5 6 7 7 8 8 9 9

mode = ...

median = ...

mean = ...

An important statistic closely associated with the mean, and calculated from it, is the standard deviation (sd), that is, the square root of the average of every score's deviation from the mean. As an example, let us suppose that a sample of schoolteachers scored with a mean of 40 on Rosenberg's (1965) self-esteem scale, and there was a standard deviation of eight. The standard deviation value gives an idea of how clustered or dispersed the respondents' scores were around the mean. If the standard deviation had been 15 there would have been more spread or variance in the teachers' scores, and if it had been four then the responses would have been tightly clustered around the mean. In the general population it is often expected that when responses are converted into data they appear in a bell-shaped curve or 'normal distribution'. The mean is a vertical line through the middle of the curve and the responses below and above this are on either side. The area in the bell-shaped curve that encompasses one standard deviation above and below the mean accounts for two thirds of responses. In the first example above (mean = 40, sd = 8), approximately two thirds or 68 per cent of the teachers scored between 32 and 48 on the Rosenberg self-esteem scale.

The sd is designated as a measure of dispersion, as is the variance, which is the standard deviation squared. Another measure of dispersion is the range, which refers to the lowest and highest scores in the sample. It is useful to compare the potential range with the actual range obtained in the sample. For instance, in Rosenberg's (1965) measure of self-esteem there are 10 questions with a score of one to five on each. If all questions are answered this means that the lowest possible score is 10 (10×1) and the highest possible score is 50 (10×5). In our hypothetical example, let us suppose that the lowest score for teachers was 25 and the highest was 47. At least one teacher was very high on self-esteem (near 50), but none was rock bottom (near 10). The pattern in the data indicates that the teachers are generally toward the higher end of the scale (the mean is 40) and the standard deviation indicates that most were not far away from this score. In contrast the score for a sample of long-term unemployed people might demonstrate that they are toward the lower end of the self-esteem scale (for example, a mean of 20 and a standard deviation of eight). If the two samples were combined they would give a distribution of responses that were fairly well spread out over the scale. Moreover by working out the midpoint in a scale (30 on Rosenberg), it can easily see be seen where the responses from a sample are in relation to this. The teachers' mean score is 10 points above this, and the mean for the long-term unemployed is 10 points below this. The standard deviation will tell whether the responses around the mean overlap the midpoint of the scale.

In concluding this section, it is clear that you can state what you expect to find in relation to your descriptive statistics if you have a basis for doing so. The expected patterns, trends and shape of the data can be stated even though these are not stated as a formal hypothesis or given an inferential statistical test. Descriptive statistics are too often undervalued and passed over as if unimportant. In reality they are an essential part of the data screening and an integral part of the overall picture. They are the starting point for subsequent tests because they show the shape and spread of each measure independently, before the statistical test between the measures is applied.

PULLING A STRING THROUGH THE PEARLS

At the end of the literature review, the series of hypotheses related to each planned statistical test should be presented in written form but not in the manner of a shopping list. The hypotheses will be much more readable if they flow in a logical and coherent manner, with one leading naturally into the other.

Exercise — Testing Olympiads

Imagine that you are to test a group of athletes in preparation during the weeks leading up to the departure for the Olympic games. What you are assigned to measure over 28 days is (increases/decreases in) time in training, quality of sleep, time in socialising, performance records and levels of fitness/fatigue. Before you commence your tests you are required to state what you expect to find in relation to each of the following:

1. What you expect to find in terms of hours training and sleeping each day.
2. Describe how you would expect performance to improve as the time for the Olympics draws nearer.
3. Describe how performance will be related to fitness levels.
4. Describe how performance should be related to self-confidence.
5. Describe how performance will be related to socialising patterns.
6. Describe how sleep quality should relate to performance.

Each of the above can be framed into a series of hypotheses, but the key would be to integrate them into one coherent whole rather than as a series of disjointed, unconnected expectations.

Presenting tables and graphs

A SIMPLE GRAPHICAL PRESENTATION

The whole point of presenting graphs or charts is to present the data in pictorial form in order to make them more readily interpretable. Therefore the graph should be a simple and clear representation of the results. Take the example below (a bar chart) that illustrates the differences between males and females in English and mathematics examinations.

Males scored higher than females on the mathematics test but the pattern was reversed in an English test. Of course it would also be necessary to describe the pattern in the textual commentary below the bar chart, but the chart itself will give a good picture of the trends in the results. Bar charts can be more simple or more complex than the one presented below, but the exercise below will give you a working knowledge of drawing bar charts.

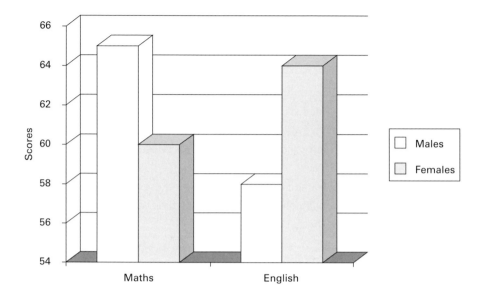

Figure 6.1 BAR CHART OF MALE AND FEMALE MEAN SCORES FOR MATHEMATICS AND ENGLISH TESTS

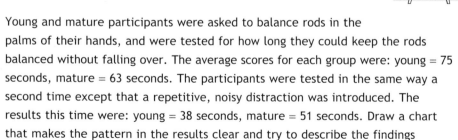

Exercise — Drawing a bar chart

Draw a bar chart like the one in Figure 6.1 for the following data:

Young and mature participants were asked to balance rods in the palms of their hands, and were tested for how long they could keep the rods balanced without falling over. The average scores for each group were: young = 75 seconds, mature = 63 seconds. The participants were tested in the same way a second time except that a repetitive, noisy distraction was introduced. The results this time were: young = 38 seconds, mature = 51 seconds. Draw a chart that makes the pattern in the results clear and try to describe the findings comprehensively in a short paragraph.

A SCATTERPLOT

In the previous example the aim in drawing the bar chart was to show the differences (or similarities) between two groups (males and females) on two tests

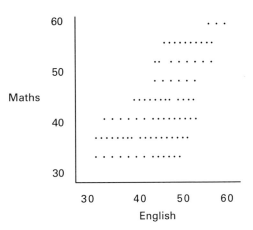

Figure 6.2 THOSE WHO SCORED LOW ON ONE TEST ALSO SCORED LOW ON THE OTHER, AND THOSE WHO SCORED HIGH ON ONE TEST WERE ALSO HIGH ON THE OTHER

(English and mathematics). However, it is also often useful to examine the association within each group on two scores (for example, male scores on English and mathematics). A scatterplot helps to show whether participants who scored high or low on the English test also scored high or low on the maths test. A scatterplot is associated with a statistic known as a correlation (this is a measure of association on two scores that ranges from 0 to one, can be positive or negative and can be weak [0 to .3], moderate [.3 to .6] or strong [.6 to 1]. The correlation is symbolised by 'r'. Let us suppose that females who scored high on English also scored high on maths and vice-versa (for example, a positive, strong correlation of $r = 0.8$). On a scatterplot this would look like Figure 6.2 above: each person's score on both tests is represented by a dot.

Let us suppose that with the males the pattern is reversed – males who scored high in mathematics, scored low in English (the correlation was negative and strong: $r = -0.8$). The scatterplot might look something like Figure. 6.3 below.

The next step is to include males and females together to ascertain what the strength of association is between English and mathematics performance. From running the test statistic the correlation was positive but weak [$r = 0.12$] and Figure 6.4 below shows that the points are randomly scattered with no clear pattern in the data.

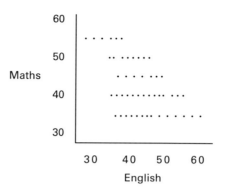

Figure 6.3   THOSE WHO SCORED LOW ON ONE TEST SCORED HIGH ON THE OTHER

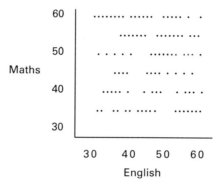

Figure 6.4   THERE IS NO CLEAR PATTERN WHEN EACH INDIVIDUAL SCORE IS
COMPARED ON BOTH INDICES OF PERFORMANCE

Sometimes a 'regression line' is drawn through the centre of all the points to illustrate central slope within the data. If lines were to be drawn to represent each of the above patterns they might look something like those presented below.

The steeper the slope on the line, the better the association between the two indices of performance. In positive correlations, the line will slope from bottom left to top right. In negative correlations the line will slope from top left to bottom right. Where there is no clear pattern in the data, and therefore evidence of a weak correlation, the regression line will be more or less horizontal, as in Figure 6.5 below. If a correlation is negative, the negative sign should be inserted, and where there is no sign it is assumed to be positive.

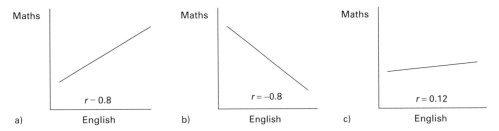

Figure 6.5 REGRESSION LINES INDICATING DIRECTION AND STRENGTH OF RELATIONSHIP IN ENGLISH AND MATHEMATICS PERFORMANCE FOR MALES AND FEMALES

PRESENTING TABLES OF RESULTS

Tables that summarise the findings from the analyses should be presented along with some commentary outlining the results. In some disciplines the comments are inserted below the table but in others they are above. The reader should be reminded of what was being tested in the study and if the hypothesis related to the particular result was supported. Three examples are presented below that are based on an actual study carried out at university (although the data are changed). The study was designed to assess the impact of a range of personality factors on academic achievement as measured by performance across a range of examinations. The personality measures were all designed for academic situations. They were academic self-efficacy (confidence), academic conscientiousness and two measures of academic anxiety in test situations (test irrelevant thoughts and worry). The first table presents descriptive statistics, the second is a presentation of positive correlations and the third summarises the measures that were negatively correlated with examinations performance.

Table 6.1 below should be described with a few descriptive observations and some minimal interpretative comment. For example the mean score for exams (63.22) is well above the required pass mark of 40 but short of grade A standard (70 +). The standard deviation and range indicate that there is considerable dispersion in students' exam performance, and this is consistent with previously reported trends. Self-efficacy scores were, as expected, toward the higher end of the scale (above the mid-point which was 40). In contrast students were not as high in self-reported conscientiousness as might be expected – the mean was below the midpoint (that is, 40) of the scale. The mean scores for the two test anxiety measures (test irrelevant thoughts and worry) were both above the midpoints (16 and 24) for the scales, indicating that many

Table 6.1 DESCRIPTIVE STATISTICS FOR STUDENTS' SELF-REPORTED ACADEMIC PERSONALITY MEASURES AND EXAMINATION PERFORMANCE

	Mean	Standard Deviation	Range
Self-efficacy	47.34	9.11	20–63
Conscientiousness	34.58	10.25	18–61
Test irrelevant thoughts	22.29	5.87	5–27
Worry	32.14	6.99	6–38
Examination results	63.22	10.72	35–80

Scale midpoints: Self-efficacy = 40. Conscientiousness = 40.
Test irrelevant thoughts = 16. Worry = 24.

Table 6.2 CORRELATION COEFFICIENTS DEMONSTRATING THE RELATIONSHIP BETWEEN SELF-REPORT PERSONALITY MEASURES AND EXAMINATION PERFORMANCE

	Exam Performance
Academic self-efficacy	0.358*
Academic conscientiousness	0.324*

* $p < .05$

students suffer from anxiety during exams. Standard deviations for all measures indicate a good spread in students' responses and index of academic performance. In general it can be concluded from the results that students appear to have healthy self-efficacy beliefs and perform reasonably well in exams but their conscientious application to study could be improved and their test anxiety levels (represented by worry and test irrelevant thoughts) would need to be reduced.

Tables are usually larger than Table 6.2 but it has been kept simple for illustrative purposes. The two correlations reported above are positive, moderate and significant (the latter is indicated by $p < .05$). Both are related to exam performance in the expected direction (that is, positively). The fact that they are significant indicates that the

Table 6.3 CORRELATION COEFFICIENTS DEMONSTRATING THE RELATIONSHIP BETWEEN TEST ANXIETY MEASURES AND EXAMINATION PERFORMANCE

	Exam Performance
Test irrelevant thoughts	−0.422*
Worry	−0.403*

* $p < .05$

relationship between the measures did not occur merely by chance. In the introduction or discussion you could elaborate on what self-efficacy and conscientiousness mean in more detail. However, at this point it would be sufficient to state that self-efficacy beliefs and conscientious practices are related to exam performance in the expected manner. It is important that the correct language is used in reporting the correlation – it is not stated that self-efficacy and conscientiousness *cause* good examination performance. The claim is that the two measures are *associated* or *related* to performance in a significant manner. The paragraph could be ended with some statement such as, 'these results suggest that the development of sound self-confidence (self-efficacy) and the cultivation of planned academic behavioural patterns (conscientiousness) are likely to impact positively on academic performance'. More detailed strategies for improving performance can be developed in the discussion.

Results reported in Table 6.3 support the hypothesis that self-reported test anxiety responses are negatively related to performance in subsequent examinations. Both measures of test anxiety, test irrelevant thoughts and worry, were moderately related to performance ($r = -0.422, p < .05$ and $r = -0.403, p < .05$), that is, they are between 0.3 and 0.6. Students who allow their thoughts to be distracted during exams by irrelevant thoughts or who divert attention to worrying about lack of preparation or how others are doing are likely to perform more poorly than those who maintain focus. In the discussion these conclusions can be elaborated on by suggesting strategies that students can use to reduce anxiety and to maintain focus during an exam.

QUALITY IN THE TITLES

Every graph that is presented in a report should have all axes clearly labelled and should be presented with a good, clear title. Tutors will give credit where care has been taken with labels and titles. These are the features that combine to give clarity and comprehensiveness to the report. Titles should contain enough information to convey the thrust of the analysis without being too verbose or unwieldy. Statistical and word processing packages may impose limits on the number of characters that can be used in titles and labels. It is well worth the time and effort to get the title right. Look back at the bar chart (Figure. 6.1) and think about the number of essential features that had to be incorporated within the title – males and females, bar chart, English and maths mean scores. These had to be framed into a simple sentence that summarised all the relevant information, and this was done in thirteen words – 'Bar chart of male and female mean scores for mathematics and English tests'.

Exercise – Practice examples

1. Try to write a short title for the hypothetical experiment with the balancing rods reported earlier in the chapter (assuming the use of a bar chart).
2. Attempt to write a title for the hypothetical arachnophobia study presented earlier.

DESCRIBING PATTERNS IN RESULTS

In a sense each table should be self-contained and self-explanatory. A careful title and good clear labelling of each variable or measure used can help achieve this. It is less likely to be achieved if any result is obscurely presented or if the whole table is too unwieldy. Very lengthy tables with excessive data make for difficult comprehension. The whole purpose behind any table is to reduce data to a manageable and comprehensible level. The reader should be able to see the trends in the results from a glance at the tables or graphs. However, it is also necessary to supply some descriptive and interpretative comment to elaborate on these, so that nothing is left to chance. More detailed interpretative comment can be given in the discussion, but it helps readers to maintain focus if they are guided through the study with succinct, incisive comments. It is also important to state whether results supported the related hypothesis or confirmed expectations. Moreover, all central and important results should be commented on as it will appear bizarre to run tests, present tables and graphs and then leave much of this without comment.

A method section

DESCRIBING PARTICIPANTS

This section of the method may simply be designated as 'Sample'. If the sample is comprised of people they should be described as 'participants' as opposed to 'subjects' – the latter term can be employed if a sample of animals is used. Background characteristics of the sample should include the total composition (for example, $n = 150$), gender, average age, nature of sample (for example, students, military personnel, the unemployed) and any other information that is relevant to the study.

EXPLAINING PROCEDURE

This section should be headed by the word 'Procedure' and should describe how/why the sample was selected for the study. Were there any ethical considerations or issues of confidentiality, and if so how were they addressed? Also describe how the study was carried out, who supervised it and what verbal/written instructions were given. If participants were debriefed after an experiment, this should be referred to. If there was selection between a control and experimental group this should be explained (for example, was the selection made randomly by choosing names out of a hat?) as should any attempts made to minimise potentially confounding problems. If any variables were manipulated by the experimenter/researcher, this process should be described. Moreover, the researcher should describe how the data were coded for computer entry, and should refer to why the particular statistical techniques used were chosen. A simple rule of thumb is that sufficient information should be provided in the procedure, and in the method in general, to allow the experiment or survey to be replicated by someone else.

DESCRIBING MATERIALS AND MEASURES

Any measures, apparatus or materials that were used in the study should be mentioned (for example, pencil, paper, stopwatch, compass, thermometer), and where necessary described in more detail (for example, Rosenberg's Self-esteem Measure, blood pressure apparatus or glass case for a tarantula). Any similar work previously published in academic journals can be consulted for guidelines. If more lengthy detail is required this can be incorporated within an appendix at the end of the report. For example, it would be useful to include a copy of a questionnaire at the end of a report, and also more detailed results that might interrupt the flow of the report in the main body of the text. If appendices are used they should be both labelled and referred to somewhere in the report.

Discussing the results

MORE THAN A RESTATEMENT OF RESULTS

A common failure with students in practical reports is that the discussion is frequently little more than a restatement of the results. The discussion must throw more light on and add further interpretation to the results. For example, the writer can show the connection between the various tables of results and demonstrate how each result builds on the previous one. The discussion is an opportunity, not merely to summarise each result, but to give a panoramic view of the complete study and show how it is woven into a coherent whole. Each result should be highlighted and discussed, and any discrepancies between expectations and findings should be addressed. Some explanation should be offered for any findings that were not predicted. Most importantly new aspects should be highlighted and directions for future research should be outlined.

Exercise — Example for practice

Look back over the three tables of examples given, and suggest ways in which Table 6.2 builds on Table 6.1, and Table 6.3 builds on Table 6.2. Also try to summarise the overall pattern in all the results and what implications these may have for students and educators.

REFER TO EACH RESULT

Another recurrent student failure in discussions is to completely ignore some important result as if it were not part of the study. Even if the result was not significant or not as expected, it should nevertheless be referred to. Such a result allows space to suggest reasons why the outcome was not as expected, what improvements future studies should make to rectify any inherent problems. Alternatively, perhaps the study is more accurate than previous studies that found different results, and this is also a matter that can be addressed in the discussion. A discussion does leave room for some speculation, but this has to be reasonable and cautious language should be used. Caution should also be applied to inferences drawn from clear results, for example, 'these results suggest that' is preferable to 'these results prove beyond doubt that'.

Exercise – Explaining an anomaly

Look at Table 6.1. Students' mean score for (academic) conscientiousness was not as high as might be expected. This may seem surprising as we might expect students to be focused and applied to their studies. Discuss. Were the students too modest in underreporting their planning, discipline, effort, sacrifice, promptness etc? Or were they measuring themselves by standards that were unrealistically high? Or could it be the case that many of the students in the study would really need to raise their standards more substantially? Or is the truth a mixture of all these?

REFER TO LIMITATIONS

An experiment or survey is not worthwhile unless it is a serious attempt to carry the research process forward in some way. No salesperson will ever do well if they give the impression that they are not convinced themselves about the quality and value of the product they are selling. Ensure, therefore, that the research is presented in such a manner that leaves the reader with the impression that the study has made a contribution to knowledge. There is no shame, in pointing to the limitations in the study. You may have been aware of some of these before the study began, but others may have emerged during the study. Humankind's first attempts to fly were limited in success, but at least the efforts pointed to the possibility that the law of gravity could eventually be counteracted. Remember that even simple and basic research, with all its flaws, can open new vistas and may trigger ideas for others to develop subsequently.

Olympic relay races

In the relay races at the Olympic games, each contestant is expected to hand the baton on to the next runner in the team until the final contestant completes the last stretch of track. No one is expected to run the complete race themselves, and this would be a disadvantage. Similarly all research moves forward in an evolutionary manner. Each new piece of research should carry the process forward, but it has to be recognised that future researchers will 'pick up the baton' and will carry the research closer to perfection by addressing the limitations in the previous research. Sometimes progress is more accelerated than others, but there is always room for more refinement. A good researcher will recognise their useful but limited contribution in the overall scheme of things.

POINT THE WAY TO FUTURE WORK

The vision for future work may be triggered in someone who reads your research, or it may be that you will be the one who points up future directions yourself. While engaged in practical studies at the early or middle stages of an undergraduate programme, students should think about what they might later do for their final year project (dissertation). Some of the vistas that open up during a practical study may give inspiration for fuller development later, or an idea may be activated as a mere aside in the study. Some of the great human discoveries (such as penicillin) came about accidentally while the researcher was looking for something else – a 'serendipity'. It is wise to always be alert for ideas that can be later developed, and to make a note of these as soon as they are activated in your mind.

At the conclusion of the practical report, it is customary to summarise the main findings in the results and to state whether these supported the hypotheses and expectations. It is also essential to suggest how the findings might be applied in practice, to highlight any limitations in the study and to point out the suggested directions that future research should take.

SUMMARY

♦ In a practical report, the abstract/summary should be written when all else is completed.

♦ A brief literature review in the introduction helps place the practical study within the context of relevant research development.

♦ A practical/lab report should be presented in a scientific manner that conforms to professional and established conventions.

♦ The frequent aim behind practical studies is to replicate or challenge previous findings and test some new facet that will carry the research process forward.

♦ Experiments, surveys etc. should be tested statistically and expectations concerning results should be formulated into clear hypotheses.

♦ Two central aspects of statistics are Descriptive (describing observable trends, patterns and shape in the data) and Inferential (the likelihood that an obtained result emerged because of some treatment, intervention or naturally occurring phenomenon, rather than by chance).

♦ Graphs and tables should all have clear titles and accurate labels, and should be accompanied by some comment to guide the reader through what they indicate.

♦ No presented result should be ignored and the writer should state whether each result was expected or not.

♦ In the discussion, all results should be woven into a coherent whole.

♦ The discussion should serve to focus on the direction the results point to, any inherent limitations in the study and how these could be addressed in future studies.

♦ The usual order for a practical report is title, abstract, introduction, method (includes participants, procedure and materials), results and discussion.

7 Acquring Numeracy Skills

KEY CONCEPTS

● ANXIETY ● SELF-EFFICACY ● INVESTMENT OF EFFORT ● NUMERACY ● MATHEMATICS ● STATISTICS ● PERSEVERANCE ● MOTIVATION ● RELEVANCE ● APPLICATIONS ● NUMBER MANIPULATION ● ADDITION AND SUBTRACTION ● MULTIPLICATION AND DIVISION ● FREQUENCIES AND PERCENTAGES ● TABLES AND CHARTS ● LEVELS OF MEASUREMENT ● HISTOGRAM ● BAR CHART ● PIE CHART ● NOMINAL ● ORDINAL ● INTERVAL

Stationary in gridlock

WELL DOCUMENTED EVIDENCE ON MATHEMATICS ANXIETY

Empirical studies have demonstrated the phenomenon of 'emotional words' – evidence shows that certain words are more likely to elicit a Galvinic Skin Response (an indicator of a stressful reaction) even when presented subliminally, while other words are neutral and elicit no such response (Hayes & Orrell, 1991). Each individual will have their own list of words that elicit a positive or negative emotional response. For many people the words 'mathematics', 'statistics' and related words are on their proscribed list of avoidance words!

Apart from the anecdotal evidence about mathematics anxiety that can be easily accumulated from individuals, the strongest evidence for it is perhaps the proliferation of scales that have been developed to measure it over the years. Similar scales have not been constructed to measure anxieties in other subject domains (or at least not to the same extent).

One example of such a measure is the Mathematics Anxiety Rating Scale – MARS (Richardson & Suinn, 1972), later revised as the RMARS (Revised Mathematic Anxiety Rating Scale). Students do not appear to report the same intense anxieties with respect to geography, history, literature etc. Numbers appear to have their own insidious way of wreaking havoc with our nerves and perceptions! Added to this is the fact that many employers and colleges are looking for a respectable pass in a mathematics subject as a basic requirement, and more students may need to do re-sits in maths than in other subjects. Negative perceptions about maths and the anxieties associated with it, are likely to contribute to students' poor performance in maths, as much as any difficulty they may have with the subject matter (Betz & Hackett, 1983)

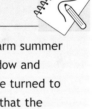

Not alone in the universe

A story is reported about a church that was poorly attended on a warm summer Sunday evening. During the service the minister looked out the window and noticed that a Methodist church nearby was also poorly attended. He turned to the scanty congregation and said, 'Well, at least we can thank God that the Methodists are not doing any better!' In a strange way we seem to be able to derive some comfort from the fact that other people suffer the same struggle as we do. That can certainly be applied in the case of maths anxieties and negative perceptions. If you start making your fears and concerns known to others, you will soon discover that you are not alone in the universe. It is a helpful start to feel a sense of solidarity with others in this, but it is most unhelpful to imagine that that is the way you are, and therefore the way you must always be.

ALL CULTURES AND AGE GROUPS

Maths anxiety is a universal phenomenon and quite pervasive in all cultures, age groups and in both females and males (Levine, 1995). It is one factor that many diverse kinds of people have in common – if you suffer from it you will be able to find others comparable to yourself in age, gender, culture etc. who suffer with you. However, that does not imply that you have to resign yourself to sticking with the status quo.

It has been claimed that in British universities generally there is fear of all things mathematical (Kline, 1994), and the relevant literature demonstrates that this fear is manifested universally at university level. In other words, problems with maths do not terminate at college entrance. Maths is the subject that many want to avoid or devote minimal attention to. In spite of the fact that the importance of maths or statistics to many courses is recognised by students, they still hope for minimal contact with the discipline.

Statistics appear to generate as much, if not more, negativity and anxiety as maths. Lalonde and Gardner (1993) suggested that the old, entrenched problems with maths lie dormant in students and are re-awakened when they encounter statistics at college. It does not take a lot of exposure to statistics at university before students become aware that the study of statistics is not an enjoyable experience for them. Whenever students fall behind in a statistics course they often suffer doubts and deficiency in self-belief, and fear that they will never master the discipline. This in turn can lead to avoidance behaviours, minimal investment in effort and speedy demoralisation. Further symptoms are a tendency to procrastinate in addressing lessons or giving up too easily when problems are encountered. All this may be related to a previous history of unsuccessful experiences, or limited and strenuous successes with maths, and persistent consequent doubts.

Compounded by the 'non-user friendly approach'

It must be very intimidating to be in an environment where not a word that is spoken is understood by the hearer, especially when some form of help is needed. When a listener tunes into a radio programme that is broadcast in a language totally unknown to them, they will hear a string of sounds that are tantamount to gibberish as far as they are concerned. Lalonde and Gardner (1993) suggested that learning statistics is like learning a foreign language – at first the communication appears to be in a code language that excludes the uninitiated. The same applies to mathematics, for it not only contains numbers (a source of anxiety in themselves), but also symbols and algebra. The numbers might be OK if they did not have to be manipulated! And the algebra and symbols might be fine if they were not associated with the manipulation of the numbers! Just as some students lose heart in learning a foreign language, so some are quickly demoralised in learning mathematics and statistics.

Why invest the effort to attempt to learn a discipline that is foreign to your natural mode of thinking when you are convinced that you are not going to master the discipline in the end. The answers are that it will be very useful to you, that it can become a natural mode of thinking for you and that it will not conquer you if you are determined not to let it. Developing confidence is all-important in the study of mathematics and statistics. This will be more thoroughly addressed in a later section of the present chapter.

THE ELUSIVE IVORY TOWER APPROACH

Mathematics was not merely designed for the proverbial white-haired professors who sit in their ivory towers navel-gazing. Nevertheless, you may get the impression that there is an exclusive club for those who have mastered maths and a larger club for the rest of us who fall short. It has been suggested that in grades of learning there are novices, advanced beginners, those that are competent, those that are proficient and those that are experts (McCarthy & Hatcher, 1996). You may get the feeling that the experts have left planet earth and are out of reach in the stratosphere. It is difficult enough to learn what seems like a foreign language, without having to learn it from those who appear aloof, unable to communicate and deficient in pitching the lessons at the right level. Students have frequently complained that part of their problem with learning maths is associated with those they have to learn it from.

Teachers sometimes move on to point 4 in the lesson when students are still trying to comprehend the second point, and the teacher is unaware of the difficulty. It may be a consolation to know that some of your problems in learning maths may not be entirely of your own making. Teachers themselves may come to expect that struggle, anxiety and confusion are a normal part of the learning process for students.

Consider again the five phases of learning referred to previously (that is, novice stage, advanced beginner, competent, proficient and expert), and realise that it takes time, patience and practise to move through the stages gradually. Do not be demoralised when you listen to the experts, but rather resolve that you will thoroughly master the phase you are at before you move up to the next grade.

THE SHROUD OF ABSTRACT THINKING

It is a sad fact of life that many students do perceive mathematics to be like a foreign language, because they imagine that it has no relevance to them other than to help them pass on to the next phase of their academic career. Why would anyone want to learn a foreign language if they have no desire to visit the country where it is spoken, or read literature in that language or communicate with others in that language? Mathematics to many is nothing more than an abstract mental discipline that has little value apart from passing a test or exam and showing off! Moreover, calculators and computers can do calculations for us, so why should we bother? However, the reality is that mathematics is probably more 'natural' to most of us than we realise, and we may be using it much more frequently than we think.

For example, when we are asked a question in everyday conversation, we may initially think of three possible answers – we quickly reject two and subtract them from the three and are left with one. Sometimes we think aloud and sometimes we quietly per-form some mental arithmetic. Or when we contemplate eating a slice of gateau, we do the mental arithmetic on how many slices we have already eaten that week or perhaps how many slices we have regularly eaten over the last few weeks. If the subject is relevant to us, and we are highly motivated about it, then all our mathematical skills will come into play quite spontaneously. This can be applied to weight-watchers who regularly monitor their calorie intake and weight loss (or gain), to holiday makers trying to barter with the salesperson or to athletes trying to improve their time.

A SNARE FOR PERFECTIONISTS

People who are perfectionists (for themselves) are sometimes in danger of setting stan-dards that they will never attain. As a result they may suffer high anxiety and their perfectionism may be a factor that impedes rather than facilitates their progress in learning mathematics (Onwuegbuzie, 1997). For those who are perfectionists for themselves, a relaxation of unrealistic standards may ironically serve to induce better progress and higher standards than they were likely to attain.

Again we can refer to the successive stages that lead to becoming an expert. These stages demonstrate that there needs to be gradual evolution and growth if a set target is to be reached. This means that it is better not to become impatient with ourselves or to become frustrated with our lack of progress. Perfectionists are likely to underestimate the progress they have already made because of one or two (perhaps small) things that they have not yet mastered. The real goal for many students would not be to become an expert in maths/statistics, but to acquire a good working knowledge that will give them confidence and competence to achieve at a good level. With the right strategy, some consistent practise and a proper attitude, that goal is well within reach of the average student.

Preparing to take off the brakes

STATISTICS NEED NOT BE 'SADISTICS'

Some students have dubbed statistics as 'sadistics'! To them, grappling with statistics is like sitting in a dentist's waiting room listening to the music for the *Omen*! Some subjects are enjoyable for students, some are neutral, but statistics are out at the extreme end of the continuum as torturous.

Maybe the best some students can hope for in the immediate future is to bring statistics toward the neutral band, but some practise, understanding and success can lead into the enjoyment category.

A simple experiment conducted some years ago demonstrated that people can come to like what they are familiar with, even if it is something quite neutral such as nonsense syllables (Zajonc, 1968). It has also been demonstrated experimentally that feared stimuli can come to be perceived as pleasant stimuli by a process of paired association. For example, if you associate statistics with mathematics, and your history of maths has been peppered with failure, confusion, lack of confidence and anxiety, then it is hardly surprising that you will want to avoid statistics as much as possible. However, if you can persevere long enough at statistics to acquire some mastery of it, this will bring you some satisfaction. Also, if you acquire some success then statistics may eventually elicit a different kind of emotion from you than that to which you have become accustomed.

You do not have to go on in the future as you did in the past. Aristotle said that if we do not learn the lessons of history, we are doomed to repeat it. Therefore we should carry the lessons of past mistakes and use them for present and future advantage. Simply put, your past experiences with maths/statistics can either be a barrier or bridge to your future progress – depending on your personal perceptions and beliefs.

Today is the first day of the rest of your life and there is no reason why you should not allow yourself the luxury of a fresh start. If you can change your mindset toward statistics, in spite of previously uncomfortable or painful experiences, then it may well be that you will go from strength to strength and discover capabilities that you never imagined you had. Such a transformation is not inconceivable and can be substantiated by anecdotal evidence from students who, after initial diffidence, have eventually achieved a good standard in statistics.

Many researchers have come to accept that beliefs and behaviours are reciprocally and dynamically associated with each other. This implies that if your personal beliefs about your own abilities are negative, your consequent behaviours are likely to be maladaptive. Conversely, if your beliefs are constructive, then the behaviours that stem from them are likely to be productive. Adaptive behaviours will then serve to confirm sound beliefs within the framework of a positive feedback loop.

Albert Bandura (1986) proposed a construct known as 'self-efficacy' which describes an individual's belief or confidence in their own ability to perform a given task successfully. Operationally, the construct is defined as the initial decision to act, effort expended in acting and perseverance in the face of obstacles. This definition describes how the beliefs (positive or negative) will work themselves out in either adaptive or maladaptive practices respectively.

Reams of empirical studies have demonstrated that positive self-efficacy beliefs are advantageous in a variety of domains such as health, education, career, sports and clinical applications (Schultz & Schultz, 1994). Moreover the construct has also been applied with the same results in the domain of mathematics (Pajares &

Miller, 1995). Students who score higher in their self-efficacy beliefs are more likely to be successful in mathematics, and in statistics by extension. They are less likely to procrastinate in their study plans, more likely to invest sacrificial effort and less inclined to give up when obstacles arise than students low in self-efficacy.

Of course it is true that high self-efficacy is likely to stem from past successes, but Ozer and Bandura (1990) claimed that when self-efficacy beliefs increase, positive behaviours increase incrementally with them. Therefore a change in personal belief system, mindset and thinking style are an important element in the process of successful mathematics/statistics application.

An important key to comprehension

Professional darts players have to be good at mental arithmetic as they have to work out the routes to finish on a 'double', or whether they are able to finish with the three darts per throw allowed to them. These players are very quick at doing their sums and can't afford to make mistakes. Their proficiency and fluency at mental arithmetic probably required much practise. However, it also doubtless came about via their love for the game and their strong desire to be winners. In other words there is strong motivation to learn all the necessary skills to give them the competitive edge. Each of us is more likely to learn particular skills if we feel that we have a personal interest and investment in what we do.

It has been asserted that students will never really become competent with statistics until they begin to work with their own data sets (Lalonde & Gardner, 1993). One male student's first practical study was on the attitudes of women to balding men and he had a great personal interest in the outcome of this study! There was good motivation to see what the patterns and trends in the statistics were suggesting. Therefore it is beneficial to find a subject that really interests you, and to try to understand the mathematics through the medium of your point of interest. There is a lot of good psychology in this approach, as your interest in your chosen subject will drive you to master the statistics so that you can understand precisely what the outcomes demonstrate.

Starting to accelerate

CONQUER YOUR FEAR BY FACING IT

Clinical psychologists sometimes use a technique known as 'implosion' or 'flooding' to help clients who are gripped by a phobia. For example, a person who has been in a car accident may have difficulty getting into a car again. The therapy here may entail asking them to enter a room where there are screens on every wall with pictures of moving cars coming toward them (Hayes & Orrell, 1991). A client's fear is likely to reach its zenith during this ordeal. However, if they can remain in the room, the only direction the fear can go after it has reached its highest point is down. Indeed the client can eventually be helped to learn to relax in the presence of the feared stimulus. Similarly, if a child falls off a bicycle, they may cope with this by immediately mounting and riding again. The longer this is left, the more difficult the challenge becomes. Mathematics/statistics anxieties and negative perceptions are not conquered by a strategy of avoidance behaviours. Yet that is the ruse that many students resort to, and that is why some questionnaires aim at detecting mathematics/statistics avoidance behaviours.

The right kind of exposure to the discipline is likely to help you reduce the anxieties and perceptions that impede your progress. It has to be acknowledged, however, that the wrong kind of exposure can prove counterproductive, so you must ensure that you have a sound strategy to conquer your fear.

WORK THROUGH EXAMPLES

There is no substitute for navigating your way through worked examples. In Chapter 6 'Writing a Practical Report', the example of Pythagorus' theorem is used to give understanding of how the theorem works in practice. With some practise at this example you can become quite competent – if you know the value of two sides of a right-angled triangle you can work out the value for the longest side of the triangle (the hypotenuse) or any of the other sides. A good teacher of maths or statistics will give you practise examples to work through. This kind of practise is invaluable because it strengthens your understanding of the principles and procedures involved in the calculations. Therefore, it is wise to look out for statistics text books that provide plenty of examples to work through. Examiners will give credit if you demonstrate that you understand these principles and procedures even if you make some mistakes with the arithmetic. It is easy enough to make a mistake by pressing the wrong button on a calculator. Mathematics is a logical subject and therefore the routines to achieve the end result follow a clear pattern. Sometimes there may be more than one route to the same end result, but the important thing is to demonstrate that you have followed a logical procedure.

In the following sections there will be opportunity to practise some simple examples. The key is not just to learn formulae etc. but to operationalise your knowledge, and soon the application will become second nature. No one ever learns to swim merely by reading books on swimming. The learner has to start by dipping their toes and then getting into the water! Watch an experienced piano player and notice that they seldom need to look down at the keys they strike. Through experience and practise they have got the feel for where the notes are. The same applies to walking into a dark and unfamiliar room – you come to know where the light switch is located even if not conscious of the processes you have used to feel your way. In the same way, familiarity through sensible practise at mathematics/statistics will ensure that you do not feel forever in the dark.

GOING OVER FAMILIAR TERRITORY

A boost to your own confidence can be achieved by going over what you have already learned and comparing this with what you knew when you started. For example, there was a time when you did not know the alphabet and now you can use many combinations of the letters (in the form of words) with great dexterity. You can now literally make the alphabet talk! Likewise, your mathematical skills can be developed until you feel at ease with the subject.

If you work your way through your maths examples, and go over them periodically, you will, through time, find that many aspects of mathematics will become more 'natural' to you than you ever imagined they would. This will require practise, patience, determination and perseverance – the latter involves not succumbing to self-doubts because of previously negative experiences. When trying to solve mathematics/statistics problems, the answer sometimes comes in a flash, as if someone had just switched on a light. At other times the answer arrives more like the breaking of dawn, as when the light gradually enters the bedroom in the morning and all the items in the room slowly come into focus.

It is a basic law of learning to use what you know to get to what you don't know. You don't need to master every fact in some proposition to grasp its intent. Indeed you can listen to and get the drift of an important speech even if you do not know the meaning of every word used. In studying maths you should not demean or demoralise yourself because you do not comprehend every fact. Go over what you do know, add any additional knowledge you have grasped, and be patient with yourself as you move toward making the picture complete.

Moving smoothly through the gears

FIRST GEAR — BASIC NUMBERS AND SYMBOLS: A RUST CHECK

Addition (symbol +)

If you can count from 1 to 10 and 10 to 1, you have made a promising start! If you can then count up to 100 and back in even numbers and then up to 99 and back in odd numbers, you have made steady progress! Now practise adding the following numbers to see how efficient you are in simple addition in terms of speed and accuracy.

$$12 + 19 = ? \ 13 + 15 = ? \ 18 + 17 = ? \ 19 + 15 = ? \ 23 + 16 = ? \ 11 + 27 = ? \ 19 + 29 = ?$$

There are three simple rules that will be helpful in developing fluency and accuracy in addition:

1. When numbers are to be added that contain tens and units, the tens can be picked out and added first. Then add the units and combine the two totals.

Example 1: $83 + 94$
$= 80 + 90 = 170$
$3 + 4 = 7$
$= 170 + 7 = 177.$

(This procedure can also be used when working with hundreds, tens and units.)

2. An alternative approach might be preferred in addition.

Example 2: 85 + 78
Round these up to their nearest 10
90 + 80 = 170
Add together the two numbers that were previously added to 85 and 78
5 + 2 = 7
Subtract this total from the previous total
170 − 7 = 163.

This process may seem tedious at first, but it is useful when the units are up near the tens:

Example 3: 78 + 98
= 80 + 100
180 − (2 + 2) = 180 − 4 = 176.

For practise try this approach with the following numbers:

87 + 38 = ? 29 + 79 = ? 37 + 38 = ? 18 + 57 = ? 39 + 17 = ? 49 + 18 = ?

3. Sometimes it is easier to round down to the tens:

Example 4: 23 + 31
= 20 + 30 = 50
(3 + 1) = 4
50 + 4 = 54

(After rounding down to ten, the units are added, in contrast to rounding up, where they are subtracted.)

For practise, try out the following examples by the rounding down procedure:

41 + 32 = ? 23 + 93 = ? 53 + 82 = ? 71 + 22 = ? 34 + 25 = ? 91 + 52 = ?

You may prefer to use one of the above approaches or combinations of them. These are the kinds of routes that help facilitate efficient mental arithmetic. Through time the procedures become 'second nature', and the skill can evolve into solving more complex problems.

Subtraction (Symbol –)

Subtraction is the reverse of addition, and the best way to become competent and confident is by plenty of practise. Try the following examples for practise and to test your current level of efficiency. The given examples will gradually increase in difficulty:

$$20 - 10 = ? \ 107 - 97 = ? \ 23 - 12 = ? \ 75 - 52 = ? \ 94 - 37 = ? \ 87 = 29 = ?$$

A couple of simple strategies can be used to help improve efficiency in subtraction:

Example 5: 94 – 27

Subtract from the identical unit immediately below the higher of the two numbers (that is, 87):

$$87 - 27 = 60$$
Then subtract 87 from 94: $(94 - 87) = 7$
Add the two composites together: $60 + 7 = 67$

Now try practising the examples below:

$$52 - 19 = ? \ 63 - 28 = ? \ 31 - 18 = ? \ 94 - 27 = ? \ 85 - 58 = ? \ 76 - 37 = ?$$

Another simple device with numbers like these is presented below:

Example 6: 52 – 19
Round the lower number to the nearest 10 (that is, 19 becomes 20)
Add the number used to round up (1) to the higher number (52 becomes 53)
Subtract the two new numbers
$$53 - 20 = 33.$$

Now try this procedure out with the last practise examples given above.

Practising the examples improves speed and builds confidence. It is wise to find a balance between using a calculator and keeping the mind active. Students may find other methods in addition to those given above that may work better for them, but the above procedures will be useful for getting the mind active and engaged with mental arithmetic. Do not resent working through the simplest examples for these are the building blocks for more complex learning. You will have difficulty with the more advanced procedures if you do not learn the basics well.

Multiplication (symbol ×)

Many students may have become rusty with their multiplication tables, especially if they have become dependent on a calculator. To check out your current fluency with multiplication, see how efficient you are at working out the solution to the following examples:

$$9 \times 9 = ?\ 8 \times 7 = ?\ 5 \times 6 = ?\ 3 \times 11 = ?\ 6 \times 7 = ?\ 10 \times 12 = ?$$

If you cannot remember all of these, then you need to give immediate and regular attention to brushing up on your multiplication tables. After that you should improve speed and confidence by working through plenty of examples.

For multiplication problems that would be tedious and time consuming it is undoubtedly better to use a calculator (especially in tests or examinations) – for example, 187×251. Another instance of this is when you are is required to multiply a series of awkward numbers, such as $11 \times 15 \times 13 \times 27 \times 19$. It is always good, however, to keep the mind fresh and active by practising simple examples by mental arithmetic.

Division (symbol ÷, or a line between the numerator [top] and denominator [bottom]).

If speed and confidence can be developed with multiplication, it will be a natural step to reverse the procedures into division, for example, $7 \times 7 = 49$. $49 \div 7 = 7$.

Try out multiplying and then dividing (by each of the 2 dividing numbers) the following examples:

Example 7: 9×7. 6×11. 12×12. 5×3. 7×12. 8×7. 4×9. 3×7.

Now try out the following examples by working in the reverse order:

$$56 \div 7.\ 28 \div 4.\ 60 \div 5.\ 45 \div 9.\ 9 \div 3.\ 132 \div 11.\ 144 \div 12.$$

If these tests reveal that you are rusty, then ensure that you give yourself plenty of practice.

Effective learning is achieved by reversing the procedures used in obtaining solutions to problems (in this case multiplication and division, and addition and subtraction). Children with learning difficulties are sometimes taught to read using a method known as 'stimulus equivalence' (Sidman, 1990). In this procedure the children first learn that A = B, and then that B = C. Subsequently, they learn to reverse these two procedures (that is, C = B and B = A). They further learn that a jump can be made from A to C (that is, A = C). When they finally learn the reverse jump (C = A), they have thoroughly mastered all possible relations and connections.

For example, they may first hear the word 'car' (A), and then see the picture of a car (B). Finally, they see the written word 'car' (C). Eventually, they can with practice make all the possible connections. In the same way principles of numeracy can be more clearly understood and efficiently mastered when the student has sufficient practice at manipulating numbers in the form of addition, subtraction, multiplication and division.

SECOND GEAR – SIMPLE FREQUENCIES AND PERCENTAGES

Frequencies

Frequencies provide very useful information when the student or researcher is collecting data. They help break the data down into a readily interpretable form and to present a useful picture of them from a variety of angles. For example, the student may want to carry out a survey on self-esteem which has ten questions (or a biology student may want to document a comparable range of contents extracted from samples of various ponds). For convenience, the self-esteem example is elaborated. If there is a sample of 100 people ($n = 100$), it would be useful to know what the gender composition of the sample is (for example, 55 females and 45 males). It might also be beneficial to know the various age categories in the group – these are presented in the table below.

This allows the reader to grasp the information about age categories at a cursory glance. These categories could also be presented in terms of gender with a separate

Table 7.1 FREQUENCY TABLE SHOWING RANGE OF AGE CATEGORIES FOR SAMPLE ($n = 100$)

Age category	Frequency
15–21	15
21–25	20
26–30	30
31–35	30
36–40	15
Total	100

Table 7.2 FREQUENCY TABLE DEMONSTRATING THE RANGE OF RESPONSES TO QUESTION 1

SA	A	N	D	SD
5	5	5	65	20

table for males or females. Alternatively they could be presented in relation to a variable that is particularly relevant to a given study.

The researcher may also want to look in detail at the responses to each of the ten questions from the self-esteem questionnaire. Let us suppose that there are five possible response options to each question – Strongly Agree (SA), Agree (A), Neutral (N), Disagree (D) and Strongly Disagree (SD).

It would be of interest to the researcher to know the pattern of responses to each question, and we will now examine a hypothetical example of the response of the sample to three questions:

Summary of response patterns. In question 1, most participants disagreed with the proposed item, but the pattern was reversed toward agree in item two. The pattern in the

Table 7.3 FREQUENCY TABLE DEMONSTRATING THE RANGE OF RESPONSES TO QUESTION 2

SA	A	N	D	SD
50	20	10	10	10

Table 7.4 FREQUENCY TABLE DEMONSTRATING THE RANGE OF RESPONSES TO QUESTION 3

SA	A	N	D	SD
15	20	30	20	15

third question is characterised by an even distribution of responses (a 'normal distribution'). A normal distribution is a pattern that would be expected in the general population and is represented by a bell-shaped curve.

Percentages

The data can be understood further by turning the above frequencies into percentages (symbol %), that is, what proportion of 100 each frequency is. In the example given above this is easily done because the hypothetical sample size was 100.

Example 8a: Females (55) = 55 per cent. Males (45) = 45 per cent.

Example 8b: In the age groups, 30 per cent of the sample fell into the category, 26–30.

Example 8c: In question 1, 65 per cent of the sample chose 'Disagree'.
In question 2, 50 per cent of the sample chose 'Strongly Agree'.
In question 3, 30 per cent of the sample chose 'Neutral'.

However, if the sample composition is more or less than 100, the target number can be converted into a percentage by using the following procedure:

Example 9: In a sample of 80 respondents ($n = 80$), 45 were female and 35 were male. What percentage of the sample was female?

$$\frac{\text{Females}}{\text{Total sample}} \times 100 = \frac{45 \times 100}{80} = \frac{45 \times 10}{8} = \frac{450}{8} = 56.2 \text{ per cent}$$

To divide two numbers where there is a zero in each, it is simpler if a zero from each is stroked out. To multiple by 10, all that has to be done is to add one zero to the number being multiplied – $45 \times 10 = 450$. To multiply by 100, all that has to be done is to add two zeros to the number being multiplied – $45 \times 100 = 4500$, etc. The solution to the above problem was 56.2 per cent. With decimals, any value at or above 0.5 can be rounded down to the nearest unit (in this case 56 per cent), and values below 0.5 can be rounded down.

The great advantage in using percentages is that meaningful comparisons can be made across groups of different sizes. For example, take a hypothetical study of surveys carried out in two cities on aggressive driving behaviour where both surveys showed that 20 drivers were observed to be aggressive in each city. However, it may have been the case that 500 people were surveyed in one city while 1000 were surveyed in the other. It would not be meaningful to compare between the two groups unless the frequencies were turned into percentages.

Exercise — Examples for practise

1. 15 students in a class of 90 achieved a first class honours degree. What percentage of the total were they?
2. Seven from 20 songs in the top twenty were new entries. What percentage were not new entries?
3. 200 from 350 shoppers surveyed in a supermarket used trolleys. 100 used baskets and the remainder carried the items in their hands. What was the percentage of each of the three groups in relation to the total number of shoppers sampled?

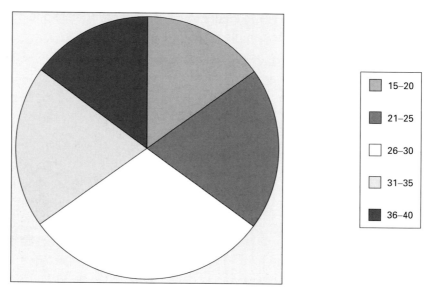

Figure 7.1 A PIE CHART DEMONSTRATING PROPORTIONS OF SAMPLE IN EACH OF FIVE AGE CATEGORIES

THIRD GEAR — GRAPHS AND TABLES

It has already been suggested that learning is likely to be more readily facilitated if the information can be turned into various modalities. The example was cited of the picture of a car, the sound of the word car and the written word car. In the same manner, clarity of presentation and understanding is achieved if numbers are broken down into categories (frequencies), turned into percentages and then observed or screened in visual form by charts or graphs.

This would be very useful for presenting percentages, and the example given above refers to the age categories previously cited. The pie chart enables the viewer to see all the information in pictorial form at a glance, and allows visual comparison of the various 'slices' of the pie. As previously cited, the frequencies, in descending order, for the above five categories are 15, 20, 30, 20 and 15, and these correspond with the percentages, given that the sample size was 100.

The same information presented in the pie chart can also, if preferred, be presented in a bar chart as illustrated below. In some cases the researcher may want to present a

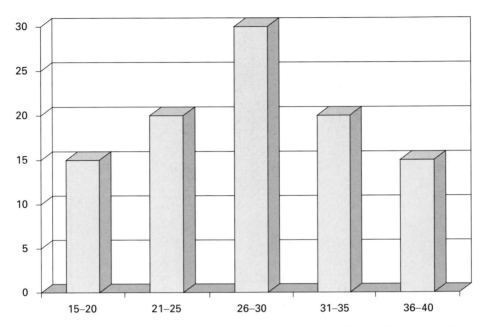

Figure 7.2. A BAR CHART PRESENTING FREQUENCIES OF SAMPLE IN EACH OF FIVE AGE CATEGORIES

number of formats in order to illustrate the data clearly from various angles. A lot of useful information is again presented in the bar chart in simple form. The observer can clearly see each category and the numbers that fall into each one.

A histogram is used when the data being measured are continuous (that is, ascending in regular, steady intervals without 'jumps' as in discrete categories – see below under 'levels of measurement'). In the hypothetical example presented below, 100 participants are timed in seconds for their ability to balance a tennis ball on top of their heads.

A glance at the histogram below will demonstrate that the shape of the data is fairly normal in distribution, that is, it resembles the bell-shaped curve. Most respondents (fictitious data used) were able to balance the ball for around eight to twelve seconds, but the two 'tails' indicate that a minority were only able to manage between four to six seconds, and a comparable minority were able to balance the ball for between 14 to 16 seconds (frequency in this case refers to the number of people who balanced the

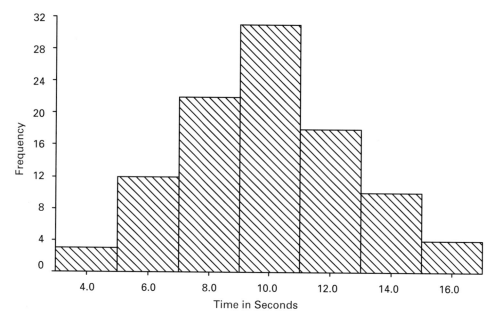

Figure 7.3 FREQUENCY HISTOGRAM DEMONSTRATING DURATION IN SECONDS
OF RESPONDENTS BALANCING A TENNIS BALL ON THEIR HEADS

ball in any given column). The large column in the middle indicates that about 31 people balanced the ball for 10 seconds, and each column can be examined in turn by glancing at the two axes that show frequency and time in seconds. A histogram is clearly useful in data screening, in that it gives a good picture of how scores are dispersed or clustered. It is used when the data being measured are continuous (that is, ascending in equal intervals), and some examples of this are time, distance, height, weight and temperature.

FOURTH GEAR – LEVELS OF MEASUREMENT

Decisions must be made about the type of statistic that will be used in an analysis, and the level at which a variable has been measured largely governs these decisions. Although tutors will frequently guide students in the choice of analysis to be used, it is nevertheless essential to understand levels of measurement before carrying out any study. There are at least three scales of measurement and each of these is described with examples below.

Nominal measurement

This simply refers to named categories that are not different from each other in rank order. For example, if gender is coded on the computer as male = 1, and female = 2, this does not mean that 1 is higher than 2 or vice-versa. The numbers could be changed to female = 1, and male = 2, and the change would make no difference to any subsequent analysis. In other words the designation of categories by numbers is purely an arbitrary convenience. Other examples include smokers and non-smokers, married and unmarried people or rural and urban dwellers. There can be more than two categories in nominal measurement, such as male, female and androgynous. There are limits on the kinds of statistics that can be used with variables measured at a nominal level, but percentages and frequencies can be applied and illustrated by bar charts or pie charts. A slightly more sophisticated approach that can be used with nominal variables is the chi-square test.

Ordinal measurement

In this approach the categories are different from each other, not only in designation but also in rank order. This means that 1 is higher than 2, which is higher than 3, which in turn is higher than 4 etc. For example, universities may be ranked by a range of indices such as teaching and research quality, achievement levels of students and employability after graduation. The other important feature of ordinal measurement in addition to rank order is that the differences between the ranks do not have to be equal. For example, in horse racing, the horses finish in rank order as first, second, third, fourth etc. The distance between the first and second horse over the finishing line may be one metre, but the distance between the second and third horses may be five metres, with the fourth horse being twenty metres behind the third. Other examples of ordinal measurement include degree classification and socio-economic status. Using the principles for ordinal measurement described above, see if you can work out why these two examples are classified as ordinal. All the statistics and charts applied to nominal variables (frequencies, percentages, bar charts, pie charts and chi-square) can also be applied to ordinal variables. Moreover, a few more advanced statistics can be used with ordinal variables, such as Spearman's ranked correlation. As a general rule it is wisest to choose the best statistic that is available for a given level of measurement. It is always a sensible strategy to choose the method that will produce the most powerful results.

Interval measurement

Interval measurement is a step above the ordinal level in an important way. Although it is similar to ordinal measurement in the sense that both have categories that are rank ordered, interval level also possesses the property of equal measurement between the ranks. A good example of this is the measurement of time where the distance between all units (whether these are seconds, minutes, hours or days) is exactly the same. Another obvious example is distance, whether measured in millimetres, centimetres, metres or kilometres. Further examples include weight and sound, but there is controversy over whether characteristics such as IQ and personality are ordinal or interval. Many academic journals will, however, publish articles where the researchers have deemed that these variables were measured at interval level.

It should be noted that some scales of measurement do not have a true zero as their starting point and a clear example of this is temperature (which can be measured above and below zero freezing point in degrees Celsius). Another example is the calendar, which has both BC and AD components. Some researchers make a difference between these kinds of scales and the interval scales of measurement considered above, but both types possess the important property of equal interval.

Interval level measurement allows the researcher to use the statistics that can be employed at nominal and ordinal levels (that is, frequencies, percentages, charts, etc.) but also facilitate the more powerful 'parametric' statistics. The basic assumptions of parametric statistics that set them apart from non-parametric methods are that the variables are measured at interval level, and the distribution of responses or observations is normal (that is, resembling a bell-shaped curve). Examples of parametric statistics are Pearson's correlation, t-tests, ANOVA and Multiple Regression.

Exercise — Revision questions (measurement)

1. What are the characteristics of nominal, ordinal and interval levels of measurement and how do they differ from each other?
2. Into which level of measurement should the following variables be categorised — degree classification, gender and distance in miles?
3. What are the essential features of parametric statistics?

SUMMARY

♦ Anxiety over mathematics has been found in all cultures, age groups, educational levels and across gender.

♦ Pre-tertiary negative perception of mathematics appears to be carried over into statistics at university for many students.

♦ Deficient teaching style associated with both disciplines may contribute to learning difficulties for some students.

♦ Students can develop their competence and confidence (self-efficacy) in mathematics and statistics by working patiently and regularly through simple examples until these are mastered before progressing to more complex examples.

♦ The ideal scenario for student learning is through working with their own data sets, which relate to matters that interest and motivate them.

♦ If students have become too dependent on a calculator, they should practise resorting to simple mental arithmetic to keep their minds fresh and active.

♦ The manipulation of numbers by a range of procedures such as addition, subtraction, multiplication and division facilitates efficient learning in relation to data analysis.

♦ Presentation of frequencies and percentages in tables and charts allows the reduction of complex data into meaningful and manageable formats.

♦ It is essential to identify the level at which a given variable is measured so that appropriate statistics can be chosen for analysis.

♦ The common levels and scales of measurement from the simplest to the more complex are nominal, ordinal and interval.

Useful symbols to know on the computer and calculator

Symbol	Computer	Calculator
Plus (+)	+	+
Minus (−)	−	−
Multiply (×)	*	×
Divide (÷)	/	÷

Multiplication rules for plus and minus signs

+	multiplied by +	=	+
−	multiplied by −	=	+
−	multiplied by +	=	−

8 Developing Memory Techniques

KEY CONCEPTS

● LONG-TERM MEMORY ● SHORT-TERM MEMORY ● RECALL ● RECOGNITION ● RECONSTRUCTION ● RE-LEARNING SAVINGS ● REHEARSAL ● LEVELS OF PROCESSING ● MEMORY MODALITIES ● PRIMACY AND RECENCY EFFECTS ● SUBLIMINAL PROCESSES ● ORGANISATION ● MNEMONICS ● STATE-DEPENDENT LEARNING ● EXTERNAL AND INTERNAL CONTEXT ● WORKING MEMORY ● MEMORY INTERFERENCE ● LEARNING AND RETRIEVAL

Your memory may be better than you think

Short term and long term memory

Imagine that you are asked to make a phone call on a night out and you are given a telephone number of 6 digits to remember. All you have to do is walk down the corridor to the nearest phone and so you decide not to write the number down. Instead you keep rehearsing the number as you walk and by the time you get to the phone you can easily remember it. You have used your short-term or working memory and it has served you very well. However, when you are asked to ring the same number a week later you appear to have forgotten the number. It does not seem to have been transferred to more permanent storage, at least in a manner that can be easily recalled. You may be able to remember the name of the person you had called, and you will remember having made the phone call, so the memory is not entirely dead. Or if someone had distracted you as you walked at the time of the first call or you had to wait in a queue for the phone you may have 'lost' the number.

It appears that some of the information evaporates at the short-term stage and other aspects are transferred to more abiding storage (long-term memory). Although this is an oversimplification of memory structure and function (Baddeley, 1999), it illustrates the point that some memories are readily retrieved and some appear to go AWOL. Many people underestimate the power of their own memory, perhaps partly because they chiefly access their short-term memory (now more commonly referred to as 'working memory'), or have not used good memory techniques or have not sufficiently focused on the large volume of information that they do remember. The human brain has an enormous capacity for remembering, and some understanding of storage and retrieval procedures will help improve memory use.

DIRECT RECALL WITHOUT CUES

There are some memories that we do not have to try to retrieve because they just spring into our conscious mind without solicitation. It is possible that these memories were important to us or we were especially interested in their content or that they were just catchy and humorous such as the following limerick:

> There once was a man from Trinity, who thought he'd
> cracked the square root for infinity;
> but there were so many digits, it gave him the fidgets,
> so he dropped it and studied divinity.

Many years ago a speaker used this to illustrate the point that perhaps some people study theology because they would fail at everything else! Because there is rhyme, humour, a moral and a context, this limerick is remembered effortlessly. You should be encouraged to know that some of the things you study at college/university will stay with you and you will be able to recall them for use whenever you need them.

Capitalising on memory

Some years ago a mature first year student went to his tutor for advice about whether he should sit his exams. He had attended many of the lectures and had completed all assignments but had been robbed of revision time because of family pressures and work commitments. The tutor's advice was that he should sit the exams because he would remember much from the lectures, seminars and assignments and all that was required in first year was a pass (40 per cent). However the student did not have enough confidence in his memory to believe that with limited revision he could recall sufficient material to attain a pass. The result was great inconvenience to himself when he really had in effect little to lose and much to gain for trying.

MEMORY BY RECOGNITION

Think back to the illustration about the phone number that you were given to remember. One week after the event you had forgotten the number completely. However, suppose someone handed you the number on a piece of paper and asked you if you could remember it. Perhaps you would instantly identify it as the number you had rung a week previously, even though you could not recall it spontaneously. It could be said that it 'rang a bell' in your memory!

For example, you have probably had the experience where you recognise someone's face although you cannot remember where and when you saw him or her before. Also you may be quite sure that you have heard a certain tune at least once before but you do not know its name, composer or performer. Indeed you may even recall a particular smell merely from one previous encounter, especially if it is distinctive.

In short, your recognition memory is probably much better than you think, and it is particularly useful to you in multiple choice tests where you are asked to identify the one right answer in the midst of wrong answers.

MEMORY BY RECONSTRUCTION

Ebbinghaus (1885) and his assistant tried to learn lists of nonsense syllables by rote in order to ascertain if they could recall these spontaneously without any cues to assist memory. Some lists they were able to recall freely but others apparently could not be retrieved. However, whenever they saw again the lists they could not freely recall, they were able to recognise if the order had been changed, and were able to reconstruct the lists into the correct order. In addition, when they went to learn again the lists they had appeared to forget, they found these much easier to learn second time round. This implied that they possessed re-learning savings. Therefore the four forms of memory that are identified from the experiments of Ebbinghaus are recall, recognition, reconstruction and re-learning savings.

A variation of reconstruction might be very useful for you in preparing for exams. You may find it helpful to take the outline of a lecture with headings and subheadings and reconstruct it into a different form. You could then try to reverse this procedure by rearranging the material back into its original form. Indeed some of the material you are given might need to be reconstructed properly into a good structured form for the first time! The general point is that making some changes to the material and re-arranging it into different forms may help learning, retention and recall.

MEMORY BY REHEARSAL

One of the best ways to remember a good joke is to tell it to someone else as soon as possible after you have heard it. People often remark that they wish they had a better memory for jokes – getting into the habit of passing them on immediately is one good strategy to start with. In this way the memory is transferred to longer-term storage and you will hopefully be reinforced by the laughter of those you tell the joke to!

A similar approach will also help you imbibe and digest your academic material. For example, during coffee or lunch break students can attempt to recall the major points they have learned from an important lecture. It would be most useful to set aside regular times to do this as it would give a lot of mutual stimulation and would not be too much of a imposition on your time.

You can also write out a few of the pointers from each lecture as 'pegs' on which to 'hang' the subject matter from the lecture. Each of these becomes like a key for a little box of information that you can open and unpack. From time to time you can take a cursory glance at your summary outlines to keep the overall vision of the module before you.

PRIMACY AND RECENCY EFFECTS

TV game show

There was a popular TV game show in which contestants were given limited time to watch valuable objects pass before them on a conveyor. Subsequently, with the objects out of sight, they were asked to recall as many objects as they could remember within about 20 or 30 seconds. The contestants got to keep all the objects they could remember, so there was a big incentive to learn and recall. According to the theory of primacy and recency effects, contestants would be more likely to remember the last objects (recency) and the first objects (primacy), and would be more likely to forget the objects in the middle. It would be interesting to test if that is what actually happened in the game show, but these effects have been demonstrated in experiments.

Primacy and recency effects are most likely to occur where there are a series of things to be learned within a short time frame with limited time for recall. Their effects are likely to kick in if you leave your revision until the night before your test. However, if you pace yourself out well, you can learn the material 'in the middle' (as well as at both ends) by going back over it and giving due attention to it. Psychologists have explained primacy and recency effects by displacement and distraction coupled with attention and rehearsal. These effects lead to the apparent loss of some material but this can be avoided if time pressure is removed. Planning your revision and allowing sufficient time for it will facilitate good memory processing and counteract primacy and recency effects.

THE ROLE OF SUBLIMINAL PROCESSES

Subliminal activity refers to the process where the mind takes in information without having given conscious attention to it. Psychologists use an instrument called a tachisto-scope to demonstrate the reality of subliminal processes in memory function. Advertisers have also attempted to capitalise on this facility within the human psyche in order to sell their products. Pleasant music in a shopping environment may help to lift the mood of shoppers, even though they may be not be consciously listening to the music. An associated idea is referred to as 'the cocktail party phenomenon'. An example of this is where you are in a crowded room at a party and engrossed in conversation with one or two friends. Although you are not paying any attention to the many conversations around you, if someone happens to mention your name it is possible that you will pick up on this and turn toward them. Even as you read this book you are monitoring sights, sounds, smells, temperature etc. around you, and although you are not diverting attention toward them, you are likely to pick up on changes around you. This understanding is very encouraging for the process of learning, for much more than we are consciously aware of goes on in the academic environment related to reading, listening and interacting with others, and we should not underestimate our capacity to learn.

Organisational aspects of learning

THE LIBRARY

Illustration

If a library is well organised and the books are kept in place, then the task of finding the book you require is much easier. For example, if each subject has a designated area in the library, you know that you should be able to find your book in that vicinity, and if authors' names are arranged alphabetically, that will further simplify the task. Moreover, if the book has a code number that you can look up on a computer, then it should not be difficult to trace its whereabouts. In short, the more efficient the organisation and coding in the library, the easier and quicker it is to pinpoint the book you want. Libraries that are well organised and kept tidy are the best public servants. Similarly, there is much you can do to organise your memory and keep it as tidy as possible. If you store the information in an organised manner, you will have the cues at your disposal to recall the information you want when you need it.

Exercise — Organised memory

Get a friend to read over Form A below and another friend to read over Form B. Give both the same time limit to memorise the list.
Give the friend who memorised Form A, a blank sheet of paper to write down as many words as they can remember, but give the friend who did Form B a sheet of paper with the four headings below, and see who can recall the most words. The experiment will only work if the time limits (for example, 30 to 45 seconds) are strict and the two people are around the same age group and have the same educational background. It should illustrate the point that good organisational strategies assist memory recall. Some participants may, however, organise the material themselves without any prompting, and if they do then this should be taken into account in the attempt to understand the results. If you have the time and opportunity, you may want to run the experiment on two groups of students from the same class.

Form A.

Potato, Pen, Car, Bus, Shoes, Shirt, Paper, Book, Cabbage, Train, Dress, Eraser, Mayonnaise, Lorry, Hat, Stapler, Pizza, Bicycle, Denims, Lasagne

Form B

Potato	Pen	Car	Shoes
Cabbage	Paper	Bus	Shirt
Mayonnaise	Book	Train	Dress
Lasagne	Eraser	Lorry	Hat
Pizza	Stapler	Bicycle	Denims

Headings:	Food	Stationery	Transport	Clothes

ARRANGING MATERIAL IN STRUCTURED POINTS

Look carefully at what you have to learn and then think of how you can make it manageable and workable. Take the typical news programme on TV or radio as an example to illustrate the point. At the beginning of the programme you are given the news headlines and these may be comprised of five or six items of news in capsule form. As the programme unfolds, all the basic headlines are elaborated on and all the necessary details are filled in. What the newsreader does at the beginning is to summarise and map out the shape and direction of the programme. You will have a very clear impression in your mind of what is about to follow. Moreover, at the end there will again be a summary of the main bullet points, so that the viewers/listeners will be left with a clear impression of all the news events. Producers of the programme also have to make a number of important decisions, for example, which items are most newsworthy and should be included in the programme? How long should each item be given? In what order should the items appear? If you are taking a written test or preparing a written assignment for college/university you will also have to make decisions about these kinds of questions. In terms of using your memory well, you need to think about the main points (your news headlines) and the order in which it is best to remember them.

SOME USEFUL MNEMONICS

The word 'mnemonics' refers to aids that are used to assist memory recall. It is a most interesting word in that it is derived from the Greek word for 'tomb' – the place that is visited to recall memories of a loved one or friend. Many people find comfort in this practice because it brings back powerful and pleasant memories. In the same way it is wise to use the full range of materials that will produce cues for recalling the subject matter you aim to learn.

One of these techniques is the use of alliteration, where a series of words are used that all begin with the same letter, for example, 'alliteration's artful aid'. In this case the retrieval cue is the common letter at the beginning of each word. Previously we made reference to the four strategies used by Ebbinghaus and described these by the use of alliteration: recall, recognition, reconstruction and re-learning savings.

Another useful mnemonic is where the first letter from a series of words is taken and one word is made from these. For example, in the personality theory known as 'The Big Five', a word is derived from the five key words in the theory. The five words are Extraversion, Conscientiousness, Openness, Agreeableness and Neuroticism. The first letter from each of these can be taken and rearranged into the acronym, OCEAN. An example that is often used in brainstorming sessions is SWOT – the four key words here are Strengths, Weaknesses, Opportunities and Threats. You can also devise your own acronyms or use nonsense words as mnemonics!

These methods are especially useful for remembering a series of key words that are linked in some way. Other strategies include rhyme – finding words or ideas that fit into a memorable rhyme, or chime – words with similar endings such as clarity, brevity, certainty or perception, sensation and reaction.

VISUALISATION STRATEGIES

An old adage says that a picture is worth a thousand words. What you might be able to do with material you find difficult to learn is to turn it into a picture, or series of small pictures, no matter how bizarre these may seem. It is reported that James Joyce could remember the names and types of shops up and down a range of streets in Dublin from his earliest days. Although he had a phenomenal memory, it was no doubt facilitated by visualisation techniques in this instance. In learning another language, vocabulary can be built by use of visualisation techniques. One frequently cited example is that the Spanish word for tent, 'carp', can be remembered by visualising a fish (carp) in a tent. The Hebrew word for the earth is 'ha-arats' and this can be remembered by 'the carrots' (sounds alike) – the earth is the place where you get the carrots! This example combines both audio and visual images!

Exercise — Memory by visualisation

Try to arrange the words below (from a previous exercise) into a simple story where you go shopping for food just before lunch time, and then for clothes and stationery in the afternoon.

Potato, Pen, Car, Bus, Shoes, Shirt, Paper, Book, Cabbage, Train, Dress, Eraser, Mayonnaise, Lorry, Hat, Stapler, Pizza, Bicycle, Denims, Lasagne.

Does this help you to remember the words?

TRIGGERS AND CHAIN REACTIONS

Students' song and dance routines

Many students demonstrate their powers of memory at a student formal when they get up to dance to the popular songs. They seem to know almost all the songs and all the words and also remember the appropriate movements to accompany each song. These are frequently the same students who complain about poor memory in relation to their academic work! When students listen to their favourite pop albums they even remember the precise sequence in which the songs appear! Even if they cannot document these on paper by direct recall, as they come to the end of listening to each track this acts as a memory cue for the next track.

That is precisely what can happen in an exam/test setting when the autonomic nervous system has been triggered and the adrenaline is pumping. Once you start writing your essay plans you are likely to find that the ideas will begin to flow. One idea triggers another in a chain reaction until you finish. Sometimes you appear to dry up for a while, but the flow will come back again. However, when you are in 'full throttle' like this, watch that you don't go off at a tangent. Keep a regular check on your planning, pacing and timing.

The little people in the brain

A psychology teacher explained memory storage and retrieval by the analogy of little people in the brain. This idea had no doubt been derived from a regular feature, called 'The Numbskulls', in a popular children's comic. The idea the teacher used was that the little people ran and searched all over our brain for the stored memories that we requested. If we used a good system of storage, we made the task easier for them, but if not then their task was harder and took longer (like the library illustration). However, the encouraging fact in the illustration is that once we commission these 'people' in our brain, they do not stop working until they find the required object! This relates back to the point on subliminal processes. You will no doubt have had the experience where you have tried so intensely to remember some item of information and it would not come. However, later when you were not thinking about it, it suddenly came forcibly into your mind. It is just as if the imaginary little people beavered away at it until they found it, even though you had forgotten that you had sent a request.

Students should not therefore be discouraged in their reading even if they cannot initially regurgitate what they have read. There is every likelihood that during an exam or assignment, some important fact will flash into the mind as if from nowhere.

Levels of processing in memory

UNDERSTANDING FACILITATES GOOD MEMORY

Research suggests that memories may be more readily retained and retrieved if they are processed at various levels and not merely by rote learning. An important aspect of this is the element of understanding, and especially if the understanding is followed by related practise.

For example, you can learn off the ingredients required for a recipe and can then understand how to add each ingredient to the mixture in a particular sequence in order for the consistency to be exactly right. However, learning is really complete when you successfully mix the ingredients together in practise. If you make a mistake in the sequencing at the first attempt then your understanding of why the ingredients should be mixed in a particular sequence is likely to be strengthened.

Part of learning the history of a war, is not only to know how many nations were involved, but also when and why each entered the fray. Learning the proper sequence of events is more easily facilitated if you understand why each nation entered the battle.

ENJOYMENT HELPS ACCESSING MEMORIES

If you learn to enjoy what you are doing you are more likely to remember it. Previous reference was made to the students who remember their favourite songs and the range of dance movements that accompany these. Ardent followers of sport often know large volumes of facts and figures about their favourite teams. Because they enjoy the games and are always keen to know how their team is faring, there is no resistance to mastering all the relevant details. Moreover, students can eventually come to enjoy subjects that did not have much initial appeal to them. The key is to be patient, to give yourself time and to work steadily.

MOTIVATION BRINGS MEMORIES INTO CLEAR FOCUS

Closely allied to enjoyment is motivation, and an illustration of the role of motivation in memory is the TV game previously referred to where contestants can win every valuable item they can remember seeing. In this case the motivation to learn is likely to be high and therefore the effort and application to learn is also likely to be high. It will help the learning process if you remind yourself of the range of prizes that stand at the end of your course. For example, there is the satisfaction of completing the task, the expertise that will have been acquired, the congratulations you will receive from family and friends and the awareness of their sense of pride in your achievement, the passport to the career of your choice etc. Use whatever you can to get yourself motivated, and try to use both long-term and short-term 'reinforcers' for learning.

MEMORY IN A VARIETY OF MODALITIES

Human memory is functional in all five senses – sight, hearing, smell, touch and taste. Many things are remembered by several of these modalities, for example, a Madras curry by its colour, smell and taste. As previously asserted, memories can be strengthened by rehearsal, because re-learning savings are operative. Memories can be strengthened by the use of various senses and by learning in a variety of contexts. You can learn the same material by reading and listening and then by reproducing this in writing and interacting with others. You can learn effectively in a library, a lecture room, in your private study room, on a bus, a park bench etc. Making use of as many modalities as are available to you is likely to be an advantage in learning. It is not good to become conditioned into thinking that you can only learn at set times and in particular contexts. In the busyness of life and with many deadlines looming it is wise to adapt learning to various contexts.

PROCESSING BY REPRODUCING MATERIAL

It is always a profitable exercise to reproduce learned material in your own words. When it comes to writing examination essays and assignments, what your educators want to see is the fruits of your own work. Of course they want to see evidence carefully and faithfully presented, but they also want to see your interpretative comments. Moreover, it is vital to acquire through practise, the ability to condense and summarise the main points from cited research because the time and space is not available to give an exhaustive account. You will be expected to cite the main findings from key studies, so it is import to learn to reproduce the material in skeleton form.

Exercise - Reviewing your career experience

Think about your own choice of career and how the sequence of events in your life has led you to be where you are at present. This should include qualifications you have acquired and opportunities that have opened or closed for you. Also included would be important life events that may have changed your intended career direction. Make a brief résumé of all the important things that may have moulded the direction you have taken to date. Ensure that each is in proper sequence. Why do you think these things are likely to be clear in your memory?

REMEMBERING THINGS IMPORTANT TO YOU

People frequently try to remember things that are important to them such as the birthday of someone near and dear. Important dates are noted in a diary so that they will not be easily forgotten. Also some important event may be recorded at the top of a diary the week before it is scheduled to take place. Students at university are seen near examination times taking notes of the dates and venues for their exams. Some then record these details in several sources so that this important information is not mislaid. Job applicants are very keen to know what the pay scales are for the vacant post and where they are likely to be placed on this scale if their application is successful. Most people will have good clear memories about these matters because they have personal implications for them. It is always encouraging to see students who have that extra enthusiasm for learning. After a lecture they come to the front to follow up on some reference, or fill in some detail they have missed or get further clarification of some point. They may be more likely to remember what they really need to know because they are focused and learning is important to them.

DRAWING OUT THE FACTS

It is clear that well-structured systems help improve learning, retention and retrieval. These give you immediate access to the cues that you need to retrieve what you are looking for. For example, if you cannot remember someone's name, it might help to work through each letter of the alphabet. When the correct letter is arrived at, the name of the person may spring suddenly to mind or you may at least remember that the person's name begins with that letter. This may indicate that memories are stored or more easily retrieved under categories. Therefore there is some value in grouping information together in sensible clusters in order to facilitate recall. Furthermore, it may also be helpful to connect clusters of information in a kind of network, such as in a flow chart or in a hierarchical structure. For example, you could write the continents of the world as the top category on your page, and a country from each, followed by the capital city from each country and then another city from each country. If you draw out a structure for the material you intend to learn, this will not only assist the memory process but will also equip you with good strategies for examinations and assignments. For an example of a structure that is drawn out in diagram form, see the plan for an essay on depression at the end of Chapter 5.

GIVING LIFE TO ABSTRACT IDEAS

In recent years there have been a variety of food scares that threaten to upset the balance between health and disease. Many people are passionately concerned about this because the well-being of humans and animals is involved. If the procedures involved in the production of food did not have such serious implications then not too many people would be interested in the results of the various pieces of research that have been commissioned. However, because of the implications for human health and animal welfare, the studies are given high profile media coverage and are the subject of endless controversial debates, with passions often running very high. The lesson learnt from this is that people are more likely to attend to and remember the facts associated with matters that have important implications related to real issues. Therefore your learning will be more effective if you can relate the subject to 'live' issues. With an essay or assignment you should always try to make an interesting story and if possible demonstrate the implications and applications from your study.

Exercise — Corporal punishment debate

What are the arguments for and against the corporal punishment of children? What are the likely implications of laws that are passed either for or against it? This is an example of how people may be able to remember the arguments because they have strong views one way or the other.

Contextual factors in memory

EXTERNAL CONTEXT

If you take a trip back to your old school you are likely to find a chain of memories are triggered as you visit the various places where significant events occurred, for example, the gymnasium, the assembly hall, various classrooms, the restaurant, the common room etc. There may be memories triggered that you would not ordinarily recall spontaneously. A similar experience may occur as you rummage through the roof space in your house and discover some old toy that you cherished as a child – a whole host of childhood memories may flood into your consciousness. The same may happen as you look over an old photograph or return to a place where you enjoyed a holiday many years previously. The memories had been well and truly stored but you suddenly found a key to unlock their treasures. This phenomenon is referred to as 'context dependent memory' and is associated with 'context dependent learning'. That does not necessarily imply that the memories will only come back if you return to the context in which they occurred. However, it might imply that there is some value in learning your material in a variety of contexts so that the material can have a variety of cues to aid recall. Moreover, you may find it useful to project your mind into the context where you learned the material, such as in a lecture room.

INTERNAL CONTEXT

Context dependent learning relates not only to the external setting but also to the internal state, that is, state dependent learning. For example it is suggested that you may not remember events that occur when you were drunk but they will come back when you get drunk again! Or when you are in a depressed or happy mood the memories associated with these may be more likely to return when you in the same mood again. Probably the best advice is not to rely too heavily on state dependent learning, especially if you cannot recreate the same state in an exam room. A calm and steady mood is more likely to be useful to you for revision and examinations. However, some students do prefer to study with the buzz of other people around them or with the sound of some music in the background. Whatever works best for you as an individual is OK, but there would be value in allowing yourself some practise at an exam room type situation so that you do not feel like an alien when you enter it for the real test! You might want to consider setting yourself some exam questions from previous exam papers and attempt them under test conditions.

LEARNING IN VARIOUS CONTEXTS

Some educators have argued that students should get conditioned to studying at one desk in one room and should ensure that they do nothing else but study at that desk. That advice was doubtless designed to help students adjust to regular and disciplined patterns of study. If that approach is working well for an individual student then there is no need to give it up, although it could also be extended to other contexts. Many students are, however, compelled to share houses and study places and are forced to compete with many distractions. Necessity dictates that they learn in a variety of contexts and this is no bad thing, provided there is rhythm and regularity in their practise.

LEARNING AT DIFFERENT TIMES

Bem's self-perception theory suggests that individuals tend to adopt certain beliefs about themselves and then feel obliged to act these out in practise: they need congruence between their beliefs and practice (see Aronson, Wilson & Akert, 1994). To do anything contrary to the image they have of themselves would cause them to experience a state of 'dissonance'. In relation to study habits, students describe themselves variously as a 'morning person', an 'evening person', 'an afternoon person' or a 'late night person'. The downside of being confined in this way is that if an exam falls outside the time when the student feels they are at their best, they start with a psychological disadvantage. For these students there is likely to be some advantage in changing their self-perception and then acting out the dynamics of their new extended self-image. A student can still, of course, have preference for a particular time of day without restricting their potential by imposing inhibiting limits on themselves.

Memory problems in learning and retrieval

INTERFERENCE IN LEARNING AND RETRIEVAL

Sometimes learning and retrieval may be inhibited because the material is being interfered with by other facts previously learned. It may be the case that either the old material is interfering with the new or vice-versa. One may dislodge and displace or confound the other. The result may be that either the information cannot be recalled at all, or else the wrong information is recalled. This is likely to happen when two words have similar meanings with subtle differences or when two words sound similar but have different meanings. In a popular TV quiz show, the contestants are asked to choose the right answer from a series of four given answers. Two of these are usually the more likely answer, but it is said by the host of the show that all the right answers are easy if you know them! However the introduction of an answer similar to the right one tests the human weakness of interference and confusion in recall. If a student has difficulty with recall they should write down the two words or ideas and try to devise some useful mnemonic to distinguish between them.

Example — Mnemonics for subtle differences

'Continual' means at regular intervals but 'continuous' means without interruption. The difference can be remembered by thinking of a dripping tap (continual) and a flowing tap (continuous). Furthermore, the difference can be remembered by thinking of the 'ous' at the end of continuous as a sound like flowing water.

SATURATION — THE DANGER OF RELENTLESS BOMBARDMENT

Earlier it was asserted that we may be taking in information even when we are not consciously aware of it (by subliminal processes). Although it is useful and encouraging to know about these processes, it would not be wise to bank on them as a primary source of learning. Good memory process is facilitated by attention, interest, motivation and by the use of good mnemonics. That does not imply that memory should be relentlessly bombarded with heavy and complex material continually. Therefore, it is important that revision strategy should be planned rather than trying to make a desperate attempt to swamp the memory on the eve of a test or examination. Such a maladaptive practice is likely to lead to interference, confusion and inefficiency. In the course of the academic semester, students can highlight the points they will later build on for revision. As the time for revision approaches, the material that was previously selected can be worked through systematically with revision sessions being spaced out to allow for adequate breaks so that the memory will function optimally.

THE NEED FOR GRADUAL MEMORY DEVELOPMENT

Work outs and marathons

Larger marathons extend over a distance of 26 miles, and no runner, no matter how enthusiastic, would attempt this distance in their first practise run. Runners set themselves much shorter targets initially and then increase these in gradual increments. If their ultimate goal is to complete a 26-mile marathon, they may aim at a 'mini-marathon' of 4-6 miles in the shorter term. Through regular practise and exercise the muscles gain strength, breathing improves and determination and discipline are strengthened. In the same way memory will improve by practise if the student is patient and determined enough. It should also be borne in mind that because re-learning savings are possessed from previous memory deposits, consolidation is easier than first time learning. If students feel that they are suffering from memory 'cramp' they should allow themselves time for a break to replenish their 'memory muscles'. While students are learning to develop the use of memory they should give themselves realistic 'work outs' and 'warm ups'.

FAILURE TO EMPLOY SUITABLE STRATEGIES

Some people are characteristically over-confident in their own memory. Most of us have at times been certain in recalling the 'facts' only to discover later that we had dressed them up considerably. Sadly, innocent people have been wrongly convicted of crimes because someone claimed to remember distinctly seeing their face at a crime scene and the accused had no alibi to vindicate their claim of innocence. The damage has often been done before the full truth can be ascertained. Therefore, although our memories are good and can be developed, it is important to remember that they are far from infallible and are prone to distort facts. Excess confidence in our memory will lead us astray but the memory techniques and strategies advocated here will serve as safeguards. Students can work at improving the use of memory by selection, attention, enjoyment, processing, visualisation, structure, consolidation and whatever else may prove effective. Realistic confidence in our memory is desirable, but reckless presumption should be avoided.

SUMMARY

♦ Memory appears to have long-term and short-term aspects, and many people have better memories than they suppose.

♦ Four functional elements in memory are recall, recognition, reconstruction and re-learning savings.

♦ Primacy and recency effects can be countered by consolidation, and recall is facilitated by organised learning techniques.

♦ Some useful mnemonics include alliteration, acronyms, rhymes, chimes, visualisation, pegs and memory cues.

♦ Memory function is likely to be strengthened by understanding and enjoying the learning material, and by processing at various levels and in diverse modalities.

♦ Memory process is enhanced where there is good motivation to learn, where the facts are important to an individual and where the learner has the opportunity to reproduce the material as soon as possible after initial learning.

♦ It may be advantageous to memory to learn and revise material at different times and in different contexts.

♦ Learning can be thwarted by continual bombardment and saturation.

♦ Memory recall can be confounded by interference.

♦ Memory efficiency can be improved by the use of sensible strategies that include breaks from learning.

9 Doing Justice to Yourself in Exams

In the lead up to the test

PLANNING FOR REVISION

Preparation for revision should begin shortly after beginning the university course. Students should always keep their 'antennae' attuned to any signals that will help in their preparation for testing. If all preparation is left until near the time of the exams there will be a steep mountain to climb in a short space of time. We do well to learn from the animal kingdom: from animals such as squirrels that store up nuts for the winter and camels that carry enough water to see them through the desert. Through the course of their academic career students can gather the material they need and compile it in a manner that will be useful to them at exam times. The thought of examinations should not be relegated or repressed, but should be maintained in the conscious mind so that when the exam season comes around there will be a good reservoir of material to draw from.

A lesson from a crocodile

It is reported that Australian crocodiles take as many people from the banks of rivers as they do in the rivers. Over a short distance they can run as fast as a racehorse and are therefore difficult to escape from. When they claim the victim in their jaws, they roll them round and round in the water until the victim is drowned. Their next step is to fasten and conceal their victim in some crevice where they can later return to eat them. The lesson here for the student is to look out for opportunities — for the material that will be needed. Make sure it is 'captured', consolidated and stored away in a place where it can be readily retrieved at the time when it is needed.

USE OF PAST PAPERS

The wise use of past examination papers is an excellent way to prepare for potential problems in subsequent examinations. A wise adage says that the early bird catches the worm, and the person who plans for their exams from the early days of the semester has a great advantage. An obvious way to do this is to dig out the previous test papers for each subject over the last few years. This does not mean that students should bank on the same questions coming up again ('question spotting'), although there may be very similar questions. However, students will be alerted to the major recurrent themes within a given topic and will acquire a good feel for the way questions are framed. If this good habit is cultivated early on, it will not only save much later strain and panic, but will also provide good templates into which accumulating subject matter can be fitted as it is absorbed. The templates can also be thought of as a series of moulds – the loose subject matter is poured into the mould where it belongs, and from which it can later be retrieved in a solid form. Furthermore, clear awareness of the central themes in a module will preserve students from wasting time in revising tangential issues.

PICKING UP SIGNALS IN LECTURES

Lecturers are required to ensure that they cover all the issues to be addressed in exams. They are not permitted to say in advance what the exams questions are and they will cover in the lectures issues that will not be assessed in the exams. A good, broad grasp of the module is nevertheless likely to be an advantage as there will be some overlap in issues and cross fertilisation of ideas. However, there will be particular themes that individual students will prefer to focus on in revision for tests.

Doing the calculations

Consider the case where there are eight major topics in a given module, with six questions in the exam, but only two questions to be answered. This means that two of the eight topics covered in the course will not come up in the exam. If only two topics are covered in revision and these do not come up then the student is in trouble. A more likely scenario is that one of the topics will not come up. What is needed in this case for adequate preparation is for four topics to be covered in revision. If the revision commences early enough then this is not as difficult as it seems. Moreover, a steady and consistent level of reading across all topics throughout the semester will pay rich dividends both at revision time and in exams. Lecturers like to see that students have a reasonable knowledge from across the spectrum covered in the module.

Exercise — Ensuring adequate coverage

It is good to get some practice on working out how many topics you will need to cover in order to be adequately prepared for a given exam. See if you can work out the following four examples:

1. Eight topics are covered and four questions are to be answered (eight questions in the exam)
2. Eight topics are covered and three questions are to be answered (six questions in the exam)
3. Nine topics are covered and three are to be answered (five questions in the exam)
4. Ten topics are covered and four to answered (seven questions in the exam)

It is probable that the person who delivers the lectures has also set the exam paper, and they will be required to help get students focused on the exam issues. Therefore, they are likely to flag up the issues where attention in revision should be directed. Although lecturers will not reveal the content of the exam directly, they may give some guidance for the selection of revision material. Students should endeavour to attend as many lectures as possible and make special note of any pointers that have been given. Some lecturers may give the clearest pointers in the lectures closest to the exam but others may drop hints throughout the semester.

POINTS TO PONDER

Many who have tried eating warm noodles with chopsticks in a public restaurant have ended up using the familiar knife and fork with cold noodles! It is always easier to work with the tools that we can use. When it comes to revision in the weeks before the exams students should ensure that they have all the right tools readily available. For example, students will need the full materials for selected topics and these will include lecture notes, extracts from journals, sections from books and notes from course work. It will be useful to keep these in a folder or pack that is clearly earmarked for revision. Anything else that is relevant can be added. Another helpful hint is to keep past exam papers always within easy reach. All these source materials can be used to draft outlines for the subject which will become the 'points to ponder'. The complete package will be like a full news programme with salient details and extended commentary. Your main summary 'points to ponder' are the 'news headlines'. These can be recorded on little pocket cards that can be carried around and used for revision and consolidation whenever the opportunity arises. The little cards are manageable tools that will enable the student to keep up to speed with revision, even while in transit. Given that the cards will only contain succinct bullet points, they will not be a heavy taxation on the mind in short spurts of study.

Pinpointing the essential issues

The story is told of a woman whose car broke down and called for a mechanic to come and help. When the mechanic came he quickly pinpointed the problem, adjusted a screw and the car started. After the woman learned the fee for this repair she was quite shocked: 'that amount of money for merely turning a screw!', was her response. To this the mechanic replied, 'no, madam, that amount of money for knowing which screw to turn!'. By the time students reach the final stages of revision they should make sure they can pinpoint the essential issues related to the topics they have selected. Indicating that you know what the crucial and relevant issues are will bring credit from the examiner.

Responding to exam-related arousal

The autonomic nervous system

In the film that celebrated the work of Diane Fossey, 'Gorillas in the Mist', a large gorilla ran at the strangers who appeared in the territory of his family. Sigourney Weaver, who played the part of Diane Fossey, pointed out that the gorilla's action was just a big bluff. The gorilla seemed to know that its large frame, deafening sound and aggressive run toward the strangers was enough to engender fear and repel danger even if the threat was not to be followed through.

Each of us will have had an experience where we have been afraid and our autonomic nervous system has been fully activated. This system gives us warning of impending danger and prepares us to take necessary action. Symptoms that follow its activation include such factors as trembling, racing heart, sweaty palms, dry mouth, nausea and headaches. These are typical signs associated with some fear stimulus, whether real or imagined. A child may lie awake half the night afraid of some unusual profile in the darkness of the bedroom only to discover next morning that father had hung up his long dark coat there the night before! For many students the fear of exams is not an illusion or a mirage – they know they have to face something that really scares them. Test anxiety is said to be likely to kick in, in a situation where a person is going to be evaluated by others. Moreover the consequences of failure may be serious and the person may feel inadequate for the task – which has been set under strict time limits (Mcilroy, Bunting & Adamson, 2000).

SURPRISING FINDINGS FROM ANXIETY RESEARCH

Over many years researchers have agreed that test or exam anxiety has a negative impact on exam performance (Zeidner, 1998). However, not all facets of anxiety are believed to be as debilitatve to performance as was once supposed and some aspects may even facilitate performance up to a certain level. The particular aspects of this kind of anxiety though might be better labelled as stress. Great sports performers have often said that they feel anxious before an important event even after many years of experience but they interpret the source of this as a flow of nervous energy (adrenaline) to channel into optimal performance. In our empirical studies we found that students who reported higher levels of autonomic arousal (bodily symptoms and tension) during exams did not perform any better or worse than students who reported lower levels. Therefore, the feeling of nervousness should not be interpreted as a signal of inevitable failure.

A REINTERPRETATION OF AUTONOMIC AROUSAL

The fido factor

A cab driver told of how he was called to pick up a fare at a house with a long garden path to the front door. As he wended his way up the path a large Doberman Pinscher came bounding toward him and it did not appear to have friendly intent! Naturally he was terrified, but he was thankful for his army days when he had worked with dogs. He knew that the twin options of running or fighting would be equally catastrophic. So he decided to stand still, and this strategy worked. The dog appeared to be confused at the cab driver's reaction and was completely neutralised.

When the autonomic nervous system is activated this can trigger various reactions and these have been described as the 'flight or fight syndrome' (the word 'freeze' could also be added with justification). The extra endowment of energy can be used to prepare for battle or to run from the perceived danger. On the other hand the energy can be 'wasted' by being turned inward in hopeless self-focus and passive resignation to fate. It seems that this is akin to what happens to some students in exams, and some even leave without making any attempt to address the exam paper. Although the cab driver in the above illustration stood still, in his case this was not quite the same as 'freezing on the spot', but was rather the most adaptive strategy available to him.

Some writers have suggested that the autonomic nervous system has evolved for our survival and should therefore be perceived as a mechanism that should be interpreted positively and deployed constructively. That entails keeping aspects of it under control and strategies will be suggested for achieving this. There is a phenomenon known as 'learned helplessness' and this has been observed, for example, in dogs that were given little electric shocks. When there appears to be no escape for the dogs, they passively resign to their plight and show signs of 'doggie blues'. For students in an exam situation there is an alternative to passive resignation and learned helplessness. If strategies to counter anxiety are well learned they will activate and function after the student has entered the examination environment.

A DOUBLE STRATEGY FOR COPING

There are effective ways of controlling the symptoms associated with the activation of the autonomic nervous system, and these strategies are commonly described as relaxation techniques. There is no need to attend full-blown therapy sessions to learn how to use simple forms of relaxation effectively. The theory behind these strategies is that a person cannot be relaxed and stressed at the same time, so that whenever an individual relaxes the stress must reduce. In the run up to the exam, the student can learn to resort to whatever proven method works in stress reduction. For example, good ways to relax include listening to some music or watching a film, especially a comedy. Some exercise is also useful, as is socialising in company where you can have some fun – humour is renowned to be an especially powerful weapon against debilitative stress. There are also muscle relaxation techniques and breathing exercises that can be used.

Biofeedback machine

This is a machine that monitors stress levels in the body, and as they go up the tone of the noise from the machine changes. When the person who is stressed is attached to the machine, they can learn to regulate their stress levels and the change in tone will signal to them that their stress levels have come down. Unfortunately we cannot carry a machine like this around with us and cannot therefore always be aware of the subtle increases in stress levels that occur. Nevertheless, what can be learned from experiments with biofeedback machines is that once we are aware of increases in stress, steps can be taken to bring these under control.

In short it is a good strategy to pull the mind away from sources of worry so that they do not constantly dominate the thinking processes. Whatever strategy (or combination of strategies) has been proven to work for the individual is the correct route to take.

Prevention is always better than cure and if the anxious arousal can be nipped in the bud then this is the best tactic of all.

In addition to having a strategy for reducing excessive stress arousal, more modest amounts of stress can be interpreted positively as previously noted. Stress can be perceived as nervous energy that is needed to prepare for meeting the demands of some challenging task that lies ahead. Therefore a good double strategy is to reduce excessive levels of stress that are liable to debilitate performance and channel remaining stress into productive, constructive activity. The problem arises when stress is allowed to mount continually without any attempt to control it and then is turned inward in passive self-focus.

Before the test

RHYTHMS OF REST AND WORK

If students revise into the early hours of the morning around exam time and drink lots of coffee to keep them awake, they are likely to throw their body clock (circadian rhythm) out of kilter temporarily. This in turn may lead to feeling tired at undesirable times and is akin to the experience of feeling jet lagged or trying to get adjusted to shift work. All this is most likely to happen if revision has not been adequately planned and has been left until close to the exam time. Another factor likely to impede exam performance is excessive use of alcohol around exam time as a coping strategy for the pressure. This is a maladaptive technique that is to be emphatically discouraged. The body and mind will function better if there is a sensible rhythm of rest and work. It is one thing at exam time to 'burn the midnight oil' but quite another to try to 'burn the candle at both ends'. This is especially pertinent if students have a series of tests within a short time frame, because there will not be sufficient time for recovery. Self-imposed sleep deprivation is a good antidote for effective performance and efficient function.

LOCATION OF THE EXAM ROOM

Almost invariably there are students who turn up late to a test because they have gone to the wrong room or have not been able to locate the designated room in time. Exams are stressful enough in themselves without this self-imposed additional and unnecessary pressure. Therefore students should ascertain the location of the exam room soon after this information is available and make a note of it in their diary or lecture note folder (rather than on a scrap piece of paper!). Confer with others to ensure that the date, time and location are correct for each subject. If you do not know the whereabouts of the designated room then ensure that you learn the route in advance of the exam. It is not unusual for a student to turn up for an exam the day after it has been completed. In summary make note of date, time, place and chronological order for each test and then ensure you can locate the venue. There is an irony in going through all the trouble of revision only to misinform yourself about exam details.

ALLOW SUFFICIENT TIME

If sufficient time is allowed on the day of the exam then even if a student has got some facts wrong the problem can perhaps be rectified. Sometimes students get time or location wrong because a friend has passed on faulty information or an initially assumed venue was not confirmed at a later stage and they had not heard about the change. Being late for a test adds to the panic factor and results in longer time taken to recover and settle. Ample time should be allowed for travelling, especially for students who do not live near the college. Allow for the possibility of punctures, break-downs, traffic congestion etc. If the exam venue is reached in good time, this will allow space for a cup of tea or coffee and an opportunity to look over revision notes. Each individual should get to know how much they should eat before exams and if parti-cular foods are likely to facilitate or debilitate performance (even if the effect is just like a placebo!). The problem with not eating at all is the tendency toward dehydration, which is compensated for by drinking more liquids that in turn leads to visiting the loo! However some students find it difficult to eat much because nerves make them feel a little nauseous.

BRING ALL NECESSITIES

Students sometimes turn up to an exam without a pen or with only one pen that runs out while writing an essay. Bring several pens and use one that you feel comfortable writing with. If it is a requirement to bring a student card for identification then ensure that this is not forgotten. Some exams require the use of a calculator and if this is the case then make sure you bring one that works. If you intend to do some draw-ing then pencil, ruler and eraser are essential. Moreover, if you are prone to feel dehydrated during a test then a small bottle of water (or a sugary drink for the energy) will be a useful part of your kit. In short, you should bring everything you need and also some reserves in case of malfunctions. The lack of these small things is a potential source for anxiety, or if you are forced to borrow from someone else, you may be the trigger for their anxiety.

Exercise — Preparing the practicalities

As a trial run for the real thing, make a list of all the things you would need to bring on the day of the exam and ensure that reserve supplies are included. Also imagine you are about to face several exams within one week. Make sure the time, venue and subject are matched against the appropriate date for each, and plan out transport strategy and journey time for each day. Practical hint — double check on everything the night before the test and leave your check list manuscript in a prominent place so that you will not walk out without noticing it on the morning of the test.

During the test

SLOW DOWN THOUGHTS AND PANIC REACTIONS

One lecturer told the story of how after sitting an exam in his student days, he was incensed at his lecturer because a given topic did not appear on the test paper. The lecturer simply pointed out to him that the question he required was actually there but he had missed it. Panic had been triggered in his mind because the wording he was looking for was not there in the expected manner. If a student turns over their test paper and finds that their thoughts are racing out of control, then a moment or two spent slowing down will be time well spent. First, remind yourself that you must slow down panic reactions, and second, use whatever strategy you can in order to slow down. As a result of reading over the questions slowly and carefully, and by starting to draft outline plans, you will help your racing thoughts to slow down and come under control. Anyone can make a mistake by misreading instructions, even in non-pressurised circumstances. Sometimes motorists are given parking fines because they failed to read the parking notices correctly. Therefore, it is no surprise that students misread questions under the duress of evaluative conditions. Time spent slowing down panic reactions during the first few minutes of a test should not be construed as wasted and will prevent questions being misread.

MAINTAIN A SENSE OF CONTROL

Each student should enter the test room fully persuaded that he or she can take control over what is going to happen for the duration of the exam. The winning team in any sports competition is likely to be the one that does not sit back and allow itself to be dictated to by the opposing team. Instead they 'take the reins' of the game and impose their own game plan. If a student has done his or her revision and learned all their bullet points (news headlines) related to each topic, then they can impose their plan on the examination.

Exercise — Taking control

Imagine that you are compelled for some reason to leave your student accommodation at short notice, and are forced to move into emergency accommodation that is more expensive. If you do not take careful control of your budget you will soon be in serious financial difficulty. Your first step in taking control is to make a list of all the things you can do to improve your income and/or manage your budget. See if you can make such a list and discover the feeling of being empowered by the sense of control you have taken.

READ QUESTIONS AND DRAFT SKELETONS

Many students enter an exam room with specific topics they intend to tackle. Once the relevant questions have been identified, they should be read very carefully, as they may differ crucially, with some new 'twist' from a similar question in a previous year. Is the question asking the candidate to evaluate or to describe and assess, and is there an emphasis on the use of empirical evidence? Does it invite the student to evaluate the strengths and weaknesses of a particular theory or to cite how the research has driven practice or vice-versa? Underline the key words in the question and ensure that all these are taken into account in the answer. Students should formulate draft plans for exam essay questions as part of their revision work. As these are written down during the test, they will slow down the panic reactions and give a greater sense of personal control over the situation. The next step in the process is to shape the points around the question. This may mean changing the sequence in which the points had been learned and also eliminating some irrelevant points. If a 'for/against' type question is addressed, then it should be decided in advance whether all 'for' points should be argued first followed by all 'against' points or if one point for and then against is followed in sequence. Also it should be decided if some conclusions should be addressed throughout the essay with a summary at the end or if all conclusions should be left to one block at the end. There are no hard and fast rules except that a clear plan should be decided upon and adhered to. The examiner will soon detect if there is a coherent strategy in the answer. Therefore, practise various formats on previous test papers and decide which is the most fluent and advantageous strategy for you.

WORK WITHIN TIME SCHEDULES

In order to perform effectively in a test setting, a skeleton outline for answers should be planned as well as the economic division of time and labour. Part of being a good student is developing a good exam technique, and an essential aspect of this is planned, controlled, time management. Some potentially good students fall lamentably short of achieving their full potential because they have not given sufficient attention to timing. When exam time arrives, students should be thoroughly conversant with the duration of the test, the number of questions on the test paper and the number that should be attempted. Moreover, students should ascertain the weighting of marks for each question and how much time should be devoted to each one. Those who overrun the allotted time span for a given question are 'scoring an own goal'. An excellent performance on one question will not contribute credit to the next question.

Exercise — Planning for time

If you have to sit a three-hour exam and are required to answer four questions, how long should you take on each question (allowing for planning)? Now focus on one question — let us assume that you have decided on five points for and five points against. How long should you take on each point (allowing for a brief introduction and overall conclusion)? You may just require a few sentences or a short paragraph for each point. If a whole page is filled with one point that occupied

10–15 minutes, then other points, and therefore marks, are bound to suffer. For practise, work on the following example (assume it is a one hour exam question and allow for planning points, introduction and conclusion):

Discuss the suggestion that smoking should be banned

Arguments against	Arguments for
Smoking causes diseases	Is only one factor in disease
Smoking is anti-social	Designated smoking rooms/areas
Smoking is expensive	Brings revenue and jobs
Smoking is addictive	Quitters substitute with other harmful habits
Is a maladaptive coping strategy	Is a necessary buffer to stress for some

Lethal weapon 1: Distraction A

FEEDING A VICIOUS CIRCLE

Test anxiety researchers concur that the real damage to performance in exams is done by the cognitive rather than the emotional components: the latter are referred to as 'bodily symptoms' and 'tension' (Benson & El-Zahhar, 1994). The cognitive elements may feed off the physiological components and vice-versa in a negative feedback loop. In other words, when a student feels anxious this feeds anxious thoughts which in turn fuel the anxious symptoms. The same negative feedback loop has been applied to such clinical syndromes as depression – depressed mood and depressed thought feed off each other in a downward negative spiral. It may not matter which one comes first if they both have a tendency to trigger each other. The important concern is to break the cycle by starving these processes of the dynamic they need for survival. It was previously noted that autonomic arousal can be reduced by relaxation techniques and can also be reinterpreted as energy that can be channelled into constructive activity.

RANGE OF EVALUATIVE DISTRACTIONS

A number of self-report instruments have been designed to assess the distracting cognition that students experience during an exam or test. Intrusive thoughts are likely to be the most lethal weapon of self-destruction during an exam, for the simple reason that they distract students from the task at hand and divert attention elsewhere. An old study demonstrated that students who looked away frequently from their script during a test did not perform as well as students who did not (Ganzer, 1963). The kinds of thoughts likely to distract candidates during an exam may be evaluative thoughts related to the exam itself. For instance, students may think about how they should have prepared better or think that the other students are doing much better than themselves. Alternatively they may wonder what the examiner will think of their feeble efforts or they may combine all these kinds of thoughts. The characteristics of this form of cognitive anxiety are persistent, evaluative and distracting. A first step in dealing with these intrusive thoughts is simple awareness of the process that is going on. Second, there should be a realisation that these may be more damaging than trembling, sweaty palms etc., and that what is needed is to focus on the task at hand rather than these evaluative thoughts. In general students should ensure that they develop a healthy cognitive exam schema (see below).

A cognitive schema

Psychologists believe that we develop cognitive schemata (plural of schema) in order to manage and make sense of the vast quantity of information that bombards us every day (Aronson et al., 1994). They argue that we develop a cognitive schema for every task we have to perform regularly such as going to the bank, the restaurant, using public transport or performing tasks such as taking a shower, doing the shopping etc. Accordingly, each of us will have an exam schema and for some of us this might be a well-established negative template — we may have nervousness and apprehension as the event approaches, partial 'paralysis' and confusion during the exam and low self-esteem afterwards. Nevertheless, although cognitive schemata can become quite inveterate, they can also be modified or transformed and imbued with a fresh energy.

LEARNED HELPLESSNESS AND LOCUS OF CONTROL

Learned helplessness describes a condition in which an individual just waits helplessly with the belief that the consequence of whatever is going to happen to them is inevitable. The person in this state is convinced that there is nothing they can do to avoid some 'punishment' that is coming their way. This powerless condition has been observed in animals that were given a series of small electric shocks without any apparent means of escape. However, the condition is also applicable to humans who become convinced that they can do nothing to change their plight. For example, a construct known as 'locus of control' refers to an individual's belief in the degree to which the outcome of their actions is under their own control or under the control of such factors as luck, chance, fate or powerful others/institutions (Strickland, 1989). Research has demonstrated that it is more advantageous to education, health, career, sports etc., for individuals to believe that they have substantial control over their own destiny.

One of the symptoms of severe test anxiety is the strong urge to leave the testing situation. Some students do this literally during an exam – they leave the test room before completing their script, and some leave without making any attempt to start. If there has been adequate preparation in the lead up to the exam, the student can begin to take some control by immediately drafting outline plans for the chosen questions, even if they do not seem at first to be entirely relevant. Students can be pleasantly surprised at how they can jumble the points they have learned around the particular twist in a given question.

DISRUPTING THE NEGATIVE FEEDBACK LOOP

Someone once composed a parody of a verse from the famous hymn, *Onward Christian Soldiers:* 'Like a mighty tortoise, moves the church of God, brothers we are treading, where we've always trod!'

A negative mindset in relation to exams is not a good frame in which to approach a new test. Individuals can resign to the mistaken belief that they have to 'tread where they have always trod', or they can take steps to reinterpret their entrenched mindset and to disrupt the negative feedback loop once it has been activated. An individual with a negative reinforcement history of exams is likely to ask, 'Why this? Why me? Why now?' The alternative is to look at the possibility of improvement and say, 'Why not? – the only way is up!' To set sights higher than previously discouraging experiences is not an unrealistic goal to aspire to.

Albert Bandura (1986) proposed a construct designated as 'self-efficacy', which he suggested reflected the initial decision to act, effort expended in acting and perseverance in the face of obstacles. The concept is further explained in terms of confidence in the ability to perform a given task successfully. Research has found that higher self-efficacy beliefs are related to better performance in sports, education, career and to better states of health with greater rates of improvements in recovery from illness (Bandura, 1997). Moreover, the experiments of Bandura and other researchers have demonstrated that self-efficacy beliefs can be increased incrementally, and the performance related to these increases can improve commensurately.

Lethal weapon 2: Distraction B

A DAYDREAM BELIEVER

Reference was previously made to the fact that some students leave the exam room quite literally. However, other students may 'leave the exam room' by allowing their minds to shift focus from the task in hand. When research on test anxiety was first initiated, the phenomenon was perceived to be one underlying construct manifested in a range of symptoms. Through time, however, test anxiety was formulated into two major components, emotionality and cognition, and the cognitive element was later subdivided into evaluative worry and test irrelevant thoughts. As previously observed, evaluative thoughts relate to such issues as better preparation, comparison with others, pessimistic thoughts about the examiner, worries about time restrictions or previous bad exam experiences. In contrast, test irrelevant thoughts are distractions that do not relate to the exam, where the mind transports itself to other interests or preoccupations. Why is it that test irrelevant thoughts have come to be classified as an element of the test anxiety construct? Perhaps the reason may be because they act as a mechanism that enables the student to escape from the pressures of the test situation. In this case they should be regarded as a maladaptive coping strategy. The 'daydream believer strategy' may have useful applications to other contexts but not for the duration of an exam!

BEWARE OF 'BENIGN' THOUGHTS IN THE EXAM

There used to be a computer game where the little pack-man with its triangular mouth gobbled up everything in its pathway, and the secret of the game was to make sure the object under control avoided the little 'gremlin'. In an exam, all kinds of intrusions and distractions are enemies that need to be avoided, whether they are evaluative thoughts or thoughts that are unconnected to the test. Some examples of the latter would be thinking of the events planned for after the exams, the meal that is prepared for the evening or the video that has been hired for relaxation. Alternatively, students may allow themselves to relive some controversial interaction they have had with someone recently or to contemplate some event that has been dominating the news in recent times or how they are going to continue managing on a 'shoestring' budget. Whatever may be the nature of the thoughts, they are distractions and intrusions that eat up precious time. Even if the physiological symptoms of anxiety (such as sweaty palms and dry mouth) are not a source of distraction, students can still do much damage to their own performance by engaging in distracting thoughts and fuelling intrusive thoughts. Research has shown that test irrelevant thoughts can be as debilitating to performance as evaluative thoughts, and both are more counterproductive than the physiological symptoms associated with the activation of the autonomic nervous system (McIlroy, Bunting & Adamson, 2000).

A SIMPLE STRATEGY FOR FOCUS

Intrusive, distracting thoughts during an exam may be far more easily controlled than is sometimes imagined. As a starting point in devising a strategy to counteract them, it is important to be aware of them and how detrimental they are. Second, if the resolution is made that these are to be comprehensively addressed, then a large part of the battle is over. Third, a simple strategy should be devised to tackle these distractions when they pop into the mind during a test. Again this comes back to the issue of believing that effective control can be taken under the pressure of an exam. It was previously noted that self-efficacy is an individual's belief in their own ability to perform a given task successfully, and internal locus of control is the belief that individuals have a large measure of control over the outcome of some event. Therefore students should enter testing situations armed with constructive and productive performance and outcome beliefs. In simple, practical terms, this should be translated into students choosing the questions they want to address, drafting a brief outline plan for each and adapting the points around the orientation of the question. Whenever students are distracted, they can go back to their plan in order to relocate their position. It might also be helpful to add a few more brief plan notes just to re-establish focus. Moreover, it might help to write down, 'beware of distractions' in large print (as rough work) to be aware of the ever present danger of tangential aberrations in thought. Finally, students should not waste thought energy lambasting themselves if recurrent distractions appear to be uncontrollable at times. The old Chinese proverb offers good practical advice: You may not be able to stop a bird landing on your head, but you can stop it making a nest in your hair!

After the test

REWARD YOURSELF FOR YOUR EFFORTS

Reinforcement schedules

B.F. Skinner was a twentieth century psychologist who emphasised the importance of reinforcers on shaping and changing behaviour. A reinforcer strengthens the likelihood that the behaviour to which it is attached will be repeated. He demonstrated 'reinforcement contingency' patterns in behaviour with rats and pigeons in a 'Skinner box'. For example, pigeons could be trained to peck a key at differing levels of intensity if they were given a food reward at regular or variable intervals or ratios (for example, at every fifth peck or at every 30 seconds). Skinner, and subsequent research, demonstrated that if animals are put on a 'variable ratio' reinforcement schedule their pecking (or lever pressing for rats) behaviour would be most steady and least resistant to extinction, even when reinforcers were terminated. Schedules of reinforcement have been applied with some success to shaping the behaviour of animals, children, offenders, clinical-patients etc. in diverse situations. Behaviour that is not rewarded (and thus reinforced) may become extinct if the reward is suddenly discontinued.

It is believed that gambling is a highly addictive behaviour because the participant is rewarded with a prize from time to time. This can be seen in the case of the National Lottery where many are addicted in spite of the financial hardships that participation may bring. Occasional, if small, rewards can be a very powerful instrument for establishing persistent behaviours. Students can take this principle and apply it to their studies, and especially with reference to revision for exams. One internal reinforcer that can be used is the sense of satisfaction that comes from achievement and the boost to self-esteem that is derived from completing a task. If students reward themselves before they know their results, then what they are reinforcing is their efforts rather than their success. Parents sometimes do this with their children before test results are known so that their children will place most value in efforts rather than outcomes. The whole point of a reinforcer is to make more likely the repetition of the target behaviour to which it is attached.

Exercise — Rewarding sound behaviours

It is a good strategy to make a list of all the rewards you can give yourself a) after each study session, b) after each assignment, c) after each revision period, d) after each exam, e) after all exams are completed.

Make a list of all the factors (external and internal) that you can use as rewards for completing your various tasks, and for reinforcers for shaping future behaviours. Some examples you may want to consider are:

A movie/A social event/Buying a new album/Listening to an older album/Extra rest/Visit to friends/Entertaining friends/Indulgence in hobby/A disco/A meal/ A sports event/A self-esteem boost/A self-efficacy boost/A dose of satisfaction/ Praise received from others.

PUTTING THE EXAM INTO PERSPECTIVE

In a pithy old adage the assertion is made that 'there is no use crying over spilt milk'. Once the exam is completed and the test room is left, students have to learn to live with the words of Pontius Pilate: 'What I have written, I have written.' For students who feel that they have done particularly well in their exam it is worth remembering that 'one swallow does not make a summer'. Conversely, for those who are convinced that they have underachieved, they should bear in mind that a college or university course is more like a marathon than a sprint, and even after lapses it is still possible to recover and achieve a good standard. In reality, one test appears to be of great importance around the time it is sat, but in time to come the student will look back and wonder why they worried so much about it. That statement is not designed to encourage complacency in students before an exam, but rather to help them maintain their balance and sanity afterwards! Of course students generally want to do their best and should not be asked to settle for less than the fulfilment of their potential at any given time. However, no student should allow themselves to slump into a negative downward spiral for that is not the optimal way to prepare for the next exam.

Working out percentages

Let us take the hypothetical example of a four-year degree course in which the weighting toward degree classification is as follows:

Year one (0 per cent). Year two (20 per cent). Year three — Placement year (20 per cent). Year four (60 per cent). Year one does not count as it is given to allow the students the opportunity to learn the system and procedures. In years two and four, there are six modules, each with one exam and two items of course work. Each exam contributes 60 per cent to the module overall. Now take year two as an example. Each module contributes about 3.33 per cent toward degree classification. The exam associated with each module contributes about 2 per cent. At this stage, if you slump in performance during one exam, it has practically no impact on your ultimate marks (especially if you perform reasonably well in your other exams and in your course work). A consistent weighting will not suffer from a few bad results at this stage. More impact is suffered from slumps in the final year where each module contributes 10 per cent toward degree classification and therefore each exam contributes 6 per cent. Even here, however, one or two lapses are not necessarily disastrous. For instance, if you achieve 65 per cent in four exams and 50 per cent in one, the overall average will be 62 per cent. The consistent weighting 'pulls' the final mark toward it. By examining the weightings you will be reassured that the system has been designed to allow for the fact that good students do not suffer irreparably when they make a few mistakes. Moreover, the system is usually designed to give students time to acquire the requisite skills before the more substantial marks begin to take effect.

TAKE A BREAK

Many students may not need to be given this advice, but some invariably do need to be reminded of it. Researchers depict the kind of person who may ultimately be in danger of coronary heart disease, ulcers and general stress-related illnesses. That type of person is profiled as hard driving, competitive, unable to 'switch off' and takes the worries of their work-related pressures home with them. With students the intense period related to their exams soon comes to an end and they can revert back to normal behaviours. However, it is also possible that students will develop strategies for exams that they will later employ in a range of stressful situations at work. The sooner efficient and effective strategies are learned, the better for the student. A good piece of advice for revision and exam times is take a break, take a rest, take time out, find something relaxing to pull the mind away from preoccupation with the worries and pressures of exams. Continuous bombardment and saturation of the mind is not the most efficient way to perform at the optimal level. Obviously, good preparation and planning for revision will leave more room in the schedule for rests and breaks. Do not fall into the trap of believing that taking breaks is going to work against you. That is only likely to happen if the breaks are totally unregulated.

An eating binge

Consider how damaging it would be to your body to go on a non-stop eating binge — somewhere along the line you would have to stop. Similarly, your mind will not be able to cope with information overload. Unless you take breaks, your faculties will not have the opportunity to renew their sharpness and freshness.

CAUTION WITH THE 'POST-MORTEM'

Some students cope in the wake of their exams by choosing to ignore any thought of the exam. They hold the view that it is done and gone and nothing that has been committed to paper or computer can be rescinded. Therefore, why worry until the result is known? Many students, however, wish to confer with other students and ascertain whether the chosen questions were correctly addressed. This can be a source of great encouragement or discouragement and can lead to high or low expectations of success. There may not be a lot of harm in this practice, and many students find it cathartic, but students should try to avoid the roller-coaster of emotions that may accompany it. Sharing with each other can produce good camaraderie and protect from isolation. Moreover, after all the interactions with friends, there are usually some in the company that can help steer the group toward solid and realistic attitudes. On balance this is probably better than repressing fears and worries, and may act as good therapy.

The advantage of attempting to evaluate performance in a test is that mistakes can be recognised and rectified for the next exam. This is a good, positive, constructive way to face up to shortcomings. The whole experience at university or college is a learning curve and if students make even modest efforts they should expect to improve their technique with practice. If an individual has experienced memory interference in an exam and has cited some study incorrectly then he or she will just have to accept that and try to avoid the same mistake next time round. On the other hand if the reason for underachievement was clearly a poor strategy then this should be comprehensively addressed. For example, a student may have sat a three-hour exam in which she or he was required to answer four questions. However, the student may have spent two hours answering the first two questions and only half an hour on the next two. In this case there was clearly a blunder in timing and planning. In effect they were probably restricting themselves to being marked out of a maximum of 75 per cent, because 25 per cent of the required material is likely to be missing.

A healed limb

It is claimed that when a bone is broken, it eventually becomes strongest at the point where it was broken. Therefore it is less likely to break at exactly that point again. In the same way, the weakest points in students' exam performance can become the strongest points when they begin to recognise and address the weaknesses. Students may feel so bad about the shortcomings that their resolution to counteract them ensures that they improve dramatically. Another example related to the body is the function of the white corpuscles in the blood. Whenever the body is cut, the white corpuscles immediately go to work to precipitate the healing process. During the first year or two at college students can spend time pinpointing the weaknesses in their learning processes, study strategy and exam techniques. They can then mobilise and channel their energies and enthusiasm into the pathway for success.

SUMMARY

♦ Undergraduates can plan for revision by use of past papers and by monitoring signals given to them in lectures.

♦ Planning a time schedule for exam questions will help maintain a sense of control over the testing situation.

♦ Symptoms of autonomic arousal around exam times can be reduced by relaxation techniques, and what remains can be interpreted as an endowment of energy for good performance.

♦ If all practicalities associated with the test are thoroughly attended to (for example, time, venue, date, stationery etc.), the exasperation of anxiety will be reduced.

♦ Reading over questions carefully and drafting brief, memorised essay plans will help counteract intrusive thoughts.

♦ Examinees are prone to the danger of fuelling a negative feedback loop that spirals their thinking away from task focus.

♦ Distracting or intrusive thoughts either related or unrelated to the exam will divert attention from the task at hand and therefore impair performance.

♦ Students should not accept a negative exam schema that forces them into a cul-de-sac of learned helplessness where they believe they have no control over exam-related events.

♦ A good strategy for when distracting thoughts encroach is to re-focus on draft plans and simply remember that distracting thoughts consume valuable time.

♦ Tests should be put into perspective by working out the percentage that each contributes to degree classification or diploma credit.

♦ Students should provide themselves with a list of rewards for their various efforts in order to reinforce their good academic habits.

10 Applying for a Job

KEY CONCEPTS

● JOB MARKET ● CAREERS DAYS ● CAREERS ADVISOR ● JOB VACANCIES
● JOB SPECIFICATION ● ESSENTIAL CRITERIA ● DESIRABLE CRITERIA
● CURRICULUM VITAE ● JOB REFERENCES ● PROFILE-BUILDING
● EMPLOYABILITY QUALITIES ● INTERVIEW PREPARATION AND
PERFORMANCE ● FIRST IMPRESSIONS ● NON-VERBAL COMMUNICATION
● PREPARING PRESENTATIONS

Getting familiar with the job market

KNOWING WHERE TO LOOK AND WHO TO TALK TO

It's never too soon for undergraduates to become aware of what is happening in the job market. A good starting point is to attend any careers days conducted within your own or another college. Find out where the university's career room is located and who the careers advisor is. This should be followed up by making a point of calling on a regular basis to see the kinds of opportunities that are available and the qualifications and experience that are required to fill the posts. In this way a clear picture is built up of what must be done to reach the aspired goals. Conversely, if this is left until near the time of graduation, opportunities may be missed because the student, may not, for example, have acquired some relevant experience via appropriate part-time work.

If a particular profession is of interest to a student, it will be most useful to speak to someone in that profession, as they will be aware of the best current routes to reach the goal. On the other hand, if a student is undecided about a future career, then it would be profitable to chat to a range of professionals in order to derive some stimulation and inclination toward a prospective profession. Even if the student has reservations about a particular occupation, it remains beneficial to sample various potential opportunities in order to get a good feel for what is available. The degree programme a student has chosen may limit their future choice somewhat, although some universities offer a basic first year course that allows progression to several career routes afterwards. Moreover, some students complete a one-year, post-graduate course that allows them to proceed in a different direction from their original intention.

Newspapers are a very important source for tracking recent job vacancies. Certain newspapers will advertise particular jobs (for example, Education, Health, and Technology) on a set day each week. A teacher or careers advisor may be able to give some guidance to steer a student in the right direction for searching out these advertisements. Another excellent source for screening job opportunities is the Internet. Companies will advertise posts on their websites and this medium provides quick and easy access to the required information. Moreover, by supplying an email address to job agencies, you can have job adverts sent daily or weekly (according to your preference) as soon as they become available. In order to get started at this and to build confidence, students can ask for the relevant information at their careers office where they will be provided with website addresses, and can access adverts both within their local vicinity and over wider regions. The habit of checking out job vacancies on websites may be much easier for a student than visiting a job centre and reading through recruitment magazines.

Preparing for buying a car

Many young people become interested in using a car before they are at the age of being entitled to have a driving licence. They watch other people driving and become familiar with the basic use of the steering wheel, clutch, brakes, accelerator, indicators etc. They look forward to the day when they can practise what they have observed. They also look around at various cars and know the particular model that they would love to own and drive. When they eventually do acquire the car of their choice, the process of driving is not entirely new to them. In a similar way, familiarity with the job market, qualifications and required experience etc., mean that the procedure for application is not totally unfamiliar territory, because the student will have already built a repertoire of knowledge along the way.

ACCUMULATING AWARENESS FOR FUTURE REFERENCE

Although an academic qualification is of paramount importance to a student, the awareness of the route to the chosen career should always be lurking in the background. Criteria for particular jobs can change and it is essential to keep abreast of any changes that occur. When a job is applied for, an application pack will be sent that includes a job-specification (or 'job spec') that is designed to guide the applicant. This lists the range of characteristics the company is looking for from applicants. These characteristics may have been previously documented on a website, and students can ask their careers officer to guide them to some examples. It is good for students to get into the early habit of looking over these so that they can give sufficient attention to developing the required qualities for the career of their choice. Below is the kind of job-spec that might be found for a one year contract for a Research Assistant at university (many graduates take jobs like this to equip them more fully for the career of their choice).

Criteria for Research Assistant post

Essential	Desirable
A good primary degree (2:1)	Previous research experience
Word processing skills	Work without supervision
Experience in statistical packages	Evidence of library skills
Ability to write reports	Good communication skills
Capable of using computer word searches	Skill in searching websites
Competence in applying research	Access to a car

Attention should be given both to essential and desirable criteria, and these are the guidelines that should be followed in preparing a letter of application. It will be helpful to prospective employers if all the criteria are clearly flagged up in the application and if the same order as specified is maintained. These criteria will also became the basis for an interview and so applicants should be ready to verbalise examples of the criteria. Desirable criteria should not be dismissed as unimportant, as employers will if necessary use these for short-listing and also for final decision about employment.

No second chance to make a first impression

It is foolish to imagine that the interview is more important than the application form, for without a good application form the candidate will not be short-listed for an interview. Moreover, the content of the application form should become the foundation for the interviewee's responses. Take time in preparing the application and make a copy in order to be reminded of what was written before entering an interview. Once the application has been despatched, the applicant is committed to what was written and there is no second chance to correct what has been indelibly recorded.

Olympic Games

In some events at the Olympic Games, competitors are given the opportunity to make several attempts at a single event and their best performance (from, say three attempts) is selected. Examples of this are the triple jump and the javelin. However, in other events competitors only have one chance for a medal — if they get through the heats and reach the finals. Examples of this are the range of running events on the track. Whenever an applicant applies for a job they are only permitted to submit one application form. Competition for jobs is fierce, and because short-listing for interviews is based on application forms, applications should aim to make a good first impression in writing.

TAILORING THE APPLICATION TO THE JOB SPEC

In the job spec just considered there were sections for both essential and desirable criteria. Applicants should attempt to demonstrate that they possess all criteria although emphasis should first be given to the essential criteria. Do not be daunted if it appears initially that you do not possess the full range of the desirable criteria. First, you may have more of the criteria than others who apply for the job, and second you may have more criteria than you imagine yourself to have and these may become apparent when you assess yourself more closely. Many degree programmes are now aimed at giving students employability skills, and these should be scrutinised in course handbooks. Students sometimes fail to be able to list the full range of qualities they clearly have. In summary, make sure that the job spec is used as the template for completing the application form, and as the basis for preparing for the interview.

Exercise — Extracting your qualities

Can you extract from your personal history information to fulfil the following criteria?

Completing projects under tight time schedules

Working effectively as part of a team

Interpersonal skills in a range of different settings

Handling conflict situations effectively and efficiently

Writing different kinds of reports

Ability to adapt to new challenges

Evidence for working in isolation when required

FEATURES TO LOOK FOR

In responding to a job advert, applicants will need to ensure that they are providing all the information requested. It may be that this information is adequately covered in a CV (see next section), but if there is a requirement to provide this in the application form then repetition should not be avoided by a statement such as 'see CV'. Qualifications should be given attention to – candidates should make sure they possess the appropriate qualifications, especially if these are designated as 'essential', and should present a clear record of these. Some applicants make the decision to apply for a job irrespective of whether they have the qualifications or not in the hope that no one who has the required qualifications will apply! That is an unlikely scenario and stretches the patience of human resources departments who have to wade through all the application forms.

If a letter of application or supporting statement is also specified, this provides an opportunity to highlight and elaborate on any particular strengths, especially those relevant to the job specification. What should be avoided here is a verbatim repetition of what was presented in the CV, but the points highlighted there can be further developed. In a supporting statement or letter of application the opportunity is afforded to take the bones and put some flesh on them, and then dress them up in a presentable fashion! The job spec should be the template for all aspects of the application.

TAKING TIME FOR MEETING DEADLINES

It is unrealistic to shelve away an application and then bring it out later and hastily fill it in at the last possible moment. That is the procedure that should be followed if the applicant is intent on avoiding that job! However, if the candidate is serious about an application, the rule to be followed is, 'never put off until tomorrow what you can do today'. An immediate start can be made by completing all the basics such as name, gender, age, address, qualifications, previous experience etc. Other aspects that may require more reflection should not be rushed into, and it will be helpful to verbalise thoughts to a friend in order to have the benefit of feedback. Good wines taste best when they are left in a cellar and allowed to mature. Similarly it is useful to read over the questions and then to go away and reflect on them for a while. They can be read over several times so that comprehensive responses are allowed to incubate. This is not like an examination or test where there are only a few hours to do justice to the material. Neither is it like an interview situation where there cannot be an indefinite delay between questions and responses. However, initial responses to questions on an application form may eventually be the ones that the applicant is most content with. Nevertheless, the fact that responses have been dismantled and rebuilt in the thought processes will equip the applicant well for the interview. It is good experience to envisage the kinds of questions that might be asked in a wide range of interview types. Try to envisage the following application situations and attempt to address the questions accordingly.

Exercise — Practice questions for job applications

A bank clerk — What special skills do you have that make you suitable as a bank employee?

A teacher — How can you be sure that you possess the requisite qualities to meet the many demands that are placed on teachers these days?

A personnel officer — What do you think are the most important qualities for a personnel officer, and what evidence can you produce to show that you possess them?

CHOOSE WELL FOR REFERENCES

Most companies will ask prospective employees to nominate two or three referees who will give a character reference and a résumé of abilities and qualities related to the post applied for. The reference usually has to be written but some companies prefer to speak to the referee on the phone. Three important points to be given attention to in relation to references are – first, referees should know the applicant well enough to be able to give a confident and comprehensive résumé of suitability for the post. Second, applicants should ensure that referees are sufficiently credible to the company to carry an authoritative recommendation to support the application. Third, as a matter of courtesy it is wise to seek permission from referees about the submission of their names for references. It may be embarrassing if they are contacted by phone and have no knowledge that the applicant has applied for the job! In some cases referees are not called upon but applicants should never bank on this. Good references can add weight to an application and may sway a finely balanced decision in favour of an applicant. Therefore start thinking early about who your referees will be, rather than making a rash decision in haste when applying for a job.

Preparing a Curriculum Vitae (CV)

Some people like to keep regular notes in diaries, not only to pencil in plans for future events, but also to look retrospectively on their previous activities and engagements. If students build their CV gradually over the course of their university career, they will find the task of final compilation much easier and they will not have missed recording important events that could otherwise be overlooked. For example, it would be easy to overlook the range of extra-curricular activities engaged in such as student committee for liaison with staff or voluntary activities outside or inside university. Many students do voluntary work with autistic children, or help with homework clubs or it may be useful to keep a note of some important undergraduate project. Lists should be made of part-time jobs, not only to illustrate the range of skills acquired but also to demonstrate the ability to complete a degree course while giving attention to other responsibilities.

Exercise — A repertoire of skills

See if you can provide written statements to demonstrate clearly that you possess the following key skills. Can you add any others to the list?

Organisational skills	Administrative competence
Interpersonal skills	Computing ability
Task-focused competence	Evidence for creativity
Applied abilities	Completion of tasks

Aspects of a CV should be general in order to demonstrate that the applicant is a 'well rounded' person who can adapt to a range of situations. Employers look for prospective employees who are industrious, conscientious, enthusiastic, co-operative, organised, trustworthy etc.

Exercise — Demonstration of qualities

See if you can provide (on the dotted lines) brief summary evidence to demonstrate that you have the qualities listed below:

Industrious ....

Conscientious ....

Enthusiastic ....

Co-operative ....

Decisive ....

Trustworthy ....

Focused ....

Good planner ....

Initiative ....

Disciplined ....

Quick to learn ....

Question — If you are planning on being involved in some leadership or management role, what kinds of qualities should you be developing and making note of? Look back at the example in Chapter 3, 'Cultivating Organisational Skills', related to managing a clothes shop.

The question about leadership/management points to specific skills that should be especially highlighted in a job application for that kind of post. Different types of vocation emphasise the need for particular kinds of skills. In third level education there is currently an emphasis on 'transferable skills', that is, generic skills that can be carried across the full range of subjects and over all years at college, and these include computing, writing, evaluating evidence and interpersonal skills. However, particular jobs may require unique features such as the ability of employees to isolate themselves from others for many hours or to work in an environment where focus must be maintained in the midst of many distractions. In some occupations employees may have to endure complaints from the public, and these can degenerate into blame or insults. Some jobs roles may require an ability to 'think on your feet', or to make the final decision in an important matter after extensive consultation. Whatever the job that is aimed for, prospective applicants should consider well in advance the range of skills that will be needed, how these can be cultivated, what practical steps should be taken to acquire them and how they should be documented on the CV. From time to time the record of achievements and experience should be re-organised on the CV into a manageable and presentable form.

Exercise — Preparing for interview questions

Anticipate the different kinds of questions you might be asked at an interview for each of the following jobs, and what kinds of skills you would want to emphasise:

Teacher

Researcher

Computer Programmer

Security Officer

Quality Control Manager

Human Resources Manager

Brick Layer

Pilot

Salesperson

Driving Instructor

COMPREHENSIVE AND CONCISE

A CV can be used as a frame of reference for completing an application form and building a supporting statement or letter of application. All the points specifically related to the post being applied for can be highlighted and elaborated upon. If a variety of jobs are being applied for, the relevant parts of the CV can be developed where appropriate. Prospective employers may not be interested in a lengthy CV where most of the points are not relevant to the vacancy they are intent on filling. At the same time it is essential to present some flavour of background and range of achievements. Too much detail may result in readers being lost and missing the really essential information. This is most likely to happen if the CV is very poorly structured, but is least likely to happen if the CV has clear headings and succinct bullet points.

Think of the task that is set before a panel of interviewers. They may have about half an hour before the first interview begins and about fifteen minutes between each interview. If someone has been interviewed before you, they may have to document some agreed evaluative statements before they have time to look at your CV just prior to your interview.

A great service will be rendered to them if they are presented with a CV in which the relevant points can be easily accessed before and during the interview. Therefore, it is a good strategy to make the CV clearly presentable, and this can be done by trimming down all the material irrelevant to the job and clearly setting out the points that relate to the job spec.

SECTIONS, HEADINGS AND PRESENTATIONS

Some computer packages provide a range of templates that can be used to type CV details into. Even if none of these is used, they may stimulate thought about devising a good alternative. Moreover, careers officers, job markets etc. may be able to provide samples of CV formats that will help to guide job applicants through the task of preparation. Headings for major sections should be placed at the left of the page and the information that relates to each heading should be inserted adjacent to these on the right. The first section should be entitled, 'Personal Details', and these will at least include, name, address, telephone number and date of birth. Following this there should be a section covering Education and this should start with what you are currently doing at university or college and the planned date of completion. From this point educational background should be traced and documented backward in time, and details of institutions attended, qualifications obtained and relevant dates should be supplied. Alternatively, qualifications obtained may be listed separately from institutions attended. Below is a sample from part of a spoof CV to illustrate layout.

Example

Education	Currently at Universtiy of Die-hards and Dare-do's, Xanadu, Burgershire. In third year of a 4-year course on Sky-hooking. (2000 — present)
	Mildred Bloggs Grammar School, Pepperville, Plunkitt Co. 1993—2000.
	Cynthia Crouton's Primary School, Poultice Ave., Skidrow. 1986—1993
Qualifications	A-Levels (1997). English & Physics (Grade B), French (Grade C)
	GCSE (1995). English, Maths, Physics (Grade A), Geog., History, French (Grade B), Computing & Chemistry (Grade C).

The above is one of many possible formats that can be looked at, and the clearer the presentation, the better for the applicant. The most important factor is that the required information is clearly seen and easily accessible. Ensure that there are no gaps in the dates and that continuity is provided in all aspects of the chronology of the CV. After all the essential sections have been covered then there may be room for 'Other Qualifications', and these can include features such as award schemes, certificates, badges, courses completed etc. It might also be useful and relevant to have a section entitled 'Other Activities' or 'Special Interests', in which can be included hobbies, summer camps and part-time voluntary work. Moreover, to enrich a CV further a section on 'Personal Skills' (see under 'Start building your profile now' and 'General and specific elements' in this chapter). In terms of general presentation, it is helpful for the reader if each new section is adequately spaced out from the previous section and if the headings are bold. The use of underlining can spoil presentation, and should therefore be used sparingly if at all. Headings can also be improved by setting them in a font size above the text.

SELL YOURSELF WELL

The 20th century ended and the 21st century has begun with a lot of emphasis on image and how individuals and companies should present and project themselves. This applies both to personal appearance and to catchy one-liner sound bites. In the world of pop music, a large part of 'the sell' is the appearance, the dance routines and novel videos that accompany the lyrics and sound tracks. A CV is an opportunity for applicants to present an image of themselves in words. Of course the whole ethos of image can be very superficial, and this can lead to disappointment when the veneer is penetrated. Therefore, no CV should be laced with fabrication and exaggeration. Conversely, modesty should not inhibit good applicants from presenting the range of qualities and qualifications that they know they have. It is not improper for applicants to assert that they have cultivated a range of social and interpersonal skills and have acquired fluency in word processing and expertise in writing skills (provided they have done so!). Prospective employers understand that this has to be done, especially if they have asked for these characteristics, and in an interview candidates can demonstrate that they have their 'feet on the ground', by expressing their aspirations to learn and develop more. Moreover, there are judicious ways of presenting achievements without making the whole thing reek of arrogance!

Exercise — Highlighting employability qualities

See if you can write a few sentences that highlight three of your personal characteristics/ skills/ achievements that could be described as making you employable. Try to do this in a way that will do justice to yourself without sounding arrogant or over-inflated with your own importance. Try this out with a friend and ask her/him to do the same. Then compare each other's answers and give mutual and constructive feedback. Now imagine that you are both in an interview and the panel is reading over your professed skills. They ask you to provide practical evidence to illustrate your skills. What can you say to support the claims you have made? Try this out on each other and ascertain if your friend feels that you can have given an adequate and satisfactory answer.

Think of the kind of job reference you would like to write for a good friend, and the kind you would like to read if you were considering employing a job applicant. Consider if this is the kind of justice you have done to yourself in the presentation of your CV.

Performing well in an interview

MAKING A GOOD INITIAL IMPRESSION

Appropriate dress is another important form of communication. A funeral director would never attend duties while dressed as a clown and an athlete does not appear on the track in formal dress. Whenever an applicant enters an interview one of the first things that will be noticed by the panel is personal appearance. It is important that dress is more formal, and that it is modest, tidy and smart (not too loud and definitely not a distraction!). Applicants will usually be introduced to the panel and should make brief eye contact with each one in turn and a little smile is not likely to do any harm. Courtesies should not be over done and applicants should not sit down until invited to do so. By this stage the interviewee can have already made a good impression and will have boosted personal confidence by following the sensible protocol just outlined.

Exercise – Breaking ground for interviews

In an interview there is every chance that you will be faced with a panel that is comprised of some people whom you may never have seen before and know nothing about. If you are not very experienced at meeting people on your own then try to get into the habit of giving yourself some useful practise. Try to speak to some students in your class that you have never interacted with before. Try asking some questions that show an interest in them that is caring but not intrusive. Listen carefully to their answers and try to develop the conversation based on their responses rather than going off on tangents. This should be done often enough to become comfortable with yourself in these kinds of situations. Similar conversations can be developed with the people who are employed in the library, the canteen and with technicians etc. It is also good to get some experience interacting with the kinds of people you might have to face in an interview. Students at college are assigned personal tutors but many don't take advantage of this opportunity. These kinds of opportunities need to be grasped in order to develop the skills that are required for formal interview occasions.

THE POWER OF NON-VERBAL COMMUNICATION (NVC)

Researchers claim that when there is ambiguity between verbal and non-verbal communication, then the NVC will be used to interpret the message (Hargie, Saunders & Dickson, 2000). NVC includes dress, appearance, facial expression, use of arms, hands and fingers, proximity, body movement, head movement and paralanguage (opening words and closure signs, pauses, emphases, hesitations, inflection etc.). Take as one graphic example, the small variations in the use of eyebrows that can send out a range of different messages. Raise the eyebrows a little and surprise is indicated, but raise them a lot and incredulity is signified. If the eyebrows are dropped a little this is a pointer toward confusion, but if they are dropped further a message of anger is transmitted.

In an interview situation, an interviewee can take NVC and use it to good advantage. Previously addressed were the issues of 'proper' dress, the use of an appropriate smile and brief eye contact with each member of the panel. It is also important to look at the person who is posing the question at any given time without attempting to interrupt before they have finished. However, it helps to give a brief nod or two while they are speaking to indicate that you understand what is being communicated. Try to regulate the pace and pitch of your speech so that the panel do not have to ask you to repeat your responses. Watch out for too many 'ums', 'ers' etc. and too much use of the same expression – for example, one person while doing a presentation repeatedly said, 'trust me on this one'. When you are invited to sit you should try to sit in a relaxed manner – too relaxed is when your hands are behind your head or when you slouch in the chair, and too defensive is when you fold you arms. Another poor NVC message is the bad habit of fidgeting or rocking back and forward on the chair. If you do not know what to do with your hands, then it may be helpful just to rest them on your knees.

Find the balance that conveys respect to the panel and confidence in your responses. Another factor to be considered is the length of the responses. A good rule of thumb is to be brief and to the point but elaborate sufficiently to demonstrate your answer with some authority. Closure is an important aspect of each response and every attempt should be made to do this smoothly. The interview panel should be clear that your response has been completed. A little glance toward the person who put the question will help to facilitate closure. If you are interrupted when you are speaking, do not display any irritation but welcome this as a helpful opportunity to harness responses.

Exercise — Altering meanings by NVC

Consider the following statements/questions and see if you can convey at least two different meanings to each of them by varying the use of non-verbal communications:

1. That was a very interesting speech.
2. It's a long time since I have tasted cooking like that.
3. I am very surprised by your reaction.
4. Do you think our mutual friend is generous?
5. We are paid enough money for working here.

All in all, make sure that body language and paralanguage are appropriate to support rather than contradict presentation and responses.

First and foremost, settle it in your mind that nerves will not hinder your performance but actually help (and remember that the interviewers will allow for some nerves). Once you get into the interview, focus on your task and get into the flow of your responses, your nerves will come under control. Probably the greatest antidote to nerves is to prepare well and wisely. This entails addressing all the issues on the job spec until you are sure that you can address all the issues adequately in a verbal manner. There is always a danger of over preparing in the sense of saturating your mind until you almost grind to a halt. This can be countered by taking breaks and some relaxation in the preparation and by giving attention to other issues not related to the approaching interview. If the company you are being interviewed by has sent you some literature about them and their background, mission statement etc., ensure that you are familiar with these and weave some of the points into your answers. It is also useful to arrive at the interview venue early, and to take a look at any displays that are presented, and then to make reference to these in the interview.

A key thought for entering an interview – what should be on your mind as you are waiting to enter the interview room? One choice is to allow yourself to be intimidated by the question, 'I wonder what they are going to ask me?' On the other hand, you can turn this right round and assert to yourself – 'I know what I am going to tell them.' You do have some control over the way you think and you can choose which of the above you want to be your dominant thought.

Ensure that you are familiar with what you wrote on the application form so that you do not contradict yourself and leave egg all over your face! Therefore, make a copy of your completed application form before you dispatch it to your prospective employers.

A very simple and direct question that interviewees sometimes stumble over is, 'why did you apply for this post?' or 'what has attracted you to this company?' These kinds of questions were so obvious that the interviewee had not thought of them! Marshal your reasons and arguments to justify your application and be ready to present them in a concise, coherent manner. If possible try to give more than one point to each answer or at least do not utter staccato responses.

Brief Exercise — Part-time job interview

Imagine that you are being interviewed for a part-time job as a sales assistant in a video shop. Address your response to the question of what drew you to apply for the job.

Another question you might be asked is if you are aware of the pressures that might be associated with the job and if you think you can cope with these. Or if applying for a part-time job you might be asked if the job is likely to conflict with your studies. It is always wise to try to envisage the kinds of questions that might be asked in relation to a specific job, and to ask friends/family if they can think of any questions that might be posed at the interview.

Exercise — Preparing outline answers

Imagine that you are being interviewed for a post as a nurse. Address the following questions:

1. Can you give us a brief outline of what you think the pressures/problems of this job are likely to be?
2. How can you be sure that you can manage these without being overwhelmed?

A panel of interviewers will be interested to hear what you have to say about the previous experiences and skills you can bring with you and use in the job applied for. Do not imagine that questions you have already addressed in the application form or letter or in your CV will not be asked again. They will be keen to see if you have your responses organised and ready at the 'tip of your tongue', and ensure that you don't contradict what you have already placed in writing. They may also ask for an outline of the qualifications you have obtained and how these might be useful in relation to the post applied for. Be ready to comment on the skills that are required for the post and how your past training and experience have equipped you for the job.

Exercise – Preparing comprehensive responses

Try to envisage being interviewed for a job as a counsellor. You are asked to describe the range of problems you may face in this job and the skills you will need to use. Also outline any past experiences that may have helped prepare you for this post.

Other questions you might be asked include whether you can demonstrate that you can work effectively as part of a team, and if you can work quietly on your own when that is required. Commonly asked questions are how you would handle conflict situations and react to insults from the public. You might also be asked what you will do to relax in order to relieve the pressures of the job. What you should always focus on are the peculiar characteristics of the particular job you are being interviewed for, and it is most helpful if you can chat to someone in a similar occupation before the interview. A final question may be what your aims, plans and ambitions for the future are and how your role in the position applied for fits in with these. For example, you might be asked, 'where do you see yourself in your career plan at this time and where do you plan to be in five years' time?'

A DIALOGUE OR A MONOLOGUE?

In an interview situation, the interviewee is likely to be expected to do most of the talking, but not all of it: an interview is not intended to be a continuous monologue. You should go into the interview armed with the thought that there will be some interaction between you and each member of the panel. When one of them asks a question you should address your response to the whole panel by spreading your eye contact around. However, it is wise to look toward the person who addressed the question as you approach the conclusion of the response to ascertain if they are satisfied or require further elaboration. Remember that an interview is two-way traffic rather than a one-way street.

The interview panel has ultimate control over the interview session in that they have set the agenda and can stop you at any point. However, that does not mean that you have no control over proceedings because you can discreetly introduce important points that they have not directly requested. Moreover, you have some control over the nature, duration and sequencing of your responses. Any use of humour should not usually be initiated by you although you should not worry if you say things that are taken as funny. The most important aspect of control for you is that you have control of yourself within the context that the panel has defined, and they want to see that you can take control in a disciplined manner. It may well be that you will have already covered some of the later questions in your previous responses, and in this case you can give a brief résumé of your previous response along with any additional points. Sometimes one of the panel members may stare at you as if you were a freak of nature! It will help you if you interpret this as a means of testing how you are able to handle pressure.

Have some questions ready

At the end of an interview a member of the panel will often ask if you have any question(s) for them and you should therefore prepare yourself with a couple of good ones. This is also an opportunity to let them see that you have read the information they have previously sent you about the job and the company. For example, a useful question might be related to something that you have read in this literature. It would not look good if you were to ask them a question that has been answered in the information pack they sent you to read. On the other hand, if it becomes clear that you have read the information sent this will send a strong message about your enthusiasm for the job. As an example you might want to ask if the company encourages further training in relation to the job or what the staff development priorities are.

Exercise — Asking incisive questions

Consider being the interviewee for a post as a sales representative selling home-based computer educational courses. Can you think of three appropriate questions to ask the interview panel in relation to keeping in touch with developing technology, promotional aspects within the company and if they are open to suggestions for innovative sales techniques and advertising?

As a rule of thumb it is good to ask questions that demonstrate that you are enthusiastic about the job, and that you want to develop within the post and envisage making a career of it in the foreseeable future. Moreover, sometimes a panel member may ask if there is another particular thing that you want to mention just before you leave the room – think of something that is important to you.

WHENEVER A PRESENTATION IS REQUIRED

In some interviews a presentation is required, especially if the job itself requires presentation skills. For guidance in this see Chapter 11 'A Skilful Presentation'. Look at the highlighted text below, which provides a checklist of the salient points you should pay attention to.

Presentations at interviews — Synopsis of cardinal points — Do's and Don't's

1. Keep strictly within any given time restrictions.
2. Tailor the number of acetates/slides to overall duration (for example, three acetates in fifteen minutes, one every five minutes).
3. Space the points out well in a good sized readable font.
4. Present the points in succinct capsules.
5. Do not block the view of anyone on the panel.

6. Do not put up a new acetate/slide while still addressing points on the pervious acetate slide or vice-versa.
7. Keep in synchrony with the points by pointing to each (with a pen or pencil) as you proceed.
8. Round off each section with a summary statement and lead into the next point.
9. Ensure that you glance round at your audience from time to time.
10. Present a brief bird's eye view of your presentation at the end.

After a negative experience

THE TOUGHNESS OF A COMPETITIVE JOB MARKET

It should be no surprise to find that a number of attempts may have to be made before a suitable job opportunity is given. The process is likely to require patience, perseverance and practise. In some cases applicants will not get short-listed for interviews because so many candidates have applied. A determined candidate must keep on knocking at doors until a suitable one opens. It is useful to talk to someone who has been successful in the pursuit of a job and try to ascertain what modifications may have to be made in the approach to the application and interview next time round. If you have had a job interview, you can at a later stage ask the company for some feedback about what you still need to do to improve your employment prospects.

VALUE IN NEGATIVE EXPERIENCES

What job seekers should not do is permit themselves to feel dejected, demoralised and disillusioned. It is understandable that an applicant will feel a little down after putting a lot of work into an application form and an interview, only to find that someone else has been given first preference on that particular occasion. An interesting point of debate is whether gloomy thoughts trigger gloomy mood or vice-versa. Perhaps both perspectives are right and it appears to be true that both feed off and into each other once they are activated. It is possible to control gloomy thoughts by gleaning positive conclusions from negative experiences and thus break the vicious circle. One good positive outcome to emerge from an application/interview is that applicants have managed to get themselves focused and arranged their material in a systematic manner as well as benefiting from the engagement of an interview. When the interview experience has been gone through once, the second occasion will be much more familiar, less anxiety-inducing and will probably require less preparation (for example, CV details will be in place). Applicants will have a clearer perception of their own strengths and weaknesses and will be better equipped to harness the one and address the other. Each time an improvement is made, applicants move further up the 'queue' in the quest to become more employable. Moreover, negative experiences can help the applicant to approach interviews with more realistic expectations and help in learning to avoid excessive euphoria and cope with disappointments.

Soldier, soldier will you marry me?

There is an old song in which a maid asks a soldier to marry her:
'Soldier, soldier will you marry me with your musket, fife and drum?' He responds, 'How can I marry such a pretty girl like you when I've got no coat to put on'. So off she goes and acquires a coat for him and returns to ask the same question again. He works his way through all the clothes he will need for the big occasion, and she goes back and forward until all his requirements are fulfilled. When the question is put to him for the last time — 'Soldier, soldier will you marry me?', his final response is, 'How can I marry such a pretty girl like you, when I've got a wife of my own!' The poor lady had been on a wild goose chase from the start without knowing it!

That may well be the way many people feel in relation to job applications. However, there are jobs available out there but success rarely comes with one attempt and sometimes not after many attempts. There is a story about a company that took out a contract to dig for gold but eventually gave up after protracted, laborious effort. Another company took over the contract and took up where the previous company had left off. Almost immediately and with just a little effort they found the gold that the previous company had been looking for and had been so close to without realising it. So do not lose heart in the pursuit of a job because you can never tell when you will be next in line.

PhD supervisors frequently have choice words of wisdom, and one offered these sound words of advice to his student – 'don't be too disappointed when certain jobs don't come your way, for it may well be the case that you are being saved from a poison chalice!' That is especially applicable if you are not suited to a job or not sufficiently prepared for it. Of course, sometimes an applicant may intend to use a job as a stepping stone to the ultimate choice. At other times, the job the applicant thought they would love does not prove to be the niche in which they would like to stay. In short, allow some open-mindedness, flexibility and a little room in your plans for some mobility. The important thing is to be well prepared and equipped. Have one eye on the goal and the other on the path toward it.

Recognising acquired employability skills

Students may fail to realise that the range of skills they have acquired at college provide them with important qualities for employment. It's useful to make a list of all the skills acquired and to place a sentence of explanation beside each one, demonstrating evidence for how the particular skill was developed. Some examples of employability skills likely to be developed at college are given below.

◆ Communication skills — **Written communication is developed through writing essays, assignments, exams and note-taking in lectures, seminars and personal study. Spoken communication is developed through interaction and discussion in small groups and by presentations.**

◆ Social skills — **These are developed by the range of friendships with students from a variety of backgrounds and by interaction with teaching and research staff, technical and administrative staff etc. On some courses social skills are taught as a compulsory module or half-module.**

♦ Organisational skills — The requirement of working toward deadlines within tight time schedules fosters the development of organisational skills. Moreover, students have to divide and balance their activities between various subjects and assignments running concurrently and often have to juggle other pressures such as family responsibilities and work commitments.

♦ Ability to focus — There is no time or room in college for 'peripherals' in academic work, and students will never achieve anything unless they learn to select relevant material and focus on salient points.

♦ Working independently — Students are required to take initiative in building on the material that has been given. For example, in assignments students are given a 'raw' title and maybe one or two key references. It is then their responsibility to do the digging and the tracing in order to build the assignment into a substantial work.

♦ Team work — Group projects, seminars and small group work necessitates working in teams and dealing with other students who may range from being very conscientious to very 'relaxed'.

♦ Analytical skills — These come from amassing and using evidence from various sources that appear contradictory. Students learn to extract strengths and highlight weaknesses from various perspectives. They learn to think critically and evaluate evidence scientifically and to avoid colouring conclusions with personal prejudices and stereotypes.

♦ Computing skills — These may include use of word processing packages, statistical and graphical packages, Powerpoint and the use of email and the Internet, as well as competence in word searches through electronic journals.

♦ Library skills — Good students learn to use their college library well and acquire efficiency in locating books, identifying periodicals, tracing references and conducting up-to-date research. They rapidly learn to compile good summary sources of information that form the basis for authoritative conclusions.

♦ Learning capacity — Students are constantly exposed to new material and fresh challenges. They are required to be rigorous in learning from computers, library, lectures, seminars and experiments, all within strict time limits.

SUMMARY

◆ It is never too early for students to become aware of the job market and sources to look for job vacancies.

◆ Careers facilities provided at university should be capitalised upon as soon as possible after entrance.

◆ Job applicants should prepare their application (and for an interview) with reference to their prospective employers job specification (both essential and desirable criteria).

◆ Students should learn how to prepare a CV and should regularly add to it as skills and experience continue to accumulate.

◆ 'Profile-building' involves taking stock of the range of employability skills and acquired experiences (for example, from university, voluntary and part-time work) and ensuring that these are clearly documented and regularly updated.

◆ In every job application, the applicant should extract and 'spin' the relevant qualities and experience toward the advertised job criteria.

◆ Some careful reflection related to acquired employability skills and qualities may indicate that job applicants have more criteria than they had first imagined.

◆ In an interview situation personal appearance should be appropriate and initial interactions with the interview panel should be measured.

◆ Non-verbal communication will either strengthen or weaken an interviewee's performance before a panel.

◆ Responses to questions should be measured to avoid the extremes of monologue and embarrassing silences.

♦ Interviewees should read any literature that has been sent to them by their prospective employers prior to the interview.

♦ When a presentation is required at an interview, a variety of simple but essential guidelines should be followed.

♦ Applicants should chose their referees carefully and request permission beforehand to use their names.

11   A Skilful Presentation

The task that is set before you

EVALUATING YOUR TASK

In bringing a presentation to a large or small audience, you have to think about a range of factors. For example, there is the time it will take, the number of overheads you will need, how your material will be structured, where you are going to stand (and move around), how you will harmonise your speaking with your visuals, how you will inter-act with your audience while keeping an eye on the time for pacing out your points etc. The purpose of the present chapter is to guide you through all the points you will need to think about and plan for.

As in all other aspects of this book, good organisation and planning are essential – these both give confidence and minimise anxiety.

Anxiety is often triggered by the realisation that we are being evaluated by others, and is compounded by the complexity of the task we have to perform. If only the task were simple and we were well used to it, we would have fewer worries. However, good preparation and careful planning will enable you to focus on the task and give you a sense of greater control over what is going on.

The fact that many things have to be thought about before and during a presentation cannot be ignored, but these can become a natural part of the routine, just as naturally as we use the bank, drive a car or prepare a meal.

A foreign holiday

Going abroad on holiday for the first time can be a daunting experience, but some careful forethought and simple planning can help to make it memorable and pleasurable. In the first place you can speak to friends who have done this before and you can read the holiday brochures and travel guides. Moreover, it may be useful to learn some essential phrases and to take out some travel insurance for your peace of mind. A knowledge of the local currency and its value in relation to yours is a must, as is preparation in terms of how you will make a transaction for purchases etc. It also helps to check out what entertainment is available so that you can make some preliminary plans when you arrive. In addition you may specifically want a hotel that has an English menu and where the waiters/waitresses understand some English. Moreover, you should prepare yourself for the hassles of some irregularities over the first few days. It would be expected that by the time you are half way through your holiday you will have learned to co-ordinate your way through most of the ingredients you need for an enjoyable holiday. At the end of the holiday you will have successfully negotiated something that is new to you and will feel more confident that you can do this again. Similarly, there is no good reason to doubt that you can stand up and give a short presentation and afterwards feel that you can continue to improve with practise.

It is also good to remember that audiences are often very sympathetic, especially your student peers who know that they will have to do the same as you. On one occasion a student was helped by a word of advice when doing a presentation that was being evaluated for a PhD transfer. Someone who had previously been on a panel that evaluates these transfers said that each panel member was as much preoccupied by the question they were expected to ask the presenter! They were concerned that they would not be construed as foolish by their peers!

OPENING AND CLOSING SUMMARIES

It has been said that you don't get a second chance to make a first impression, so you need to ensure that your introduction is good. If you can get some catchy, gripping idea to open with, this is very useful but important features to concentrate on are brevity and clarity. A few well chosen and clearly focused sentences can immediately give a good impression of what your presentation is about. Give a brief summary map of where you are going, and don't waste time with a lot of unnecessary preliminaries (sometimes described as waffle!). Prepare your brief introduction really well so that you can get off to a confident start and get used to the sound of your own voice in public. It may be helpful to use some humorous remark in the introduction just to put yourself and your audience at ease, but watch out that it is not the kind of humour that goes down like a lead balloon!

A brief summary to help remind you of the need for brevity, clarity and focus is: Tell them what you're going to tell them; then tell them; then tell them what you've told them.

Similarly, your conclusion is vital and it should be designed to leave an impression of what the presentation was about. Therefore you will need to include some clear summary pointers of what you have said. It has been said that a long speech can be given at short notice, but a short address requires great preparation. Part of your preparation will be to hammer into shape a good clear introduction and conclusion. It is necessary to perfect these after all your other preparation in order to ensure that these incorporate all the facts in your presentation.

Exercise — Necessity of independent study skills

Practise designing a short introduction on why third level students are likely to need to learn independent study skills. Try to make three or four points.

In readiness for your delivery

THE WORK STARTS BEFORE YOU BEGIN

Full preparation has to be done before you stand up to begin your presentation. When you become more experienced, you will be more able to 'think on your feet' and to introduce points that occur to you as you speak. Initially, however, you will probably feel more comfortable adhering fairly strictly to what you have prepared. There will be some flexibility for you to introduce new material in a question session at the end of your presentation. In general you will, in your early experience with presentations, feel much more comfortable and confident being innovative at the preparation rather than at the delivery stage.

Tracking your position

It was alleged that a former British Prime Minister, Sir Winston Churchill, used to learn his parliamentary speeches verbatim. The opposition became aware of this and therefore frequently interrupted him to throw him off track. After addressing the question, the premier had to retrace his position by going back three or four sentences prior to where he had left off in order to get back into his flow.

If you have any interruptions (such as for questions) during your delivery, you can return to exactly where you left off, provided you are working your way systematically through well structured points. Good preparation and structure that is accompanied by clear visuals helps you keep track of where you are in your speech.

SELECTING MATERIAL FOR PRESENTATION

Selection and focus

The story is told of a farmer who went to church on a cold, snowy, winter Sunday morning. To his dismay, no one else turned up for the service with the exception of the preacher. The farmer fully expected that the preacher would deliver a short, summary address but he just continued with the sermon he had prepared for a full congregation. When the preacher asked the farmer afterwards what he had thought of the message, he replied: 'Well, let me put it to you like this: if I prepared a bucket of food for my chickens, and only one came for feeding, I would throw a handful of the fragments to it, but not the whole bucket load!'

Remember that a presentation should not be designed to tell your audience everything you have ever learned about a given topic. The key words are selection and focus. You have to make choices between what you really need and what amount to nothing more than trimmings and trappings.

SELECTING THE POINTS TO FOCUS ON

In the process of selecting your material, it will be beneficial if you can make a list of all your important and central ideas. At this stage you can discard any ideas that are not relevant, points that you feel are strained and are only likely to add 'noise' to your presentation. A special danger is the inclusion of unnecessary controversial points that will pull your listeners' minds away from you want to say. Some audience members may have their own agendas or pet subjects that are likely to emerge in question time anyway, so watch that you do not lose control of what the presentation has been about. Each point that you make should be like a tributary that leads into the central stream of your presentation theme.

SHORT CAPSULES FOR EACH POINT

Major and minor headings should not be comprised of lengthy sentences. A few words are usually enough such as the heading used above: 'Short capsules for each point'. You may need some practise before you fully develop this skill but the effort invested will more than repay itself. Your various headings will become pegs on which you can hang the material you want to develop in your talk.

Exercise — Preparing bullet points

Try to summarise the following sentences into a few words useful for headings:

1. You are going to describe how shop assistants and customers have a mutual influence on each others' behaviours and reactions.
2. You want to explain a range of factors that are likely to contribute to the maintenance of good friendships.
3. You intend to discuss the manner in which past experiences on holidays influence the choice of subsequent destinations.

After some practise you will develop a capacity for doing this economically, efficiently and effectively.

ARRANGING A FLOWING SEQUENCE

It is difficult to follow a presentation that has no clear structure and no flowing sequence. Presenters should not assume that, because of their own familiarity with their subject, all their listeners share their level of expertise. If your audience is hearing a lot of new things for the first time, your arguments will be better digested if these are presented with a clear and organised structure. Previously it was asserted that you should select your material and points to focus on. Make a note of your points and decide which are major headings and which are minor ones. Second, see if you can arrange all your minor points under appropriate major headings. Third, try to look at how the major points are best arranged in sequence so that one flows naturally into the other and that there is progressive development in the overall theme. When you have finished that, you can apply the same to the minor headings. Try to rearrange the following example into three major headings with three minor points under each, and then arrange the three major headings into a good sequence (the three major headings are in bold):

Exercise — Changes across the life-span

Restrictions in physical mobility	Bonding with wider circle of relatives
Challenges in childhood	Impairments in hearing and sight
Keeping up with modern changes	**Obstacles in declining years**
Learning the rules of language	**Maturing into adulthood**
Settling into a career	Finding a permanent partner
Balancing savings and expenses	Learning novel tasks independently

Preparing the overheads

CHECK OUT BEFORE YOU CHECK IN

Ensure that you check out all the facilities in the room where you are speaking before you check in to do your presentation. Knowing all these details in advance will help to settle your nerves and to combat potential sources of anxiety. For instance, it is useful to know how to turn the Overhead Projector (OHP) on and off, and whether you will need to turn on and off the lights for the main room during your presentation. If you are using PowerPoint you will need to ensure that an appropriate projector is in place for you. In general, check out that you can focus your acetates clearly on the screen, and that you are comfortable with where you will stand. You will need somewhere to set your acetates both before and after you use them – ensure that you have a place (such as a desk or chair) and a strategy for doing this. Also practise peeling the acetates from their covers as this can be tricky if you have never done it before. If you only start to think about all these things after you have commenced your presentation, you will waste time, heighten your anxiety and shake your own confidence.

USE AN APPROPRIATELY SIZED FONT

The size of font you use will depend on the size of the room and whether the people who sit at the back can see it clearly. You will need a very big font size for a long room and where there is a large audience. This is why it is important that you should have some idea of the room, for what is the point of using overheads if many in your audience are exasperated because they cannot see them? Moreover, there is little sense in typing out a lot of text in a small font that your audience cannot read.

SPACE THE BULLET POINTS OUT ADEQUATELY

Probably the best strategy is to make all your headings and subheadings the substance for your overheads, with a few additional pointers here and there (for example, illustrations). For your own guidance while talking, you can fill in the details with additional notes that you can read from small cards in your hands. If you read from a large A4 notepad this looks rather awkward and unwieldy, but using small cards makes it easier for you and gives you something to do with your hands when you are not changing the acetates around. Unless you space the bullet points on your overheads adequately, your audience will have difficulty keeping in touch with where you are in the presentation. If you keep your points well spaced out they will have a 'bird's eye view' of how your points are related to each other and developed into/from each other.

MONITOR THE NUMBER OF ACETATES/SLIDES TO USE

Many presenters fall into the trap of running out of time when they are only half way through the range of points they intend to cover. This may be because they have far too many acetates. In a short talk of 15 minutes you should only need about three and this allows about five minutes to cover each one. Remember that the details are for your personal notes, not for presentation on the OHP. Students often give themselves a lot of work preparing masses of detailed information on their acetates, and then stand up and find that their audience can't read it and they do not have enough time to present it all.

A golden rule to remember is that it is better to finish a little early with some time left rather than run over your time, and be reluctantly forced to cut out important details. If you plan the number of overheads you can use within the allotted time span, these will guide you in balancing and pacing out your use of time.

It is wise to use the range of facilities available to you on your word processor in order to give variety, emphasis and contrast to your presentation. As a rule, block capitals do not make for an attractive presentation. Even in a simple word processing package you can vary font size, use italics, bold, underline etc. to create good effect. You can also use lines with arrows, ellipses, and text boxes to aid clarity and readability. Too much use of bold text or underlined text does not look good and loses the desired impact. What you should do is play around with various presentation styles and also listen to the feedback from others. Moreover, you can learn from watching experienced presenters and take the opportunity to attend seminars where such people present. With good packages you can also use background colours and clip art. However, your visual presentation is intended to support your verbal content and can never become a substitute for it.

Exercise — Shaping the structure of the points

Look back at the Exercise, 'Changes Across the Life-span' on page 243. Consider how you might present the 12 points on acetates, for example, numbering main points as 1, 2, 3 and labelling subheadings as a, b, c. Also consider where you would use bold, italics and spacing, change font size and also how many acetates you would need. Furthermore, work out a time schedule for your points, based on the knowledge that you have been given 15 minutes for the presentation, and 5 minutes for questions.

In harmony with the visuals

If your presentation is well structured and ordered, you may be able to do without additional notes, because your headings and subheadings will act as triggers for the information you need to recall. You can use your pen (rather than your finger) to point to each of your headings as you move through each one. Also it is useful to remember to make the connection between one point and the next as you move along. At the end of each overall heading you can summarise the subheadings under that point and lead smoothly into the next point. For example, 'having described the features of early childhood development, we can now turn to consider various aspects associated with development in adolescents'. In doing this you summarise what you have said and make a connecting lead into your next point. This helps maintain a sense of continuity and flow and keeps the overall picture and direction before your audience.

UNCOVER EACH POINT AS YOU PROCEED

It is probably better to keep the points on acetates covered until you reach them one-by-one. In this way your audience does not run ahead of you but can keep in touch with where you are at any given point. If you allow them to read too much in advance you may lose some attention, especially if they see some particular point of interest ahead. Also it is not a bad strategy to keep them in a little bit of suspense as you whet their appetite for what follows (although you may tantalise them with a few tasters!). Every good story teller likes to do this.

AVOID OBSCURING THE VIEW

When you are nervous it is easy to inadvertently block the view of your visuals for some of the audience. Whenever you see some listeners looking like the Leaning Tower of Pisa, you should be alerted to this problem and take remedial action! Audiences can get frustrated when they can't see your presentation, so you should try to exercise sensitivity in this matter. Again it is useful to enter the room before the scheduled presentation so that you can work out your strategy in this regard and anticipate potential problems.

SYNCHRONISE THE WORDS WITH THE OVERHEADS

It is a rather peculiar experience to watch sport on TV and simultaneously listen to the commentary on the radio! The spoken commentary kicks in after the action has occurred, and at best this is humorous. In the same way it is not helpful to observe a presentation where someone is well into the content of the second acetate while the first one is still on the screen. Therefore, it is an important aspect of the art form to ensure that the verbal and visual aspects are carefully synchronised at each stage.

ARRANGING THE ACETATES IN SEQUENCE

Again, as a result of nerves, it is easy to shuffle your acetates into the wrong sequence before your presentation. This can result in you being quite frustrated, especially if you have just peeled off the protective covering. If you are very nervous this can be a disaster as your talk will proceed out of sequence if you are not aware that you have made this mistake. Panic is likely to set in when the realisation eventually dawns upon you. A simple way to help prevent this is to ensure that your acetates are correctly numbered and that you get into the habit of checking these as you move through the presentation. Also check immediately before the presentation that the sequence is correct. Many embarrassing moments would have been avoided if these simple steps had been taken.

In synchrony with your faculties

DISCREET USE OF EYE CONTACT

It is not easy to keep eye contact exactly right when you are anxious about your presentation, but it is something you should be aware of and attempt to work at. At one extreme there is the presenter who focuses on one person in the audience and appears to speak to them alone throughout. This is a distraction to the audience and an embarrassment to the person focused on. At the other extreme is the person who looks at the ceiling, the floor, the wall, or focuses just above the heads of the audience or who closes their eyes when they face the audience. The best strategy is to spread your eyes around the audience so that everyone feels you are speaking to them and including them. None should feel that they are excluded by no eye contact or embarrassed by fixated eye contact.

BALANCED USE OF THE VOICE

It is essential for your audience not only to see your visuals clearly but also to hear your voice distinctly. Again there are two extremes to be avoided: sounding either too soft or too loud. A practise run in front of a few friends may be a useful way to learn to pitch your voice at the right level. You should take into account the fact that various rooms will differ in their acoustical properties, and if you are expected to use a microphone watch that you are not too close to it. Acoustics also differ according to the size of the audience in the room. Ultimately the acid test is when you stand up to speak, and it is wise to ascertain if those at the back can hear you clearly.

A common weakness with many presenters is to drop their voice at particular points (such as toward the end of a sentence or summary or when making a humorous remark). You should practise ensuring that all your words are clear and distinct, and beware that you do not rush to such an extent that your voice degenerates into almost incomprehensible garble. The importance of pacing yourself for time also has consequences for your clarity of speech.

Exercise — An informal presentation

Meet with a few student friends and each of you give a short speech, even if only for a minute, on some simple task like replacing a light bulb, changing a fuse, preparing an omelette or selecting a suitable video for Saturday night. Open yourselves up for constructive feedback, not in relation to content and structure, but in relation to clarity of sound, pace of speech and suitable pauses. Also look out for distractions such as repeated use of the same word as a stop gap — such as too many 'wells', 'ahs' etc.

MEASURED USE OF NON-VERBAL COMMUNICATION

Non-verbal communication is a vitally important part of communication and researchers have concluded that where there is an ambiguity in a message, listeners will opt for the non-verbal cues. One important form of non-verbal communication is paralanguage – the various characteristics that accompany the spoken message. These include tone, pitch, inflection, pauses, hesitations etc. Careful attention to all these and discreet use of them can have a powerful effect. Sometimes the use of rhetorical questions can sharpen the effectiveness of the communication. Other features that can be used to good effect include a smile, eye contact, raised or lowered eyebrows or holding out open hands.

Exercise — Consult a book chapter

A worthwhile exercise would be to look at a relevant chapter
from a book on communication so that you can become aware of
how you can effectively use body language and non-verbal communication (for
example, Hargie, Saunders & Dickson, 2000).

It certainly contributes to the avoidance of monotony to use some inflection in the
voice and some non-eccentric movement of the body (unlike the old clergyman who
was reported to have pirouetted on one foot as he was speaking, and at other times
moved one foot up and down his leg!). Try to avoid distracting eccentricities and to
ensure that your non-verbal communication supports and harmonises with your presentation. A variety of studied approaches using appropriate non-verbal communication will enhance the quality of your presentation and help to harness any natural flair
you possess.

CIVIL RESPONSES TO QUESTIONS

It is not always the hard questions that are most difficult to answer, but sometimes the
naive ones. There is always the temptation to become impatient and dismissive of
these, but you must not lose your cool or your aim to become as professional as
possible. Try at all times to remain calm, even under provocation, and respond to all
questions in a civil manner. Do not be drawn into a particular agenda that someone
has come with but you can offer them more extended personal discussion after the
session is over. If it is evident that someone has asked a question because they did not
listen attentively to your presentation, remember that it does not add anything to your
authority to embarrass them before others. Conversely, when someone is hell-bent on
embarrassing you publicly then maintain your dignity, civility and courtesy at all
costs. A powerful proverb says that a soft answer turns away wrath.

PROVIDING SUPPLEMENTARY MATERIAL

It is not sensible to present reams of (for example) statistical tables, unless you highlight a few points of interest (for example, by drawing a circle around them) to illustrate patterns or trends in the data. What you can do is come to your presentation armed with supplementary material that you can make available to anyone who requests additional information. You can either allow them to inspect your detailed information more fully or have some handouts ready to give to those eager souls who want them. When there are tight restrictions on your time, the best you can hope to do is to highlight the main trends in your argument, yet condense these in a way that does not make them look emaciated.

DON'T TELL IT ALL

We have seen that the decision to leave out some material is an important part of your preparation for the good and simple reason that you will not have sufficient time to include all you would like. There is another important reason: this practise leaves you room to furnish additional details in the question session that follows. Furthermore, you can use a little bit of subtlety by deliberately leaving out some aspects where you feel your audience will be likely to ask you some questions. Your audience will then feel good because they have asked sensible and relevant questions that have clearly elicited such good quality 'off the cuff' responses, and they will also be left with the impression that you have a good command of your subject. On the other hand, if you leave no stone unturned in your presentation, you may force them into awkward questions and yourself into strained answers.

In tune with your limitations

THE FEAR OF AWKWARD QUESTIONS

More often than not the fear beforehand of being asked awkward questions is worse than the experience of being asked them. However, there are several considerations that will help to prepare you for the eventuality of these. The first is to ensure that you have a good presentation that clearly demonstrates that you have done your ground work, then by the time you reach the question session, you will already have won the respect of your audience. You are not going to lose that respect if you do not know the answer to one or two questions. Second, most audiences are sympathetic to the pressures of giving a public talk, especially if they know you are inexperienced at this task. Moreover, it is good to remember that a deliberately awkward questioner is likely to look worse than the speaker, especially if the speaker treats them with civility.

STRATEGIES FOR HANDLING QUESTIONS

In general there is nothing wrong with admitting you do not know the answer to a particular question. Honesty will gain you more respect than attempting an answer that is patently flawed. You can thank the questioner for raising some important issue that you will address in the near future. Or you can offer to investigate further and send an answer to the questioner as soon as possible. Sometimes the answer may be already implied in your presentation and you may just need to go over this again and clarify what you meant. As previously suggested, your answer may be in the material that you deliberately chose not to use. It may help you to ask the questioner to repeat the question if you are not crystal clear about what you are being asked. Questions are sometimes very badly framed and you will be helping the audience too by asking for the repetition. It is also most important that you monitor and keep control over the duration of your responses, as your listeners will already have had a lot to digest by this stage, and may have to listen to other presentations after yours. This is especially a danger to watch out for if you feel strongly about some controversial point. Finally, if you are calm enough to 'think on your feet' and suggest various possible brief answers, then all the better for you.

IF YOU ARE A PERFECTIONIST

A good old adage says that if you will settle for perfection or nothing, you end up with nothing every time! Do not expect over much of yourself while you are learning, and do not be too hard on yourself. At the same time you will want to learn regularly, change purposefully and grow steadily. No one has ever stepped into a car and driven it perfectly through heavy traffic at their first driving lesson, and no one jumps into the water to engage in advanced synchronised swimming and sophisticated tumble turns at the first time of asking.

In any discipline, there is an art in doing a presentation that is cultivated by practise. A few mistakes are not an irreversible disaster and other people will forget about them a long time before you do! Remember the old story of how Robert the Bruce was allegedly inspired to win his battle by watching the spider make many attempts to climb the wall in the cave before it eventually succeeded.

STRATEGIES FOR COPING WITH NERVES

A little nervousness may not necessarily be a bad thing, and even seasoned, gifted speakers can be nervous. However, some people fear that their nerves about speaking will so overwhelm them that their performance will be diminished. The first thing to establish in your mind is that you can take and keep control, and the primary strategy is to prepare well and keep focused on your task. Have your points well structured, ordered and clear, and rehearse them until you are sure of your ground. It may be helpful to rehearse your presentation with some friend(s) – see later, 'a dry run'. Furthermore, some simple relaxation techniques in the lead up to your task will be helpful. These are not full-blown therapies but simple procedures that you have proved as effective in relaxation. They may be listening to music, watching a film or doing some simple physical exercises and some breathing exercises. A well-proven servant in this respect is humour: try to watch a funny movie or socialise with friends who help to make you laugh. In theory, you cannot be relaxed and stressful at the same time as one is likely to displace the other. Finally, you can think in terms of some nervousness being a sign that energy is available to help you accomplish some task. Try to channel this energy into the productive purpose of a good presentation by focusing on the task rather than on your nerves.

WHENEVER THE PLOT IS LOST

The best way to ensure that you do not lose the plot is to ensure that you prepare a good structure, and then move steadily through the points, pacing yourself for time. What you should not allow to happen is for someone to have to tell you that your time is up when it is clear to everyone that you are only starting to get to the heart of your argument. Too much preliminary padding (which can include excessive courtesy, modesty, compliments, thanks, apologies) is a temptation many speakers cannot resist. The consequence of this is that they 'live on borrowed time' that is rapidly running out. A former radio presenter and interviewer used to say, 'never mind the pleasantries, just get on with it!'. There is room for pleasantries, but don't over do them. Ensure that you avoid lengthy, irrelevant distractions at every stage of your talk. If you do find yourself drifting then walk over to your acetate, point to where you are in your speech and move on with more focus!

A DRY RUN

A final piece of very useful preparation is for several friends/fellow students to give their presentations to each other in a 'dry run' where they can allow for a little 'friendly fire'. An amateur theatre company may prepare for their live performance by daily practise leading up to a full dress rehearsal. This allows them more control over timing, positioning, movement, voice projection etc., and enables them to discover and address potential problems. The exercise of reading a book on swimming will never be the same as actually attempting to learn to swim, and knowing all there is to know about giving a talk is helpful. However, giving yourself some 'hands-on' experience will be the greatest teacher of all, especially with some constructive feedback.

SUMMARY

♦ A presenter is required to juggle with many aspects of a presentation in order to blend them into one coherent and effective delivery.

♦ The preparation of preliminary practicalities such as checking acoustics, visuals, standing position, strategy for manipulating acetates etc. is indispensable for the achievement of a smooth presentation.

♦ A few good opening sentences and a clear outline of where the delivery is going will give confidence to the speaker and reassure the audience that the presenter will deliver an authoritative talk.

♦ Presenters should ensure that bullet points are well spaced out and clearly legible to all the audience.

♦ Good presenters will limit their material to essential points and will present these in clear, succinct, summary points.

♦ Discreet eye contact will add to the effectiveness of the presentation.

♦ Controlled projection and inflection of the voice will augment overall effectiveness.

♦ Bodily movements and non-verbal communication provide variety for the audience, but their studied use should be complementary to the presentation rather than a distraction from it.

◆ It is vital for the presenter to ensure that the verbal and visual aspects of the presentation are synchronised with each other.

◆ If the points to be covered are carefully paced out for time, no injustice will be done either to any particular part of the talk or to the presentation overall.

◆ Supplementary information that might be too tedious for the presentation can be provided on handouts.

◆ Time should be left for questions, and the presenter should handle these with courtesy, civility and brevity.

THE LEARNING CENTRE
TOWER HAMLETS COLLEGE
ARBOUR SQUARE
LONDON E1 0PS

References

Aronson, E., Wilson, T.D. & Akert, R.M. (1994). *Social psychology – The heart and the mind.* New York: HarperCollins College Publishers.

Austen, J. (1775–1817). *Pride and prejudice.* London, England: Oxford Press.

Baddeley, A.D. (1999). *Essentials of human memory.* Hove, UK: Psychology Press, Ltd., Publishers.

Bandura, A. (1986). *Social foundations of thought and action: A social cognitive theory.* Englewood Cliffs, NJ: Prentice Hall.

Bandura, A. (1997). *Self-efficacy – The exercise of control.* New York: W.H. Freeman & Co.

Barrier, T.B. & Margavio, T.M. (1993). Pretest-posttest measure of introductory computer students' attitudes toward computers. *Journal of Information Systems Education,* 5 (3) 1–6.

Becker, H.S. (1963). Outsiders: Studies in the sociology of deviance. Cited in P. Worsley, (1987). *The new introducing sociology.* Middlesex, England: Penguin Books,

Benson, J. & El-Zahhar, N. (1994). Further refinement and validation of the Revised Test Anxiety Scale. *Structural Equation Modelling,* 1 (3), 203–21.

Betz, N. & Hackett, G. (1983). The relationship of mathematics self-efficacy expectations to the selection of science-based college majors. *Journal of Vocational Behaviour,* 23, 329–45.

Bouffard, T., Boisvert, J., Vezeau, C. & Larouche, D. (1995). The impact of goal orientation on self-regulation and performance among college students. *British Journal of Educational Psychology,* 65 (3), 317–29.

Brosnan, M.J. (1998). The impact of psychological gender, gender-related perceptions, significant others, and the introducer of technology upon computer anxiety in students. *Journal of Educational Computing Research,* 18 (1), 63–78.

Brosnan, M.J. & Davidson, M.J. (1994). Computer phobia: Is it a particularly female phenomenon? *The Psychologist,* 7, 73–8.

Bunyan, J. (1622–88). *The Pilgrim's Progress.* Introduction and notes by R. Sharrock (1987). London: Penguin Books Ltd.

Cattell, R.B., Eber, H.W. & Tatsuoka, M.M. (1985). *Handbook for the sixteen personality factor questionnaire (16PF).* Institute for Personality and Ability Testing, Inc., Champaign, Illinois.

Colley, A.M., Gale, M.T. & Harris, T.A. (1994). Effects of gender role identity and experience on computer attitude components. *Journal of Educational Computing Research,* 10 (2), 129–37.

Colquitt, J.A. & Simmering, M.J. (1998). Conscientiousness, goal orientation and motivation to learn during the learning process: A longitudinal study. *Journal of Applied Psychology,* 83 (4), 654–65.

Costa, P.T. Jnr & McCrae, R.R. (1992). *Revised NEO personality inventory (NED PI-R) and NEO five factor inventory: Professional manual*. Odessa, FL: Psychological Assessment Resources, Inc.

Deffenbacher, J.L. (1980). Worry and emotionality in test anxiety. In I.G. Sarason (ed.). *Test anxiety: Theory, research and applications* (pp. 111–24). Hillside, New Jersey: LEA.

Dickens, C. (1812–1870). *Great Expectations*. Edited by R. Gilmour (1994, third reprint 2001). London: J.M. Dent.

Dyck, J.L. & Smither, J.A. (1994). Age differences in computer anxiety: The role of computer experience, gender and education. *Journal of Educational Computing Research*, 10 (3), 239–48.

Ebbinghaus, H. (1885). *Memory: A contribution to experimental psychology*. New York: Columbia University Press.

El-Zahhar, N.E. & Hocevar, D. (1991). Cultural and sexual differences in test anxiety, trait anxiety and arousability. *Journal of Cross-Cultural Psychology*, 22 (2), 238–49.

Eysenck, H.J. (1998). Trait theories of personality. In S.E. Hampson & A.M. Coleman (eds). *Individual differences and personality*. London and New York: Longman.

Ganzer, V.J. (1963). Effects of audience presence and test anxiety on learning and retention in a serial learning situation. *Journal of Personality and Social Psychology*, 8, 194–9.

Hargie, O., Saunders, C. & Dickson, D. (2000, 3rd edn). *Social skills in interpersonal communication*. London and New York: Routledge.

Hayes, N. & Orrell, S. (1991). *Psychology: An introduction*. Essex, England: Longman Group.

Hembree, R. (1988). Correlates, causes, effects and treatment of test anxiety. *Review of Educational Research*, 58 (1) 47–77.

Hoshmand, L.T. & Polkinghorne, D.E. (1992). Redefining the science-practice relationship and professional training. *American Psychologist*, 47 (1), 55–66.

Kline, P. (1994). *An easy guide to factor analysis*. London: Routledge.

Lalonde, N.L. & Gardner, R.C. (1993). Statistics as a second language? A model for predicting performance in psychology students. *Canadian Journal of Behavioral Science*, 25 (1), 108–25.

Levin, T., & Gordon, C. (1989). Effect of gender and computer experience on attitudes toward computers. *Journal of Educational Computing Research*, 5 (1), 69–88.

Levine, G. (1995). Closing the gender gap: Focus on mathematics anxiety. *Contemporary Education*, 67 (1), 42–5.

Liebert, R.M. & Morris, L.W. (1967). Cognitive and emotional components of test anxiety: A distinction and some initial data. *Psychological Reports*, 20, 975–8.

McCarthy, P. & Hatcher, C. (1996). *Speaking persuasively: Making the most of your presentation*. Australia: Allen & Unwin Ltd.

McIlroy, D., Bunting, B. & Adamson, G. (2000). An evaluation of the factor structure and predictive utility of a test anxiety scale with reference to students' past performance and personality indices. *British Journal of Educational Psychology*, 70, 17–32.

McIlroy, D., Bunting, B., Tierney, K. & Gordon, M. (2001). The relation of gender and background experience to self-reported computing anxieties and cognitions. *Computers in Human Behavior*, 17, 21–3.

Onwuegbuzie, A.J. (1997). Writing a research proposal: The role of library anxiety, statistics anxiety and composition anxiety. *Library and Information Science Research*, 19, 5–33.

Onwuegbuzie, A.J. & Daley, C.E. (1999). Perfectionism and statistics anxiety. *Personality and Individual Differences*, 26, 1089–102.

Orwell, G. (1903–1950). Cited in O.M. Thompson (1978, ed.). *Essential Grammar*. London: Oxford University Press.

Ozer, M. & Bandura, A. (1990). Mechanisms governing empowerment effects: A self-efficacy analysis. *Journal of Personality and Social Psychology*, 52, 472–86.

Pajares, F. & Miller, D. (1995). Mathematics self-efficacy and mathematics performances: The need for specificity of assessment. *Journal of Counselling Psychology*, 42 (2), 190–8.

Pancer, S.M., George, M. & Gebotys, R.J. (1992). Understanding and predicting attitudes towards computers. *Computers in Human Behaviour*, 8, 211–22.

Pavlov, I.P. (1927). *Conditioned Reflexes*. London: Oxford University Press.

Paxton, A.L. & Turner, E.J. (1984). The application of human factors to the needs of novice computer users. *International Journal of Man-Machine Studies*, 20, 137–56.

Peers, I.S. & Johnston, M. (1994). Influence of learning context on the relationship between A-level attainment and final degree performance: A meta-analytic review. *British Journal of Educational Psychology*, 64, 1–18.

Purdie, N.M. & Hattie, J.A. (1995). The effect of motivation training on approaches to learning and self-concept. *British Journal of Educational Psychology*, 65 (2), 227–35.

Ramsden, P. (2000). *Learning to teach in higher education*. London and New York: Routledge-Falmer.

Richardson, R. & Suinn, R.N. (1972). The Mathematics Anxiety Rating Scale: Psychometric data. *Journal of Counselling Psychology*, 19, 138–49.

Robson, C. (1994). *Experiment, design and statistics in psychology* (3rd edn). London: Penguin Books.

Rosen, L.D. & Maguire, P.A. (1990). Myths and realities of computerphobia: A meta-analysis. *Anxiety Research*, 3, 175–91.

Rosen, L.D. & Weil, M.M. (1992). *Measuring technophobia. A manual for the administration and scoring of the Computer Anxiety Rating Scale, the Computer Thoughts Survey and the General Attitude Toward Computers Scale*. Chapman University, USA.

Rosen, L.D., Sears, D.C. & Weil, M.M. (1987). *Computerphobia measurement. A manual for the administration and scoring of three instruments: Computer Anxiety Rating Scale (CARS), Attitudes Toward Computers Scale (ATCS) and Computer Thoughts Survey (CTS)*. Dominguez Hills, CA: California State University.

Rosenberg, M. (1965). *Society and the adolescent self-image*. Princeton, NJ: Princeton University Press.

Schultz, D. & Schultz, S.E. (1994). *Theories of personality* (5th edn). Pacific Grove, California: Brooks/Cole Publishing Co.

Selwyn, N. (2000). Researching computers and education – glimpses of the wider picture. *Computers and Education*, 34 (2), 93–101.

Shakespeare, W. (1564–1616). *Complete works of Shakespeare – The Alexander Text*. Edited by the late professor, P. Alexander (1994). Glasgow: HarperCollins.

Sidman, M. (1990). Equivalence relations: Where do they come from? In D.E. Blackman & H. Lejeune (eds). *Behavior analysis in theory and practice: Contributions and controversies*. Hove, Sussex: Lawrence Erlbaum.

Simpson, C.L., Premeaux, S.R. & Mondy, R.W. (1986). The college level introductory computer course: a student turnoff? *The Journal of Computer Information Systems*, 24–7.

Strickland, B.R. (1989). Internal–external control expectancies: From contingency to creativity (presidential address). *American Psychologist*, 66 (1), 1–12.

Weil, M.M. & Rosen, L.D. (1995). The psychological impact of technology from a global perspective: A study of technological sophistication and technophobia in university students from twenty three countries. *Computers in Human Behaviour*, 11 (1), 95–133.

Wilson, B. (1999). Redressing the anxiety imbalance: Computerphobia and educators. *Behaviour and Information Technology*, 18 (6), 445–53.

Wolfe, R.N. & Johnson, S.D. (1995). Personality as a predictor of college performance. *Educational and Psychological Measurement*, 55 (2), 177–85.

Zajonc, R.B. (1968). The attitudinal effects of mere exposure. *Journal of Personality and Sociology Psychology*, 9, 1–27.

Zeidner, M. (1991). Statistics and mathematics anxiety in social science students: Some interesting parallels. *British Journal of Educational Psychology*, 61, 319–28.

Zeidner, M. (1998). *Test anxiety: The state of the art*. New York & London: Plenum Press.

Index